Praise for *The Lord*

"Dr. Rawlings has been my mentor for forty-eight years. He taught me the sanctity of the local church and the centrality of the local church in the enterprise of world evangelization. He is the greatest visionary I know. He has always been ahead of his peers. He is a man of great wisdom. He is an obsessive reader. He is unbelievably progressive without ever compromising truth and principle. Humanly, I owe him more for the success of my own ministry than any other mortal."

> JERRY FALWELL, *Chancellor, Liberty University*
> *Thomas Road Baptist Church, Lynchburg, VA*

"American original. Visionary. God's own preacher. Volumes of words can hardly describe Dr. John Rawlings's near 72-year ministry of the Gospel of Jesus Christ around the world. Yet, this brilliant, comprehensive, and exuberant biography achieves what few first biographies do: it captures the many-layered portrait of Dr. John's life and impact, beautifully rendering the man who ministered almost daily up until his 99th birthday. You're in for an adventure, reader. Saddle up. Kaitlyn O. Rawlings honors her great-grandfather with this story. And the story glorifies God even more."

> JEFFREY S. HILLARD, *Associate Professor of English,*
> *College of Mount St. Joseph, Cincinnati, Ohio*

"Having known Dr. John Rawlings as Pastor, Teacher, Mentor, and Friend, he was truly a Giant of the Faith of the 20th Century. His understanding of human nature and physical creation gave him a true understanding of life situations. His knowledge of church history, especially Baptist history, is unparalleled. His leadership abilities and motivational skills thrust him into an un-measurable leadership role. His love for God; the Bible; people; ministry; and evangelism, and his World Vision was a challenge and encouragement to all who knew him. He left a great legacy. Anyone who reads this book and learns more about this man, John Rawlings, will be greatly enriched."

> LELAND R. KENNEDY
> *Former President of Baptist Bible College, Springfield, Missouri*

"My friend, Dr. John Rawlings, whom I admired tremendously, was one of the great Christian leaders in America. While holding uncompromising biblical convictions, he did so graciously and could work with all other Bible believers effectively to present the Gospel. His gracious spirit and effective communication of the Gospel are reflected in this outstanding book. Through it, he will continue to be an inspiration to many. This book is a must-read for every believer."

> JUDGE PAUL PRESSLER

"There are several descriptive words that come to mind when I think of Dr. John – courageous, convicted, committed, confident, colorful, and even controversial. His great-granddaughter has done an incredible job of capturing these and more of the outstanding attributes that my dear friend John Rawlings possessed. As he made an impact on my life while he lived, this book will be used of God to allow his life to impact generations yet to come. Thank you, Dr. John, for your friendship, and thank you, Kaitlyn, for keeping his memory alive!"

DANNY L. MOODY
President of Arlington Baptist College, Fort Worth, Texas

"Every time I heard Dr. Rawlings was on the phone I knew I was about to be encouraged and challenged at the same time. He 'being dead still speaks' through this wonderful volume, penned by his own great-granddaughter. Now, future generations will be inspired by his unique and God honoring life. Read it and reap!"

O.S. HAWKINS, *President/CEO GuideStone*
Former Pastor First Baptist Church Dallas

"Few pastors, preachers or church leaders have exercised such lasting influence on evangelism, church growth, Christian education, world missions, the ministry or mentoring as Dr. John Rawlings. This well documented account of his life tells why. His passion! Dr. John's passion to make a difference for Jesus and His church glowed until the very end of is 99 years. This book should be required reading for all pastors, young and old."

L. D. CAMPBELL
Pastor, First Church, Burlington, KY

"Dr. John Rawlings was a visionary, a pioneer, and an innovator. He was focused on the Great Commission. He could analyze a situation, immediately distinguish the end from the means and cut right to the heart of the issue. He lived unselfishly, using his every resource for the cause of Christ. He was the ultimate motivator—challenging (and chiding) everyone around him to greater heights. I miss him!"

BILL MONROE
Pastor, Florence Baptist Temple, Florence, South Carolina

John Rawlings was a hero to me; in a sense, bigger than life. His messages touched and challenged my life beginning in 1976 at my first church. It was a dream come true to become his personal friend later in his life while serving on Liberty University's Board. He was a Preacher, Church Builder and, most of all, a Man of God.

PASTOR JOHNNY HUNT, *First Baptist Church, Woodstock, GA*
President of the Southern Baptist Convention 2008-2010

The Lord Is Not Through with Me Yet

The Story of Dr. John W. Rawlings

Named by Jerry Falwell as the "Baptist of the Twentieth Century"

KAITLYN O. RAWLINGS

CROSSBOOKS
PUBLISHING

CrossBooks™
A Division of LifeWay
1663 Liberty Drive
Bloomington, IN 47403
www.crossbooks.com
Phone: 1-866-879-0502

First published by CrossBooks 7/19/2013

ISBN: 978-1-4627-2823-7 (sc)
ISBN: 978-1-4627-2825-1 (hc)
ISBN: 978-1-4627-2824-4 (e)

Library of Congress Control Number: 2013910516

Printed in the United States of America.

This book is printed on acid-free paper.

Certain stock imagery © Thinkstock.
Any people depicted in stock imagery provided by Thinkstock are models,
and such images are being used for illustrative purposes only.

Photo on page 121 by Henry Allen.

To Daddy, for his loving dedication to me and this project

CONTENTS

ACKNOWLEDGEMENTS

Because of the wide scope and reach of Dr. John's legacy, there are so many people to whom I owe sincere thanks. Many testimonies have been shared, countless stories have been told, and multiple people have had a hand in the molding and formation of this book through which Dr. John's legacy will live on. First and foremost, I would like to thank my father, who never left my side and never wavered in his support of this project. Without him, I would not be writing these acknowledgements. Special thanks also belong to my family for their love, support, and forbearance throughout this long but rewarding process.

I also want to thank my great uncles, George, Harold, and Carrol, as well as my grandparents, Herb and Pat, for their and my Uncle Harold's tireless editing efforts. They, along with my father, helped gather research, do fact checking, and altogether make this a better rendering of my great grandfather's life. My appreciation also belongs to Dr. Leland Kennedy who, like my great grandfather, taught me the importance of remembering who you are. Thanks to R. L. Jacobs, Bill and Phyllis Aven, Johnnie Stewart and his lovely family, and Don and Patsy Walker. I would also like to extend a heartfelt thank you to Jackie Reynolds and Jeff Hillard for their kind words of encouragement and investment of time in providing feedback throughout the editing process.

Thanks to Doc Humphreys and the many others who sat down with me to share stories and laughter, reminiscing about Dr. John and his ministry. Most of all, thank you to Granddad, who shared many a meal with my family and me, telling stories with amazingly vivid details while enjoying my mom's grilled salmon that he loved so much. Granddad, thank you for allowing me the honor of recounting your life and ministry through writing your biography. I have a great example to follow. I promise to never stop reaching for my potential.

I love to tell the story
Of unseen things above
Of Jesus and His glory
Of Jesus and His love
I love to tell the story
Because I know 'tis true;
It satisfies my longings
As nothing else can do
I love to tell the story
'Twill be my theme in glory
To tell the old, old story
Of Jesus and His love.

FOREWORD

"John Rawlings was a giant."

— ELMER L. TOWNS

John Rawlings was a giant among men, a giant among preachers, and I believe a giant with God.

I first met John Rawlings when I was writing the book *The 10 Largest Sunday Schools And What Makes Them Grow.* I first interviewed Harold Henninger of Canton Baptist Temple; he helped me understand large churches. The second person I interviewed was John Rawlings; he helped me understand pastors of large churches. The very fact these ten pastors had built the ten largest churches in America made them giants. All the pastors of these ten churches were larger than life, and John Rawlings was perhaps the largest among them all. I am not saying he had the biggest physical frame, or the biggest church; I am suggesting he had a larger view of the pastorate than the others.

I knew John Rawlings for 44 years, since 1968. He did not change in all those years. He was as big as Landmark Baptist Temple from the beginning. He was big in evangelism, and there are many he personally won to Christ, not counting those who came to Christ under his preaching. He was big on Gospel music, the music that moved the hearts of those who came to his church, or attended his evangelistic crusades. But most of all he was big on serving the Lord. No one ever doubted his obedience to Jesus Christ. Those of us who knew him could say he loved the Lord his God, with all his heart, with all his mind, and with all his strength.

John Rawlings was big on helping young preachers. He always had time for them when preachers visited his church. He wanted to help them build a bigger church. He had time for this writer. When I visited Landmark for the first time, he spent morning, afternoon, and evening with me, explaining how and why his church grew.

John Rawlings was a giant, and when a giant walks, he shakes the ground under his feet. John Rawlings shook the neighborhood of Greater Cincinnati, picking up children in old school buses, and bringing them to Landmark Baptist Temple to hear the Word of God and to be saved. There are people all over Cincinnati who were saved at Landmark, also including those who heard the message across America through his radio broadcast.

John Rawlings was a giant who shook up pastors' meetings. He spoke at many Baptist Bible Fellowship meetings, both state and national, not to mention other denominations and interdenominational meetings. When he spoke everyone got his point, whether or not they agreed with him. He shook up lethargic preachers; sometimes they determined to go build a great church, and sometimes they crossed their arms and rejected what he said. But John Rawlings was a giant who could not be ignored, just like no one can ignore a giant when he walks into a room.

John Rawlings shook up the Baptist Bible Fellowship in the mid-70s. The Baptist Bible Fellowship had been founded and built by giants such as Beauchamp Vick, W. E. Dowell, and himself. But when the early giants of the Fellowship began dying and their leadership positions were vacant, Rawlings's personality guided the re-writing of the Constitution of the Fellowship to reflect what he called a New Testament approach of "one-church, one-vote." The way the Fellowship does business today has John Rawlings's fingerprints on it.

Another good thing about a giant: they defend their family and friends. The Baptist Bible Fellowship and fundamentalism in general have lost a great giant who was a staunch defender of the fundamentals of the faith, the integrity of the local church, and the American right to life, liberty and the pursuit of happiness. As this giant leaves us, who will defend the truth, and who will take his place?

Also, giants are taller than we are; people look up to them. They stand tall and tower above us. John Rawlings stood tall for Christ. He was a prime example of integrity and righteousness. There was never a doubt left in the mind from anything John Rawlings said. You knew his life backed up his walk, and his words were never spoken timidly. He did not stutter, stammer, nor did he speak with a forked tongue. You always knew where he stood!

When John Rawlings left the local church, this giant began building youth camps around the world. He knew that many came to know Christ through youth camps, so he built them and supported them through the Rawlings Foundation.

But even giants must die. God has given a lifecycle to everything that grows. There is conception, growth in the womb, and then birth. There are lessons to be learned of walking, speaking, running, and in school lessons of fighting for survival. John Rawlings learned these lessons well. There are lessons about work, love, marriage, children, and plans for the next generation. John Rawlings also learned those lessons well. He grew greater than most men, and more influential than most pastors, and he lived 99 years, longer than most . . . and then God took him home.

I think there was a great welcoming committee for John Rawlings on the other side of the Jordan on January 30, 2013. Beauchamp Vick led the welcoming committee; John R. Rice was there to count all those baptized by Rawlings; Earl Smith sang; and Reg Woodworth, who was dean of men, kept all the boys in line. W. E. Dowell was there to buy coffee, and Jerry Falwell was there to keep the majority moral.

A giant died and was buried on the grounds of Landmark Baptist Temple.

Long live John Rawlings.

ELMER L. TOWNS
Co-Founder and Vice President, Liberty University
Dean, Liberty University School of Religion and
Liberty University Baptist Theological Seminary and Graduate School

INTRODUCTION

Many biographies refer to their subjects by their last name. But Dr. John W. Rawlings was such a personable character that that just doesn't do him justice. To many, he was more than a preacher; he was a confidant, an advisor, a mentor, and a friend. To me, as my great-grandfather, he was a master storyteller and spiritual role model.

Dr. John W. Rawlings has been called by many names, such as John, Brother Rawlings, Dr. Rawlings, "Doc," and the lovingly bestowed nicknames, "Father John," "The Bishop" or "The Preacher." But the name that was most recurrent during his lifetime was quite simply Dr. John and was most commonly used during the later years of his life. While we refer to him as John in writing about his early years, Dr. John is the name that will be predominately used throughout this book. His loving wife of nearly seventy-five years was most often fondly and respectfully called "Mrs. Rawlings."

The name John, derived from the Hebrew, means "God is gracious." God was certainly gracious in the life of Dr. John W. Rawlings, a namesake of John the Baptist and the apostle John, and, as a result of his ministry, countless numbers of lost people were brought to the saving knowledge of the Lord Jesus Christ. According to Ephesians 2:8–9 in the King James, the version beloved by Dr. John and used throughout this book, we know that "by grace are ye saved through faith; and that not of yourselves: it is the gift of God: not of works, lest any man should boast." Dr. John was respected and revered for his unashamed proclamation of the Gospel. He spent nearly his entire life preaching the inerrancy of Scripture. His belief in the power of the

Word of God is reflected by Hebrews 4:12: "For the word of God is quick, and powerful, and sharper than any two-edged sword, piercing even to the dividing asunder of soul and spirit, and of the joints and marrow, and is a discerner of the thoughts and intents of the heart." For believers, the Bible nourishes and is a comfort; but for those not committed to Christ, it brings judgment. Dr. John preached this with certainty, not opinions or conjecture. As did the Apostle John, Dr. John brought people back to the basics of Christianity and taught the fundamentals of the faith. He followed the Lord with all his heart and never looked back.

Second Peter 1:16 says, "For we have not followed cunningly devised fables, when we made known unto you the power and coming of our Lord Jesus Christ, but were eyewitnesses of his majesty." As the last remaining apostle, John enjoyed close association with Christ during His earthly ministry, death, resurrection, and ascension. John's ministry was highly respected among the churches of his day. In the same way, Dr. John W. Rawlings was admired and respected for the success of his radio, television, music, youth camp, and Bible college ministries. As a visionary, Dr. John exuded a confidence and passion that drew people in and beckoned them to join him on his journey to reclaim lost souls for Christ. In this circle of soul winners, he promoted a spirit of unity, and as a strong leader, he always sought to surround himself with other strong Christian personalities. He was not afraid to invite great pastors, evangelists, motivational speakers, and trendsetters in the music industry to fill his pulpit.

Dr. John's creative approach to evangelism motivated others to join him in his mission to spread the Gospel. "I'm an original," he described himself. "I do my own thinking." Rather than blindly accepting the ways of the world, Dr. John based his beliefs on Scripture and developed his own style of preaching accordingly. Because of this, he was able to preach with the power and authority that comes from God's Word alone. "God called me to preach," he said. "Preaching is my business. Preaching is my forte. Using street language ... it is my 'cup of tea.' That is what God called me to do. That is what I excel in ... I wake up at night dreaming of when I can preach again. I would like to preach every hour; I never grow tired of preaching. When God calls a man to preach, he puts preaching in his soul! It is just like singing. If God puts a song in your soul, you will never be happy unless you are singing!"

Dr. John built one of the largest churches in East Texas in what many considered a very small town. "The vastness of the Lone Star State influenced his life's philosophy as expressed in his personal motto: 'Plan it big—keep it simple.'"[1] He planted churches all over Texas and later across the country and founded a Bible college and youth camps around the world. He started and built a successful radio and bus ministry, maintaining a fleet of over one hundred buses. He was also a driving force of the Gospel music industry. During his time in Cincinnati, he led a church to become one of the ten largest in the United States with over ten thousand members.

Dr. John could certainly be described as the definition of a visionary, for he never missed out on an opportunity to proclaim the truth of God. He truly did not only dream a dream, but inspired others to catch the vision and, in the process, changed the world. We hope through this account of his life that you too will catch the vision and be inspired to change your world with the saving knowledge of Jesus Christ, just as Dr. John's everlasting commitment was to serve Christ. Even to the time of his death at ninety-nine years of age, he continued to evangelize and through his legacy carry out the Great Commission around the world. Therefore, the stories that lie herein are but a portion of his full life story. As Dr. John used to say: "[We are] writing a book about part of my life. The rest of it hasn't happened yet." Although he passed away on January 30, 2013, one day after his ninety-ninth birthday, he lived according to the principle that there is always more of our potential to reach, and we must never stop reaching. He would say, "The Lord is not through with me yet."

---

1   James L. Adams, "Landmark Baptist Temple: Plan it big, keep it simple," *The Cincinnati Post*, (August 21, 1976): 1, 31.

1

Keep Breathing

I am a work in progress at ninety-five, dreaming big dreams. I have a holy determination that I'm going to finish this trip with victory.

—DR. JOHN RAWLINGS

"Have you done this before?" Dr. John asked his surgeon Dr. William H. Cook in a voice grown quite raspy after decades of fiery preaching. "I don't want to be your first patient."

Soon, Dr. John would undergo a four-way bypass heart operation, though he and his family had already faced an eventful previous month. Several days before, during the first weeks of February 2010, Dr. John and his wife, Mary, had journeyed to Texas with Dr. John's second son, Harold. Dr. John and Mary had been married since November 1, 2008, one year and eight months since the death of Dr. John's first wife, Orelia.

Harold recalls from the long drive cross-country that when one truck would pass another, and it would take several minutes for the truck to pass, Dr. John would become irritated. When Harold would catch up to the passing truck, his father would look out the window, try to get the trucker's attention, and shake his index finger as if to lecture, "Move on, and get out of my way." Harold thought how humorous this might appear to the truckers, who must have been amused by this older gentleman with a black ivy cap pulled down over his forehead sitting low in the passenger seat. Dr. John was accustomed to doing his own driving and had been doing so for over eighty years, including the time spent on the family farm where he grew up. His fearless driving skills were thus legendary to whoever rode with him or watched him drive.

Harold had reserved rooms in a Texarkana hotel, for the drive from Kentucky had been a long one at just over eleven hours. However, as they approached Texarkana, Dr. John insisted on driving on to Henderson, Texas, that very evening. With a sigh, Harold relented, although he had to call and beg the hotel to cancel the reservation for the two rooms.

During their time in Texas, Dr. John, Mary, and Harold stopped in Texas City to visit Mary's sister Billie. Afterward, the three of them traveled on to Houston for the mid-winter Baptist Bible Fellowship International (BBFI) meeting for pastors, which was one of three annual BBFI meetings that were to take place from February 17–19, 2009. During one of the assemblies, a missionary from the Philippines spoke. After he finished, although without invitation and without being on the itinerary, Dr. John strode down the aisle determinedly and stepped up to the microphone. Harold wondered whether or not he heard gasps from the other audience members as Dr. John took the podium.

He began sharing his thoughts regarding mission work in the Philippines and abroad. Then he switched gears and, as part of his impromptu speech, went about lambasting the preachers in attendance for "playing too much golf and spending time on trivial matters. I never played one golf game in my life." He must not have recalled the story he used to tell about the particular time he did play golf: when he drove his ball into the woods, he walked over to retrieve it, and while his playing partner was looking for his ball, Dr. John carried his own back to lay it upon the green. His playing partner, who had not witnessed this, said in amazement, "John, how did you do that?"

Dr. John further reproached the preachers, "You need to get back to business and quit all the foolishness and return to your calling." When he concluded his message, the spectators applauded respectfully, although he may have taken some fun out of their golf game. After the meeting, they returned to Henderson, Texas, for the evening.

During the evening hours of Sunday, February 22, Dr. John woke Mary, complaining of chest pains and shortness of breath. Mary hurried to Harold's room and rapped urgently on the door. "I think your father is having a heart attack," she said.

Quickly, Harold answered, "We should call 911."

Mary called, and in about seven to eight minutes, the paramedics arrived. They immediately entered the room to assist Dr. John, and as they transferred him from his bed onto a stretcher, he muttered, "I can't believe the incompetence."

They wheeled him out to the emergency vehicle and assisted Mary into the back of the truck so she could be with her husband. Harold followed them in Mary's SUV Lexus on the thirty-five minute drive from the hotel to Trinity Mother Francis Hospital in Tyler.

Right away, the hospital staff began tending to Dr. John in the intensive care unit. As they worked, Dr. John wistfully remembered aloud to Harold, "You know, son, this is the same hospital where my father died in 1948, sixty-one years ago." Would Dr. John's life end in the same hospital where his father had passed away?

It was later determined that Dr. John had suffered a minor heart attack during the night, but his condition had stabilized. He demanded a *USA Today*. Harold felt compelled to comply and walked from one end of the hospital to the other to purchase one for his father. The newspaper, however, was left unread, as Dr. John was released from Trinity Mother Francis Hospital the following day when his youngest son George had him flown home to Kentucky in his company jet.

Dr. John drove himself to his office on Tuesday, February 24, where he worked a full day. But his chest pains persisted, so on March 2, their daughter-in-law Pat drove Dr. John and Mary to Mercy South Hospital in Fairfield, Ohio, north of Cincinnati. Mercy Hospital was where Dr. John's family physician of many years, Dr. Dennis Humphries, practiced. Dr. Humphries was a dedicated member of Dr. John's church for many years, serving as a Sunday school teacher and involved in the television and radio ministry. Dr. John insisted on wearing his charcoal-gray Ralph Lauren robe over his suit for warmth with matching gray Puma sneakers. For decades, Dr. John had worn a suit and tie every day of the week; although comfort now held precedence, he would still wear his dress pants and coat. On the way to the hospital, Dr. John also requested they stop at Bob Evans, where he ate a sausage biscuit for breakfast.

On March 3 in Room 9 of Mercy Hospital, Dr. John received his diagnosis from heart specialist Dr. Babbitt. Three of his arteries were 99 percent blocked, and a fourth artery was over 90 percent blocked. Dr. John quickly decided to undergo open-heart surgery, medically termed as a coronary artery bypass graft times four. Later, Dr. John stated, "I didn't have any choice." Mercy Hospital was where Dr. John's family physician of many years, Dr. Dennis Humphries, practiced. Dr. Humphries was a dedicated member of Dr. John's church for many years, serving as a Sunday school teacher and involved in the television and radio ministry.

Dr. Cook, who was to perform Dr. John's operation and whose team had performed between fifteen to sixteen hundred heart surgeries, told the family he had previously operated on patients who were up to ninety-three years old. "But I believe you are my oldest," he said to Dr. John's satisfaction.

When Dr. John's son Carrol was later told of a friend's grandmother having open heart surgery at ninety-three years of age and then subsequently living to be 107 years old, Carrol joked, "Oh no, don't tell me that!"

Dr. John's four-hour, four-way bypass operation was scheduled for Wednesday, March 5, from 1:00pm – 5:00pm. During the preparation for the operation, Dr. John was up to his old tricks. "Hurry up, I've got to go," he rushed Dr. Cook.

The procedure was successful, and by the following morning, Dr. John was already well on his way to recovery, sitting up in bed and talking to friends and family. That same day, he walked the circuitous route around the intensive care unit. Dr. Cook proclaimed the operation and quick recovery a miracle and said Dr. John was "doing circles around some of his patients in their fifties." Dr. John even asked for a coffee and a *USA Today* that morning but was given only decaffeinated coffee, which would have been against his better wishes had he known this was the case. The following day, Dr. John ate all of his food for lunch, including an entire hamburger, and walked twice round the corridor in the hospital. Dr. John's son George said, "Dad thinks he is an athlete. He had to do everything twice over what they told him to do."

Dr. John was released from the hospital on Sunday and was home by noon, as quickly as or sooner than many younger heart patients. On Monday, visitors found him sitting at his kitchen table with an unbuttoned shirt, "airing out" his scar.

When Dr. John's son Carrol was asked about his father's operation, he answered, "Dad is as tough as boot leather" and wondered aloud if his father would later claim to have actually performed his own heart surgery.

Despite Dr. John's rapid healing, not all was behind him quite yet. On

Thursday, March 26, he awoke from his sleep with difficulty breathing. He slept the rest of the night sitting up, and in the morning, his oldest son Herb drove him to his heart doctor's clinic where it was determined that he had 1.2 liters of fluid on his lungs, a condition not unusual for a patient who has previously undergone major heart surgery. Sleeping upright the night before just might have saved his life.

After having the fluid removed, Dr. John left the clinic and went to the hospital for X-rays. Herb described his father's exit from the hospital as quick and effortless, as Dr. John scurried out on his feet, saying, "I feel 100 percent better." He even went grocery shopping that evening with Mary. With the aid of his walker, he followed her through the supermarket, but later proclaimed, "She's not good at grocery shopping," and so he had to do it all. It has become one of his favorite pastimes. He enjoys asking lady shoppers to help him locate the items on his grocery list.

For dinner the next day, Dr. John ate pork sirloin and a salad. He weighed 167 pounds before having the fluid removed from his lungs and about 157 pounds two mornings after.

Before a follow-up doctor's visit, Carrol asked Dr. John if the doctor would release him to work after the checkup. Dr. John, quick-witted as always, responded tongue-and-cheek, "I found out you can get by without working." As an afterthought he added, "I think I'll just coast in from here."

On Saturday, April 4, Dr. John walked one and a half miles on his treadmill—three-fourths of a mile in the morning and three-fourths in the afternoon. By Saturday, April 25, he was walking four miles a day. Also by that date, he was lying in the sun for forty minutes to replenish himself with vitamin D, twenty minutes on his back and twenty on his stomach.

The next day, Mary drove him to his former church, Landmark Baptist Temple, for a visit. On the way home, they stopped at the local Cracker Barrel for a long-desired country meal.

Dr. John showed up at his office at about 2:30 p.m. on April 10, 2009, the first time in weeks. The employees working that day stood at the window and watched Mary gently turn her SUV into Dr. John's usual parking spot, with Dr. John probably directing her from the passenger seat. Carrol commented wryly, "No matter what seat he's in, he's always driving."

As coworkers watched him climbing the steps of the front stoop, Carrol dialed his father's extension and chided him, "About time you got back to work."

"That wasn't very nice," Dr. John responded matter-of-factly, his feelings quite unhurt. He spent nearly two hours in his office that day.

Two days later, Sunday, April 12, Dr. John experienced pains in his chest as he had before and was readmitted to Mercy Hospital. His diagnosis showed he had excess fluid on his lungs again, and the doctor drained the same amount as he had before, 1.2 liters. Mary said she couldn't believe they filled multiple containers of excess fluid.

While recovering in the hospital, Dr. John enjoyed bantering with the staff. He asked his attending nurse if she was married, and when she answered that she was not, he said, "Then we need to find you a rich husband."

On April 15, Mary and Herb's wife, Pat, visited Dr. John around four o'clock. Believing the hospital had already provided him with lunch, they hadn't brought him anything. Earlier he had requested country ham and biscuits from his attending nurse, but she replied that that was a no-no for a recovering heart patient.

"Did you bring me anything to eat?" Dr. John asked when his family arrived.

"Why didn't you call us if you were hungry?" Pat asked.

Offended, he jutted his index finger at the phone as if to say, "You could have called to see what I wanted." He asked specifically for a meal from Cracker Barrel, so Pat went to the restaurant and came back later with his order of pinto beans, chopped onions, relish, and sourdough white toast.

Soon after being released from Mercy Hospital on Thursday, April 16, Dr. John met with three of his sons, Herb, Carrol, and George, for breakfast. Harold had gone to New England, and Herb told his father that he, too, would be out of town for a while, as he was leaving for Africa the following night. Dr. John then asked George if he would be traveling soon, and George replied that yes, he was leaving for Florida. Dr. John considered for a moment and then turned to Carrol and said, "I guess you're going to have to take care of me."

"You're in big trouble now," George interjected.

Carrol said to his father, "You'll just have to call 911!"

During this time period when Dr. John would go to the doctor's office, on more than one occasion he was asked for his health coverage card. When he handed them his card, the employee would peer at him and ask, "You're still working?"

"You're probably one of the oldest social security recipients still working and still paying into social security," George told him.

On Tuesday, April 21, Dr. John again returned to his office. Mary drove him to work and stayed with him throughout the day. George teased him, "Quit bringing your wife to work." The next day, Dr. John followed George's orders and drove himself to the office in his gray Cadillac, the first time he had driven since his surgery.

Dr. John's dry wit, reflective of his quick thinking, was an ability never lost in any way over time. After so many years as a pastor and an evangelist, Dr. John's sense of humor certainly made itself known. But despite all his accomplishments and lifetime experiences, he never forgot his humble beginning as a cotton farmer's son growing up in the foothills of the Ozark Mountains of Arkansas. "Remember who you are," Dr. John would often say.

Reflecting upon his heart attack, he said, "When I had my heart attack, I didn't know whether I was going to make it or not. But I had perfect peace because I know whom I believe, and I am persuaded that He is going to take care of everything until He finishes with me. I am a work in progress at ninety-five, dreaming big dreams. I have a holy determination that I'm going to finish this trip with victory."

Some may think Dr. John's late-life experience would be difficult for anyone to bear, but if they had asked ninety-eight-year-old Dr. John how he lived so long, he would merely reply with a shrug, "I just keep breathing."

2

Foothills of the Ozarks

Train up a child in the way he should go: and when he is old, he will not depart from it.

—PROVERBS 22:6

The Birthplace of Dr. John W. Rawlings

John William Rawlings was born on his father's homestead in the upper Mississippi Delta in the foothills of the great Ozarks outside Mobley, Arkansas, on January 29, 1914. He was the only son of George Washington Rawlings, a cotton gin operator, and Amanda Evelyn James, born into a family of twelve children from the "James Tribal People," who migrated from England to America. On his mother's side, his grandfather William James was English and Irish, and his grandmother Martha Lewallen James was German. His grandmother on his father's side was part Comanche Indian, and his grandfather was English. Two of his brothers, George and Amos, were Baptist preachers. George was known throughout Independence and Sharp Counties in Arkansas as an able and distinguished preacher who was often invited to conduct revival services and meetings.

It was part of family lore that the Rawlings family was related to the infamous Jesse James, the notorious outlaw. A familiar quote in John's Grandfather James's family was, "If you were a James, you were either a preacher or an outlaw." Jesse James's father, Robert S. James, was a Baptist preacher and one of the founders of William Jewel College in Liberty, Missouri.

The Rawlings had a blood connection with the family of George Washington through his mother, Mary Ball Washington. The family had originally come from Loudoun County, Virginia, traveling "with the Ball family on a wagon train in 1828 from Virginia to Arkansas."[2] From Virginia, they journeyed westward but due to lack of supplies settled in Independence County, Arkansas. The Rawlings clan were among the original pioneer families to settle in the area of Cave City, Arkansas, still named today on the Cave City Chamber of Commerce's website for settling in the city before it was eventually named for the cave in the center of the town:

> The cave supplied the drinking water for the local school, as well as serving as a veritable "town refrigerator." Many families stored their milk, butter, and other produce in the cool cave to prevent them from spoiling. The cave was both a great asset to the community and a source of mystery. Over the years, various attempts have been made to explore the cave and to determine the origins of the Crystal River, which flows under the town of Cave City. No one has ever been able to show where the river begins or where it eventually ends. Although the town of Cave City is

---

2   *A History of the One-Room Schools of Sharp County.* (Windmill Pub., 1986), 99.

some 150 miles from the Mississippi River, it has been said that the Crystal River rises and falls with the Mississippi River.[3]

The early pioneer families made their homesteads along the creeks and waterways and farmed the sandy terrain. This earth, composed of the perfect balance of sand and soil, produces the world's sweetest watermelons, according to the Cave City Chamber of Commerce.[4] Their annual Watermelon Festival is not just well known for drawing large crowds or for large watermelons, but for the sweetness of the fruit.

Among the pioneers, a woman by the name of Susannah Ball took an interest in educating the children of the group:

> She organized one of the first schools, which she called the Ball School … The love of learning and educating their descendants was passed on to other generations of the families, and years later, Warren Ball gave land for another school, which he named Promise Land. The families of Rawlings, Ball, Mobley, James, Pinkston, Dethrow, and Brewer sent their children to this one room school.[5]

John's parents also instilled many values in him from an early age. Growing up in those times, during the days of far less technology and prior to modern distractions, family life was vital in building character. John's father was farming and running a sawmill at the time of his son's birth. He taught John the importance of character and virtues such as never being late, including the importance of performing everyday chores around the farm, such as how to harness the family's fine team of horses with the leather shined and the horses curried. He learned to pull the Spaulding hack to the front of the old farmhouse, tie the horses, and wait on his mother and sisters before going into town.

There was the ritual every weekend of washing, and so his mother taught him the importance of cleanliness. But if ever there was a wild bronco, it was young John. Having to wash him was a task his mother dreaded, and so did

---

3   "A Brief History of Cave City, Arkansas." *Cave City Area Chamber of Commerce:* *http://www.cavecityarkansas.info/history.html* (February 21, 2013).

4   "A Brief History of Cave City, Arkansas." *Cave City Area Chamber of Commerce:* *http://www.cavecityarkansas.info/history.html* (February 21, 2013).

5   *A History of the One-Room Schools of Sharp County.* (Windmill Pub., 1986), 11.

John. He never did like her scrubbing his ears, and later in life, he attributed this to their being so large. His mother would grab him by the ear and say, "Now, son, you might as well hold still!"

He would flinch at the roughness of the washcloth in his ear and shy away.

"Wait!" his mother said. "I don't have it all out."

Thus went the weekly pre-Sunday school ritual.

As he grew older, John's parents taught him many lessons, things that at the time seemed insignificant but stayed with him in his memory into adulthood. His mom might pull ears, but his dad pulled something else!

First Samuel tells the story of the woman Hannah who was barren until she prayed to God that if she could have a son, she would give him back to the Lord. In the same way, Dr. John's mother made a similar vow, that if God gave her a son, she would give him back to God. And that's exactly how it happened. Later, as an adult, John described his mother as "the sweetest any boy could ever have."

She was a virtuous, devout Christian woman who was married to an unsaved man for many years until later when she herself led her husband, George Washington Rawlings, to Christ. Before that, John's father came from a nonreligious background, a wanderer traveling the frontier country because he had no real roots. Despite having only an eighth grade education, he read everything he could get his hands on, which exposed John to good literature. John's father was an unusual person.

John's mother had fallen in love with and was engaged to be married to a man who was killed in an accident. Later, she and John's father were brought together, but John was never sure if they were deeply in love with one another or not. John described his mother as a beautiful woman with coal-black hair, large brown eyes, a smooth complexion, and dimples in her cheeks. His father loved her, but John was never sure if she loved her husband so entirely. She had a deep religious conviction about her family. Some people at the time may have believed she made a mistake marrying an unsaved man.

Life was always a little tough in those days, even for John as a little boy. As one of the first men to bring a modern cotton gin to the area, close to the time of the Eli Whitney days, John's father operated a cotton gin, dairy, blacksmith shop, and two sawmills, as well as cut and floated virgin timber to New Orleans. Before, they would pick the seed from the cotton, and the country women would make batting, which they put on the spinning wheels and made into clothes. They did the same thing with the wool from the sheep. John's father didn't make much money, but he worked hard and was also chair of the Aetna school board.

At the age of two years and four months, John was stricken with a disease prominent in those days, of which about twenty-three children his age in their area died. John was one of three children who survived and the only boy. John's body was swollen. The country doctor came to their home and told John's mother that her son wouldn't live. John's father was working at the sawmill and came home that night to learn from his wife what the doctor had said. Being unsaved, he was frustrated because his only son was going to die. He then left home, leaving his wife alone with their three children.

John's mother paced all night, carrying John and praying. At about four o'clock in the morning, she gave him a very primitive treatment, and by daylight, his fever had abated. At about ten a.m., the doctor arrived on horseback. "Amanda, God has answered your prayer!" he said.

John was weak, and it took several months before he learned to walk again. His godly Christian mother taught him to read the Bible at the age of two and a half. By the time he was four, she had led him through the entire Bible. Because of his two older sisters, he begged to go to school and was enrolled at four years old.

When John was almost eight years old, his father was shoeing a horse in his blacksmith shop. John remembered to his dying day the smell of the coal smoke on that warm spring day as he played in the back of the shop. Suddenly, his father said, "Son, come here!"

As usual, John didn't argue with his pa. His father never had to tell him anything twice; once was enough to prompt obedience. He stood in front of his father, who stood with one leg resting on the anvil, his elbow on his knee. "Son, I want to ask you a question."

"Yessir?" squeaked John.

"Son, what is your name?"

John was trembling, but he knew better than to break down and cry in fear in front of his father. The tears were on his cheeks because he didn't understand what was taking place and was afraid this meant trouble, and trouble meant punishment. John said, "My name is John William."

His father said, in his quiet way, "That's right. Where did you get that name?"

"Well, it's my Grandpa Rawlings's name, and it's Grandpa James's name, and it's Uncle John James's name."

"That's right," his father approved, "but what is your *other* name?"

After a pause, John said timidly, "Rawlings."

"That's right. Where did you get that name?"

Now John was shaking, and his tears were flowing freely. "It's your name."

His father said one last time, "That's right." He went on this time: "now look at me," which John did. With steel-blue eyes and in a soft voice yet with a ring of steel, he went on, "That is my name, and don't you *ever* bring shame or reproach on that name."

Barely above a whisper, John promised, "Yes, sir. I never will."

His father put his big, strong arm around him, pulled him close, and then kissed his brow. "You can go play now."

John was an entrepreneur at seven years of age. The family had a sow with eight piglets, four little boars and four little sows, but the mother had cholera or some kind of disease and because of this, she had to be put down. John's father was going to put the piglets down as well.

But being a country boy, John loved animals and everything on the farm and didn't want the little piglets to die. Even before he was saved, he knew in his heart he would be a preacher someday. Whenever a little chicken, kitten, or other animal died, John would preach a funeral.

"Papa?" he asked his father. "Give me those pigs."

They didn't have bottles and nipples in those days, so he had to improvise. He found a white cloth, went out into the field and milked a cow, warmed the milk, and absorbed it in the cloth. In a matter of minutes, he had coaxed the little piglets into sucking the cloth.

As the piglets got older, John castrated the boars and built a pigpen in the yard. Once they were grown, he traded his three boars and was on his way in the hog business. His mark was a split in the right ear and a bit in the left ear. It wasn't long until he had dozens of hogs and then a couple of horses. The environment did not dictate to John; rather, he dictated to the environment!

Growing up on a farm, animals were important to him. "Anything that wiggled, I had as a pet," he would say later to his grandchildren. There were goats, possums, rabbits, and red squirrels on the farm, as well as typical farm animals. His favorite pet was a little goat; they were good friends. Every summer, his mother would buy him a straw hat, and the little goat would always eat the brim off. His mother would give him a "shellacking" for it!

John even trained a cat to hunt with him. First he would use his dog to track a rabbit in a hollow log and then take his hunting cat and sit her in the opening of the log. After she chased the rabbit out, he would catch it. He caught squirrels this way as well.

For a time, John had a "toad-frog" for a pet that he named Sally and fed bugs, ants, and other creeping things. Sally lived under the porch; to call her, he made a sort of whistling sound, and Sally would come out. At that same time, he had his own BB gun with little round pellets. One day when he was playing with Sally, he casually flipped a little round pellet for his BB gun toward his toad-frog. She licked it up, so John tried another one. Sally ate that too. John continued until he got all of his little pellets into her. Feeling somewhat guilty, he got his dad's old razor and his mother's needle and thread. He knew how to paralyze frogs and now had the chance to put his unusual talent to use. He turned Sally over onto her back and gently scratched her belly. Then he took his father's razor, carefully split her belly open, and began to pull out his BB pellets. When he had them all in his hand again, still stroking her belly, John sewed her back up with the needle and thread and put a salve over the stitching. Sally lived and healed nicely, and John "became a surgeon, formally."

Even though he worked hard and kept busy, John still managed to get into trouble. He got along well with his two older sisters, Audi and Nona, though he did quarrel more with Nona. In fact, he later admitted with a wink and a chuckle, "Nona beat me up all the time."

Once as a little boy, John was playing cowboys and Indians. He happened to stumble upon his sisters' dollhouse unlocked and open, and the idea struck him that he could be just like a real Indian. Excitedly, he took out his sisters' dolls, scalped them, and with pride hung the scalps from his belt. But soon the voices of his approaching mother and sister startled him.

"The Spirit of God moved me to start running," he tells the story, so he took off, but to little avail. His sister caught up with him about a half mile down the dusty country road and "beat [him] into a pulp!"

John and his sisters attended Aetna School, a tiny one-room schoolhouse located halfway between Mount View and Cedar Grove churches about seven miles east of Cave City. "Aetna School produced some well-known persons. There were many schoolteachers. There were nurses, bankers, dentists, doctors, preachers, an Air Force colonel, and many well-known cattlemen and farmers."[6]

John liked school; he made friends with just about all the other students. When he grew into his teenage years, Glenn Cobb became his best friend. The Cobb children would often visit the Rawlings family home, and he and Glenn spent many hours together, especially double-dating with their sweethearts. Often they went to parties together on Saturday nights.

John loved to play baseball at Aetna; his position was second base. At sixteen, he was also a local long-jump champion, and at seventeen while attending Cave City High School, he was offered a basketball scholarship to an Arkansas junior college but was unable to attend because he was needed on the farm.

It was not as a teenager that John first learned adult lessons. When he was only nine years old, he learned how to drive. This happened one particular day when he took the family's Model T without permission and ended up running through a white picket fence. When his father discovered this, he said, "Well, you got it in there, you can get it out." And John did. Three years later, at twelve years of age, he drove that same Model T all the way from Cave City to Batesville and back, a distance of twenty-six miles. Even at ninety-eight, he continued driving. Surely he must hold the world record for longest-driving man!

Growing up on the farm and attending Aetna School surely helped build John's character as he grew older. His chores on the farm varied. The horses and hogs needed to be fed, the cows needed milking, the corn had to be picked, and the ears had to be thrown into the trough for the animals. The Rawlings family grew cotton as well as corn, beans, potatoes, peas, peanuts, and hay. John grew up around folk in the logging, woods, and timber businesses. Down in the Delta country, he saw men injured and killed, which matured him quickly.

As God prepared David of the Bible as a young shepherd boy to later become king, the Lord used John's humble upbringing and a praying mother to prepare him to become a great soul winner. Growing up on the farm taught him virtues and a work ethic that would stay with him as he became the man the Lord wanted him to be.

---

6   *A History of the One-Room Schools of Sharp County.* (Windmill Pub., 1986), 3.

3

The Glorious Gospel

*From that home and that teaching today I stand, a man
of God, called to preach the glorious Gospel.*
—DR. JOHN W. RAWLINGS

As a little country boy, John would lay on his stomach for hours, watching the ants toiling in the sun. He would wander through forests and valleys, watching birds and other animals. He would get on his horse and with his dogs trotting alongside ride out into the big woods for hours and sometimes stay overnight. He loved the big woods and its nighttime sounds. He would listen "and hear sounds that the human ear is not really supposed to hear.

"I owe today to my parents and to the generation in which I was born my love for nature," Dr. John later said. "From infancy to adolescence, until I reached the age of accountability, I did not have one single doubt that God had created everything." This universal truth that we can connect with our Creator through His Creation is found in Romans 1:20, "For the invisible things of [God] from the creation of the world are clearly seen, being understood by the things that are made, even His eternal power and Godhead; so that [men] are without excuse." One can realize the existence of God merely by observing the beautiful complexities of nature. How could everything be made from nothing?

Much of the godly influence in John's young life came from his devout Christian mother, who was a living testimony of God's love. She would often read to the family sermons by J. Frank Norris, the famous and controversial Baptist preacher from Texas. His paper, *The Searchlight,* arrived at the Rawlings's household each week. This paper was first introduced to the Rawlings family by an itinerant preacher and John's great-uncle on his mother's side, John Robert Lewallen. The front page of this newspaper portrayed Norris victoriously gripping his Bible in one hand and a searchlight in the other while Satan cowered below.

John Robert Lewallen visited the Rawlings family when John was about thirteen years old and sat down with them in their living room while John's mother cooked in the kitchen. He pulled out an issue of *The Searchlight* and suggested they subscribe to it also. At that time, in the community there was only one church service per month, so beginning after Lewallen's visit, the family would read from *The Searchlight* on Sundays when there were no services. The introduction into the family of Norris's paper was one of those defining moments that would change the direction of John's spiritual walk and the course of his life.

The Rawlings family also owned an old Silvertone radio and would listen to Norris's sermons on the radio. John dreamed of hearing him preach in person. By coal-oil lamplight, John's father would read sermons by famous preachers, such as Charles Spurgeon, to the family on Thursday nights. John's mother never missed a church service and did everything in her power to ensure her family went with her. In those days, circuit-riding preachers were the lifeblood of the church community. If the Methodist preacher was preaching at the Methodist church, John's family would go there; similarly, when the Baptist preacher was in town and conducting services at the Baptist church, they attended there. Still, as a young boy, John sometimes didn't take things like church attendance very seriously. He did go to Sunday school—his teacher was a Methodist, teaching in a Baptist church.

In those days, according to Dr. John, the "hillbilly mountain men" didn't go to church much, and when they did visit, they would remain outside so they could smoke and chew their tobacco. They were referred to as the "Spit and Whittle Club." Sometimes during the sermon, members of the congregation were startled to see the men's faces peering in the windows to see what was going on inside. Most men in the Spit and Whittle Club were not believers, but John's father enjoyed talking with them about crops and things. John, who wanted to be strong and important like his father, thought it was a big deal to skip church. But if he tried to, his mother would take care of that. His father had a razor strap about three inches wide that he sharpened his straight razor on that his mother used to discipline her son, or as Dr. John put it, "To put whelps on my little butt when I skipped church to hang out with my daddy and those hillbilly mountain men."

But the Lord's hand was on John in both mountaintop and valley experiences. One such valley experience came to the Rawlings household one fateful morning.

Eight-year-old John and his family were up early for chores. Sitting at breakfast table as John's mother bent over the old cookstove, preparing the meal, they suddenly heard sharp barks and growls in the distance. The children looked up in alarm as their father leapt out of his chair and took the shotgun from above the door. He hurried outside; John held his ears as shots echoed outside the little house across the open range of the farm. John's mind immediately went to the sheep, particularly to his little pet lamb, which was crippled, and he feared for its life.

Audi, Nona, John, and their mother went outside. When they opened the door, a flock of sheep fought their way to the barn.

John just knew the dogs outside had already killed several of them. Dreading the worst, he followed his mother outside. In the yard, there was his little pet lamb, following its mother. John's heart sank when he saw the blood streaming from its neck. One of the dogs had torn the flesh all the way to the vein. The mother sheep came near John and his mother, and the baby fell to its knees and then to its side.

As farmers, John and his family were very close to the animals, and it always broke their hearts to see one of their pets wounded. John began to cry as his mother knelt beside him. She put her arm around him and told him about another lamb, the Lamb of God. Jesus Christ died and shed His blood for the atonement of mankind's sin.

"I didn't need to be told that a second time," Dr. John remembered. "It stayed with me. It's with me today, more precious than ever. [Jesus] died that I might live. I didn't ignore what Mama said. She implanted it in my mind and heart."

Still, it was not at this age that John personally received Jesus Christ as his own Savior, even though the message was always near his heart. Even before he was born, his mother had dedicated his life to the Lord to be a preacher, and John was aware of this calling even before experiencing salvation.

At age thirteen, John performed saddle bronc riding in an adult men's rodeo. Saddle bronc riding, rodeo's classic rodeo event "evolved from the task of breaking and training horses to work the cattle ranches of the Old West. Many cowboys claim riding saddle broncs is the toughest rodeo event to master because of the technical skills necessary for success."[7] John rode a mean bronco that had been brought in off the range. The bronco was rearing up on his hind feet, swinging John like a lasso. As John's head spun inches away from the corral fence, ten thousand things ran through his mind. He knew he would die if his head struck the fence. With superhuman effort, the cut-off horse rider was able to stop the horse from whirling for a moment, and John freed his foot from the stirrup. Other than bruises, he was unharmed. Nonetheless, the experience troubled him because he realized that, had he died, he would have gone to hell. So after arriving home that evening, John stormed up into the hayloft in the barn to vent his frustration and confusion. He knew he should repent of his sins and accept God's gift of salvation, but he pushed the thought aside yet again.

Two weeks later, a revival was held at the little country Baptist church where John's family attended. John was under deep conviction, and his father, though he himself was unsaved, recognized this. John's Methodist Sunday school teacher played an important role in leading him to Christ. One afternoon during the week of the revival, John's father found him on the old tire swing behind the house. "Son, if you need to go to the altar tonight, I'd like for you to go." He spoke from his heart, even though he himself had not yet been saved.

During the church service, John's father said in his strong, silent way, "Son, I'm impressed that you seem to think you need to go forward when Brother Wilkerson gives the invitation." With tears in his eyes, his strong chin trembled. "Would you for my sake go forward?"

"I did business with God that night," Dr. John testified, and he was born again.

The third night of the revival, under deep conviction, John left the building at the time of the invitation and stood at the foot of the hill below the church. In the beautiful moonlight and starlight, it seemed the whole world was weighing upon John's soul. He looked up into the starry sky and said to the Lord, "God, I can't run away from you." The voices of the country congregation carried down

---

7   "Rodeo Events: Saddle Bronc Riding." *101 Wild West Rodeo*:
     http://www.101wildwestrodeo.com/info/saddlebronc.htm (March 15, 2011).

the hill from the small church, singing the words of an old Methodist hymn, "O Why Not Tonight":

> O do not let the Word depart
> And close thine eyes against the light;
> Poor sinner, harden not your heart,
> Be saved, O tonight.

As quickly as his thirteen-year-old legs could carry him, John ran back up the hill and into the church building to make his way forward to the altar. He told the preacher, Brother Edgar Wilkerson, that he wanted to be saved.

"John," said the pastor, "you've been coming forward every night."

"I know it," John said. He confessed that the last two nights he had been telling God how good he was. That he had seen men killed in the logging woods, had been in the livery stable where men who hauled freight in wagons had fights, played stud poker, and shot dice … but on that third night, sitting on the home-built church bench with his elbows on his knees, he prayed, "Dear God, if you don't save me, I'll go to hell." Something glorious happened then. John thought he heard music from heaven like voices of angels, a song in his heart. He went outside and sat in the driver's seat of his father's Model T, and the stars had never seemed so bright. His family came out, and he drove home. When they arrived home, John stood in the dining room doorway and knew he would never forget his mother's radiant face and sweet smile when she said, "Son, you've been saved."

His father was saved during the same year. When John was fourteen years old, one year before the Great Depression, his father suffered a terrible accident in a sawmill. While installing a drive belt on a wheel, he became locked in the wheel, which struck his chest, broke some of his ribs, and punctured his lungs. He was near death as he rode in a Model T Ford to a clinic twenty-four miles away with blood running from his mouth. He remained in this near-death state for a month. John's mother stayed with him, and John assumed the responsibility of running his father's business and farm. Immediately thrust into the role of an adult, John "became a man."

One of the men John worked with at the sawmill was a foreman who, for four days, challenged John, calling him names and declaring he would refuse to take orders from a "fuzzy-faced so-and-so." John realized he could either go home and cry or assume leadership. In those days, men carried switchblades and guns, as self-preservation was the first law of life. John withdrew his switchblade and said, "In ten seconds, I'm going to cut you to pieces." He counted to five before the foreman threw up his hands with an apology and said, "You're the boss." There were about twelve to fifteen other men standing around to whom John demanded, "Anyone else have anything to say?"

They all replied, "No, you're the boss."

That's when John believed he grew to manhood. He did admit, though, that on many nights he cried himself to sleep. He was mentally and physically exhausted from filling his father's role as head of the house and provider. He had to get up at 4:00 a.m. each morning to be at the cotton gin by a little after daylight. On the farm, all of the cows had to be milked, the horses fed, and cotton pickers assigned to their work. Thus John's childhood was rather short-lived. He sold and bought cotton, transacting business by the age of fourteen according to all that his father had taught him.

That year, cattle robbers passed through their part of the country. The cowboys were driving the cattle after they purchased them. A herd of cattle of about two hundred passed through the delta country. John and his father were out working the farm, and they could hear the cowboys yelling and the whips cracking. His father said, "Son, those cattle that we have—you go to the corral and sell them."

"Dad, I don't know what kind of price!"

"Some of these cattle are yours," he answered his grownup son. "You'll never learn any younger."

John got on his horse and rode to the corral to transact business with the three buyers. John showed them the fifteen head of cattle, five of which were his and ten his father's. He told them what he would take for them, but the buyers laughed, saying the price "was out of line." John asked what they would be willing to give, and once they had negotiated a price, John had successfully sold the cattle. With pride for his accomplishment, he rode back to where his father and the other men were working in the field and gave his report of the sold cattle. His father praised him saying, "Son, you did a good job." Whether he actually got the full value of those cattle he was never sure, but he was proud to have his father's approval. He felt like a real man.

The years of the Depression took their toll on the Rawlings family's business until nearly everything was lost. Like many other families, they survived by living off the land. During this time, John considered different options for his future, but all the while, in the back of his mind, he knew he was going to have to preach. Though he was saved at thirteen years of age, he did not follow in believer's baptism until he was fifteen. Because of his Methodist background, no one told John he ought to get baptized, as no one explained that baptism is an act of obedience after salvation.

Edgar Wilkerson, pastor of Mount View Missionary Baptist Church, baptized John in a creek. Once the preacher had baptized John and lifted him out of the water, he proclaimed, "I just baptized a Baptist preacher!"

4

Orelia

Cheers to a memory of friendships made, that lasted, and lasted, and lasted!
—MRS. ORELIA RAWLINGS, "OUR COUNTRY SCHOOL"

At Aetna School, John met his wife, Orelia, when he was but five years of age. She was a year ahead of John in school, but they were attracted to one another from the beginning.

Even before John began attending Aetna school, his mother taught him how to read, and he also knew the alphabet and multiplication tables by the time he was four-and-a-half. In the cotton country, communities had summer school, the two months between the harvest of the later crop and the time when farmers began picking cotton. On John's first day of school, he went with his sisters, Audi and Nona, and sat with Audi in the double-seated school desk. Little Orelia came by, put her hand on John's head, and prophesied, "I'm going to marry you when you're old enough." She was six years old at the time.

Orelia was born on August 16, 1912, the third of four children to Henry and Ethel Mobley. Like John, Orelia had two older sisters, Letha and Amy. The Mobley family had been hoping for a boy when Orelia was born, which may have been the reason her parents gave her the middle name of Willie. Three years later, Orelia's mother delivered a baby boy, whom she and her husband named Clark.

The Mobleys owned a farm about eight miles east of Cave City, Arkansas, and about 120 miles northeast of Little Rock. Mobley, Arkansas, named after Orelia's family, remains today a sparsely populated ranchland.

Orelia was twelve years old when she received Christ. The defining moment in her young life took place at an old-fashioned Brush Arbor revival meeting sponsored by Mount Tabor Methodist Church. Her parents were staunch Methodists and insisted that Orelia be sprinkled as a young child according to the custom of the church. About ten years later, after she had married John, she was baptized by immersion in the Curia Creek by Edgar Wilkerson, the pastor of Mount View Missionary Baptist Church and the mayor of Cave City, Arkansas. In later years, John would often jest, "When Orelia married me, she saw the light and became a Baptist!"

In the old country schoolhouses, they did not have the luxury of restrooms or even an outhouse. "You just got behind rocks and trees," Dr. John recalls fondly. The boys would chase one another around one big rock in particular, and some of them would sneak around when the girls would go down to the "rest area." John never participated in this mischief, though.

The one-room schoolhouse had tongue-and-groove walls with gaps as wide as two inches. The girls sat on the right side of the room, and the boys sat on the left. Because the boys and girls were divided, John and Orelia sat two seats apart. Notes were passed across the aisle, and John would hide his in a knothole in the wall.

During one particular summer, bumblebees had built a nest underneath the weatherboarding. A few devilish boys pulled the boards loose, and John's love notes from Orelia fell out for all to see. The boys giggled as they read the letters and passed them around the room for the other students. The teacher, Clyde Puckett, quickly collected the notes, and when recess had ended, said, "I think before we start studying, John William will come up front and read some of his notes."

Poor John turned scarlet with embarrassment even though, as he said later, "There wasn't anything too sexy about them." But as John read the notes from Orelia expressing her love for him, his classmates clapping and shouting, "Carry on!" John was compelled to read about a half dozen of his notes. "I wanted to either commit murder or hide!" he would laugh when telling the story. "Orelia and I were both popular, so anything the kids could get on us was real gossip."

Many years later, Orelia sat at her kitchen table with her grandson Steve and typed out on her old black Royal manual typewriter a poignant poem for her grandchildren, based on her memories from her school days at Aetna in Sharp County, Arkansas, 1920:

"Our Country School"

In the Ozark hills by the roadside stood,
A schoolhouse dear to us children.
So quaint, so small, yet boasting it could
Of two trails, a bell, and a cistern.

No spacious views, no well-mowed lawns
Or playgrounds with swings and fences.
Out of bounds for us was the huckleberry bush,
Or, "just where the hill commences."

No tile on the roof, or paint on the door,
But hearts that were eager for learning.
No halls, no stairs, but that didn't matter.
'Twas for knowledge that we were yearning.

Kids walked to the school, many miles some of them.
Two miles, three miles, and four
With books in their arms, and smiles that would charm,
Some came with feet that were sore.

On cold winter days when children arrived
With frostbitten toes and noses,
We rushed each one to the old cistern shed
And bathed them till cheeks looked like roses.

But once inside with each at our desks,
We settled for a long day of learning.
Or for turns we strove, by a potbellied stove, to stand
While pine logs were burning.

The best time of all when the teacher would call,
"Recess! But be in at two."
You hurried to stand, to hold a friend's hand
And wait for the team to choose you.

The games that we played were simple and gay
Like horseshoe, softball, or just hiding.
Then girls chased the boys,
And boys chased the girls,
Steal a kiss if no one was looking

How well I remember our first basketball
That arrived in a mail order kit,
When I close my eyes I sense the surprise,
And the smell of that leather yet.

We had no gym or basketball court,
So hurriedly we all went to work,
With axes and saws, and hatchets and hoes,
We soon were down to the dirt.

We smoothed, and smoothed, till the place looked to us,
Fit for a major league game.
Then we watched with pride as our teacher chose sides,
And began the pupils to train.

We brought our lunches in pails and satchels,
And set them in corners so neat.
It seemed that noon never would come,
Then alas we were ready to eat!

One day a pig from a nearby farm
Decided to invade our lunches.
While out for recess the unwelcomed guest,
Ate them all with oinks and crunches!

I still remember the well-worn path
That led to the old hollow stump.
At last recess we raced down that path
As our heart gave a thump, thump, thump!

You see in this stump the boys had hidden
Crumpled notes to each of us girls.
As we would read ... to tell you no need,
They sent all our heads in a swirl.

Sometimes there were rhymes, but most of the time,
For words there were only a few,
But the line from the start that captured our hearts,
Was the special one, "I love you."

Some left from this school for lives of success,
While others had hopes and plans blasted.
But cheers to a memory of friendships made,
That lasted, and lasted, and lasted![8]

Things went well for John and Orelia as children, but several years later, as adolescents, they experienced their first breakup. It happened during a revival one hot summer evening in August. After the meeting, John began the long walk home, deep in thought about the breakup. At one point along the path, there was a ditch about twelve feet deep, and those who took this path had to turn left to avoid the waterhole in the ditch. John was so disturbed about the breakup that he "failed to negotiate the turn" and fell into the waterhole. "I thought I was going to hell until I fell into the water!" he says.

At this time in his life, John was attending Cave City High School. His neighbor, Mr. Bowers, who was quite "well-to-do for those days," owned a Ford, which John borrowed to drive to school in Cave City. He had completed all of the available grades at Aetna, but he still visited often because he loved to play basketball. One Sunday afternoon, Glenn Cobb, John, and a couple of other boys were out driving. They came within a quarter of a mile of where Orelia and her family lived, and John spied a car parked in front of the Mobley family's home, which he recognized as belonging to the father of one of the boys

---

8   *A History of the One-Room Schools of Sharp County.* (Windmill Pub., 1986), 3.

on John's basketball team. Apparently, the young man had a date with Orelia. John didn't like this at all. He still had a crush on her but had not seen her since August. Now it was February, and he had been busy at school during the week and on the farm on the weekends.

Several days later, Glenn Cobb came by to see John. "We're rehearsing a play," he said. "Why don't you go with me?"

John had just arrived from basketball practice at Cave City and was finishing his chores. At first he hesitated, until Orelia's name happened to come up. Apparently, she was playing the queen of the production. Immediately, John's interest was piqued; he liked the idea of Orelia being the star of a play. He walked to Aetna School with Glenn, but when they arrived, they discovered only about half the cast had come to rehearse. "That's how country people do things," Dr. John laughs.

But Glenn's girlfriend was there and Orelia too. John followed Glenn into the schoolhouse and was given the role of the king. When Queen Orelia touched his hand during the play, Dr. John says, "That's where it all started."

Orelia, known as the foremost beauty in the neighborhood, was considered quite a catch. During their courting, her father made a great impression on John. Though he didn't like this young boy very much at first, John liked Orelia, and that made a difference.

John, 17, and Orelia, 19

Mr. Mobley was a music teacher, and one of John's favorite activities at the Mobley home was the music. The family would gather around their old pump organ and sing together. "They were singing all the time," Dr. John reminisces.

Other families would visit to sing with the Mobley family as well. Orelia's brother Clark wrote music, taught piano, and published several songs each year. All of John's family members were also musicians; the James family once had a choir and an orchestra. John's uncle Porter James could play "just about anything" and organized his own dance band. Porter was the brother of John's mother. According to Dr. John, he was a wonderful man. "He was about six two and one of the most handsome men you'd ever see with dark, curly hair, dark eyes, and olive skin. He played violin, guitar, banjo, mandolin … he could play anything."

By the time John was eighteen, he thought it was time to settle down, get married, and become a prosperous farmer. Orelia, nineteen years old at the time, accepted his proposal of marriage, and on February 13, 1931, she and John were married. It was a simple ceremony at the little Aetna School, performed by Justice of the Peace, Burl Crabtree. It cost the nervous groom $2.50. Four witnesses were present: Orelia's sister Amy, Amy's future husband Earl James, and two friends, Christina Pinkston and Owen Lewallen.

John and Orelia in 1931

Earl James was one of John's best friends as a teenager. He later became fondly known as "Uncle Spot" because of a speck in his eye. Earl was the eldest of five boys. His dad was John James, a younger brother of John William's mother. At the age of thirty-two, Earl's father died from a ruptured appendix. His wife, Sara Lee, was expecting their fifth child when he died. This meant that young Earl, twelve years of age at the time, had to assume the responsibilities of a father. John married Orelia Mobley and Earl James married her sister Amy. Earl and Dr. John remained friends for many years, and kept in touch. Earl lived past the years of a centenarian to the age 103.

John never went to college, for his father had been in a terrible accident, and from then on, John provided almost all of the household income. Like Earl James, John had to assume a great responsibility at a young age. At age twenty, he was Sunday school superintendent and teacher.

John and Orelia, now Mrs. Rawlings (as she was called for most of her life), settled on a cotton farm. At age eighteen, John made a commitment to preach the Gospel, but it was not until age twenty-three that he followed through with his decision to pursue full-time ministry.

5

Herb and Harold

Behold, children are a heritage from the LORD, the fruit
of the womb is a reward.

—PSALM 127:3

John and Mrs. Rawlings were blessed with their first son, Herbert Max, in 1932. Herb was born at home, as the closest hospital was in Little Rock, 120 miles away. "Women had babies at home. You were fortunate if you got a country doctor there," Dr. John explains.

When Mrs. Rawlings went into labor, John's neighbor Charlie Cordell rode his horse to alert John, who, with his mother, hurried to the house.

Mrs. Rawlings was struggling. No one, not even the doctor, could think of a solution, so John took the lead and told them, "I'm going to get on the bed with her and turn my back to her face so she can put her arms around my back and hold on. I want a midwife on each knee to put her foot on the bed and hands on her knees. And I'm going to place my hands on her stomach, and when the birth pains hit, I'll push gently. With all of us working together, the baby will be born."

Dr. John smiles. "And that's what happened."

He was still just a teenager at that time. Yet he was already exhibiting his natural leadership skills. "I don't mess around with those things," he laughs.

Two years later, in 1934, there was a period of time of frequent storms and floods. One blustery Thursday morning, Mrs. Rawlings was in the throes of labor, and the midwives said the baby had turned the wrong way. John knew he would have to brave the storm raging outside the small farmhouse to call a doctor.

It was over seven miles to Cave City, Arkansas. John mounted his favorite horse, Tony, and rode heavily toward town to fetch Dr. Layman. Once he arrived, John hurried to the barn behind the house and saddled the doctor's horse while the doctor collected his things.

Together John and Dr. Layman started the difficult return trip. By the time they had traveled one mile back to John's house, the creek had risen substantially. On the first leg of the journey, Tony had swum the creek successfully.

Dr. Layman's horse plunged into the water up to his chest, but he panicked, whirled around, and lunged out of the water and back onto shore. John tried to lead the horse, but he balked. John and the doctor tied the horse to a tree, and John told the doctor to get his saddlebags with his equipment. The doctor would have to ride Tony.

"See that tree on the other side?" John yelled over the raging storm and creek. "Keep that between the horse's ears. He'll swim!" John could hardly swim himself but said he could hold onto Tony's tail. "But if you let him drift and we get down below that bank, we'll all drown."

Tony sank into the water up to his chest, and it grew even deeper. John guessed this was the deepest point, probably about twelve to fourteen feet deep. Tony began to swim, and the doctor held his saddlebags up to keep them dry. John held onto Tony's tail with the hair wrapped around his hand.

The current was swift and Tony drifted, but they made it successfully to the other side with about six feet to spare. Tony's muscles rippled as he lunged out of the water and onto the bank. They felt as though they had barely made it. John told the doctor, "I'll walk, and you go on."

By now, Tony had traveled nearly fourteen miles. When the doctor arrived at the Rawlings household, the baby's navel cord was wrapped around his neck. The doctor later said that if he had gotten there even five minutes later, the baby would have died of suffocation. John gave his wonderful horse Tony all the credit for saving baby Harold's life.

6

To Die Is Gain

For to me to live is Christ, and to die is gain.
—PHILIPPIANS 1:21

In a recorded tape entitled "Memories" by John's cousin-in-law, Earl Lewallen describes living on "cotton-field farms" and on property adjoining his cousin John's farm during his childhood. He recalls as a young boy walking to church services with John's mother, whom he referred to as "Aunt Sis." She was also often lovingly called "Aunt Sissy." Earl loved her, and she fondly called him her "preacher boy" even though he was just a boy at the time. As an adult, Earl became a Baptist preacher.

Mrs. Rawlings's father and Earl's mother were siblings. Also, John Rawlings's grandmother James was a Lewallen and a sister to Earl Lewallen's grandfather. Therefore, John's relation to Earl Lewallen was twofold. Earl graduated from Oklahoma Baptist University and was a member of the American Missionary Baptist Association.

Earl and his family attended Mount View Missionary Baptist Church. He and his family would walk about a mile and a quarter, and then Aunt Sis would meet them down about "half a quarter" from their house, and they would walk together to church. That was back when they didn't have gas to run the "old T Models." Sometimes there would be as many as three cars in the parking lot, yet the church was full. "Aunt Sis was one of the greatest, most spiritual, sound ladies," Pastor Lewallen says.

However, Aunt Sis's son-in-law "was wicked," according to Pastor Lewallen. He was cruel to the horses and to his wife, Aunt Sis's daughter. Aunt Sis was so burdened; she would go down to the stalls when there was nobody around and pray for those abused horses and for her son-in-law to find Jesus.

During the service on a Sunday Morning in 1937, Aunt Sis, as a respected prayer warrior, was called on to lead prayer. A large crowd was in attendance.

Her twenty-three-year-old son John was saved, but according to Pastor Lewallen, "He was backslidden, oh, how backslidden he was! He wouldn't surrender to preach."

Pastor Lewallen describes her ardent prayer. "Lord," Aunt Sis pleaded, "whatever it takes in my family, get them right with You. If it takes my life, take it. I'm ready."

That was on Sunday. On Monday, she became ill, and a doctor was called. On Tuesday, she was still sick, and they called in another doctor.

On Wednesday morning, Earl looked across the field where he was plowing to Aunt Sis's farm and saw many cars parked in the yard. "I tied up my team, walked over there in my plow shoes and straw hat on, wet with sweat, and the yard was full." There were fifty to seventy-five people there. Earl worked his way through the throngs of people and went into the house. He wasn't there five minutes until Aunt Sis died. It was never known what caused her death. She was fifty-five years of age.

Her son John, kneeling at her side, sobbed, "Alright," he cried out to God. "I'll preach!"

In praise to the Lord for John's commitment, shouting broke out in the room, on the porch, in the yard, and down to the barn—and were heard from everywhere. Everyone remembered Aunt Sis's prayer, and although they would miss her dearly, they trusted in God's plan.

The death of John's mother had a profound spiritual impact on his life. In a sermon he preached many years later on July 9, 1978, he spoke of the day his mother was buried. "That hot May afternoon that I buried my mother, we turned and drove back to my dad's old place. That old log house, those grounds; I had always loved them. It was home. I walked down in the back pasture. I couldn't stand it.

"I thought I was alone, but suddenly I realized someone was nearby. It was my father. He, too, had gone to walk around. There were horses grazing in the field. One of my favorite horses was in that field, and I tried to pet him. He seemed to understand. He put his nose up against me and fondled my face. I had cried every tear I had in my soul.

"I sat down on a big rock in that pasture, and my dad sat down with me. I said to my father, 'I don't believe I can stand it.'

"'Son, we will have to,' my father answered.

"Have you ever been like that? You say, 'I have never had to give up my mother.' If you love your mother like I loved my mother, you would know what I am talking about.

"The time came when I could stand at her little grave—that little old tombstone that has one verse of Scripture on it—'To die is gain'—and I could look up and say, 'Someday, Mother, I will see you again.' The desert is past, the flowers bloom, and the birds sing.

"Peace, oh, thank God for peace!"

Aunt Sis was buried on a Thursday. And also, just as she had prayed, her son-in-law was also saved.

Earl Lewallen tells the story of his own mother and her life's prayer: that one of her children would become a preacher. "Lord, if it could please You, give me at least one preacher boy." Between her sons and grandsons, God granted her seven! He answered her prayer as specifically as He had Aunt Sis's.

Earl Lewallen surrendered to preach under John's ministry. He heard John's first sermon, and John heard his first sermon. During a revival meeting they organized together, Earl surrendered to preach and John invited Earl to preach his very first sermon. Dr. John mischievously states, "Before the service, the Holy Spirit moved me to steal [Earl's] sermon notes."

When Earl nervously stepped forward to speak, he saw that his sermon notes were nowhere to be found. "Well, folks," he said uncomfortably. "I've lost my sermon." So he had to rely on the Holy Spirit to speak through him for the remainder of the service.

Once, John brought a revival meeting to the 104th District Schoolhouse. There were very few Christians in this community; in fact, there were "just a few ladies." John preached sermons for a week and a half, and although he preached his heart out, he never had one convert. However, because he had opened this new church, Earl Lewallen was able to preach there a year later. During the first and second meetings, there were just a few in attendance. During the following meeting, one extra person showed up. But by the end of the week, the church was full; children sat on the floor at Pastor Lewallen's feet.

Seventeen grown men made decisions for Christ, in addition to several women and children. John was faithful in forming the church, and Pastor Lewallen followed in his footsteps until many lives were changed.

Thus, Aunt Sis's legacy lived on through John and his family as well as Earl Lewallen and his family. She trusted in the Lord and prayed a prayer that changed the course of the Rawlings family history.

7

Miss Huckaby

*Let brotherly love continue. Be not forgetful to entertain
strangers: for thereby some have entertained angels
unawares.*

—HEBREWS 13:1–2

In 1939, *The Searchlight*, the newspaper first introduced to the Rawlings family by
John Robert Lewallen, announced the founding of a new school for "preacher-
boys" called the Fundamental Baptist Bible Institute (later called the Bible Baptist
Seminary and then Arlington Baptist College) by J. Frank Norris. John had for
a long time been impressed by Norris's writings in *The Searchlight*. Instead of
furthering his education at the Little Rock School run by Dr. Ben Bogard where his
family expected him to attend, he decided to pursue studies at Norris's new school.

Known as the "Texas Tornado" and the "Texas Cyclone" because of his
flamboyant style as a "hellfire and brimstone" preacher, Norris often encountered
controversy in his ministry. At one point during his career, he shot and killed a
man, but he was soon exonerated in the name of self-defense. "No other event in
Norris' long career brought him such national notoriety as did the tragic killing
of D. E. Chipps, 49, on Saturday afternoon, July 17, 1926."[9]

---

9   Homer G. Ritchie, *The Life and Legend of J. Frank Norris: The Fighting Parson*, 1st ed.
     (1991), 155.

Norris's life and his family had been threatened repeatedly, and his church had even been burned twice. Because he had been fighting the gambling syndicate in Texas, he had faced all kinds of adversity. One of his opponents, Mr. Chipps, had been to the saloon one time too many, and when he stumbled into Norris's office on Saturday afternoon and reached into his pocket for a handkerchief, Norris thought he was reaching for a gun. Before Mr. Chipps could draw, Norris fired his own gun first.

As one of the most controversial fundamentalist preachers during his time, Norris's church, First Baptist Church, was the first to be excommunicated from the Southern Baptist Convention, which marked the beginning of the Independent Baptist Church movement. Norris served at First Baptist for forty-four years until his death. With the announcement of the founding of the Fundamental Baptist Bible Institute, John became the first male to enroll as a ministerial student at the seminary, which he referred to as the Bible Institute, in Fort Worth, Texas.

When John surrendered to the call of the ministry, he realized the need for preparing himself for this great work. He was like Elisha, who wanted a double portion of the spirit of Elijah and also his mantle. John knew the teaching of experienced men who had labored for the Gospel for twenty, thirty, and even forty years would be the most profitable of all schooling for him, echoing the old adage: "A man can chop faster and better with a sharp axe than with a dull one, although it does take time to grind it." With the opening of the Bible Institute in October 1939, John hoped it would be the kind of school he so desired.

As Bible teacher and Sunday school superintendent at his church, John would have gone into training then, but he wanted to wait and go to Norris's seminary. Dr. Benny Beaugard, a friend of the family, had spoken at John's church and said he was going to start a school, which he wanted John to attend in Little Rock and "wear his mantle." But after reading Norris's paper, John had a feeling in his soul that Norris's school was where God wanted him. Beaugard told him, "You've got the personality to be a debater," but John couldn't head in that direction. He had his heart set on attending Norris's new seminary, the Bible Institute.

However, 1939 found John struggling to leave his farm in order to transition into ministry. He faced the difficulty of limited funds, as there was a recession in the country during that time, and that part of the country was especially affected, as many citizens were still feeling the effects of the stock market crash of 1929. Despite these hardships, John and Mrs. Rawlings had been successful;

they owed no debts and owned horses, hogs, and sheep as well as cattle on their own farm and in an adjacent county about eight or nine miles away. John still had Tony, his beautiful saddle horse.

One day, during the return journey from visiting his cattle, John stopped by his brother-in-law's farm, where he and John's sister were picking cotton. Mrs. Rawlings was expecting their third child, who would later be born on Herb's seventh birthday, September 2, as Carrol Clark Rawlings.

After visiting with his sister and brother-in-law, John remounted his horse and set off for his father's farm. He passed by the house but didn't stop, even though he was supposed to leave Tony at that barn. Instead, he took the lane around the house that led back to his own farm, just a quarter of a mile away.

Mrs. Rawlings was sitting outside in the yard on a quilt under a shade tree. John rode Tony to the picket fence, dismounted, and sat down next to his beautiful wife. "Sweetheart," he said. "I'm going to Fort Worth. We're leaving the farm. I've made my decision." He paused. "Let's go down to Granddad and Grandmother's."

Mrs. Rawlings's parents lived about a mile away. So John lifted Herb and Harold onto Tony's saddle, and together they walked to Mrs. Rawlings's parents' home.

Her father was none too happy to have a Baptist preacher for a son-in-law; he already wasn't too fond of John anyway. But after telling the Mobleys their plans, John and Mrs. Rawlings went to John's father's house that evening and shared their news with him. John also needed to speak with his grandpa and grandma who lived four or five miles away. "They were very fragile," he remembered.

John rode Tony to his grandparents' home and greeted them. They were his mother's parents, William and Martha James. She was "a dark-skinned Dutch German from the Blacklands (the Black Forest) of Germany. John's granddad was blind and had long, white hair and a beard that reached to his waist. He had memorized a lot of Scriptures and often would sit in his house and quote Scripture with a fixed expression in his eyes. "My old granddaddy was such a giant in the Bible and committed so much of it to memory long before he lost his eyesight that he could sit and quote Scripture by the hour and would shout and rejoice and praise God while a wheelchair victim for eighteen years. He taught me more than they taught me in theological seminary," Dr. John said.

When John told his grandparents he was leaving for Texas and came to say good-bye, his granddad said, "Son, come over here." He was sitting in the shadows of the log house. After John came beside him, he said, "Get on your knees." He put his wizened, crippled hand on John and murmured, "I want to pray for you."

As he prayed his wonderful prayer, "that little grandma" was standing over John, and when he felt something wet falling on his face, he realized it was her tears. Her arm was around him as she stood, crying.

Later in life, with a glimmer in his eye, Dr. John would tell this story to his grandchildren, imparting to them the wisdom that "a child that has something like that as an inheritance from his granddaddy can't help but have some success."

He later had one regret about his grandparents. When he returned home from Fort Worth at Christmastime later that year, he was so busy preaching and the weather was so bad that he didn't make time to visit them, and they both died during the last of January. His grandmother died ten days after her husband of pneumonia she had caught at his funeral.

Within two weeks, John had taken care of much of his business. He sold some of his livestock and bought a ticket to Fort Worth. Granddad Mobley, John's father, and John's brother-in-law took him to Batesville. By this time, his third son Carrol had been born, an event that took John's eldest son Herb by surprise. His parents came to him and said solemnly, "Herb, we have a surprise for you."

Overjoyed, he asked, "What is it? A watermelon?" He hadn't even noticed his mother's pregnancy over the past months and was shocked (and perhaps a little disappointed) to find out the surprise was not a juicy watermelon but a new baby brother, Carrol.

From Batesville, John caught a train and had a layover before changing trains to head to Newport. He then had to change trains yet again to Little Rock before he could get on the train to Dallas, Texas, and another from there to Fort Worth, where he arrived at four o'clock on Saturday afternoon. He was already homesick, carrying nothing but a little cardboard suitcase and a shoebox at his side. He had brought some biscuits with country ham and little jars of molasses and butter.

When he arrived at Fort Worth, all he knew was he had to get to First Baptist Church, the nation's largest Baptist church at the time with about five thousand in attendance where J. Frank Norris pastored. John looked up at the stoplights; he had heard of them before but had never seen them until now. He asked a man nearby, "Could you tell me where First Baptist Church is?"

"Yeah," said the stranger. "Go up this street about sixteen blocks to Fourth and Throckmorton." The light changed, and the man was gone.

John hesitated for a moment before setting off to walk the sixteen blocks to First Baptist Church. When he arrived, he was dismayed to find everything locked. As he walked around the outside of the huge building, he began to pray. Of all things, he found the side door unlocked.

After letting himself in, he walked down the long hallway into the large auditorium. He paused and stood in awe, overcome with emotion. He had read J. Frank Norris's paper and listened to him on the radio, and now he felt like Moses standing on holy ground. But the great room was empty. John walked to the back of the auditorium and sat down in a lonely pew. Overwhelmed, homesick, and uncertain, he began to cry. Suddenly, he heard a voice ask, "Young man, what are you doing?"

John glanced up, startled, to see Miss Jane Hartwell, "an old maid" and one of Norris's personal secretaries. "I'm here to enroll in the school."

She blinked down at him. "What are you doing here?" she repeated.

He was beginning to feel somewhat agitated. "I don't know anybody, and I don't know anything. I'm just looking for somebody to help me with some information."

Without smiling, she stared down at him. "Come with me."

He rose from the pew, trailed behind her through the auditorium, and followed her into the office.

"Do you want to stay in a hotel?" she asked.

"I don't have money." He had a little left over from his travels but not enough to pay for a hotel room.

"Well, let me think." She made two or three calls while John waited uncomfortably. One of the calls was to a woman with whom the secretary chatted for a while. But John wasn't paying attention to what they were saying; he was too busy thinking about his dilemma and what could be done about it.

Then Miss Jane Hartwell hung up the phone and said, "Young man, there's a tenement house down this street about six or eight blocks. There's a vacant room, and she's just cleaning it. And she can take you."

"Well, I appreciate it." He paused. "How much?"

The secretary answered, "She'll tell you."

John picked up his little cardboard suitcase and started out on Fourth Street and then turned right onto Fifth Street where the tenement house was located. By then he had learned green lights and red lights!

He went into the tenement house to find the owner, a short, heavy-in-the-middle, apron-wearing woman named Miss Huckaby. "Young man," she told him, "I'm cleaning this room. My tenant just moved out." Other that that, six or seven people lived there.

Miss Huckaby led John to his new room. It had a straight chair, one little table, a bed with wheat straw as the mattress, a quilt, a pillow, and a little forty-watt bulb. The restroom was down the hallway.

Emotionally and physically exhausted, John sat down in the chair while she was making the bed and started crying again. Miss Huckaby came over to him, put her arm around his shoulder, and cried with him. "Honey, don't you cry," she murmured. "I was going to charge you a dollar and fifty cents for this room, but I will knock a quarter off, so it will only cost you a dollar and a quarter a week." She bent over and kissed him.

"My mama died, and I left a wife and three little boys," John managed to say.

"Well, I'll be your mama."

That was the start of a beautiful friendship. John lovingly recalls Miss Huckaby "was like one of those angels that you encounter."

Three years later, when J. Frank Norris was having a Bible school at First Baptist Church, John preached before the great T. T. Shields. He arrived early and asked one of the janitors, a black man, "Could you tell me where a woman by the name of Huckaby lives?"

"Yeah. She's down here in the [nursing] home. She's blind."

John walked about four or five blocks down from the church and went into the home. "I'm here to see Miss Huckaby," John said to the woman at the desk.

"She's down this hallway in room six."

"Thank you. I'm a friend of hers—an adopted son."

After knocking on the partly open door, he went into Room 6 and said, "Miss Huckaby?"

"Yes?"

He smiled. "You know who this is?"

The familiar, kind voice answered, "Yes! It sounds like my boy!"

"Yes, it is your boy."

Miss Huckaby was sitting in a little old rocking chair. John kneeled, put his arms around her, and kissed her.

"Oh, honey," she said. "It's so good to see you."

John kissed her hand, and she rejoiced to be reunited with her "son." He told her how much he loved her and what she had meant to him.

8

Seminary

And every one that hath forsaken houses, or brethren, or sisters, or father, or mother, or wife, or children, or lands, for my name's sake, shall receive a hundredfold, and shall inherit everlasting life.

—MATTHEW 19:29

The Bible Baptist Seminary

John said good-bye to his wife and children, left the Arkansas farm, and headed to Fort Worth, Texas, arriving friendless and uncertain. The first person to make him feel welcome in his new environment was Miss Huckaby.

After settling into his new room at the tenement house, John went to First Baptist Church and met with Dr. Louis Entzminger, Norris's Sunday school superintendent. An Old Testament professor at the Bible Institute, Entzminger was a driving force in the modern Sunday school movement in America as well as an associate of J. Frank Norris for many years. Entzminger at that time had led the reorganization of twenty-three of the twenty-five largest Sunday schools in America, and he and John became good friends.

Working with Norris, Entzminger established a Sunday school that set an example for churches throughout America.[10] He became famous for the Six Point Record Keeping System, which was later implemented by the Southern Baptist Convention at large.

Norris used to tease, "Entz couldn't preach his way out of a wet paper sack," but his accomplishments were many. Not only did he lead in the Sunday school movement, he also developed an administrative system to equip churches to establish successful Sunday school programs and instruct Sunday school teachers to keep good records of their class attendance. Records included names, addresses, and phone numbers typed out on an old manual typewriter. If someone missed class, their Sunday school teacher would visit them in their home based upon the information in the records. Entzminger printed "The Berean Banner," which was described as "the uniform, whole Bible lessons for the whole family." Teaching timely truths of Scripture, these lessons empowered teachers to grow their classes from a firm biblical foundation.

On his first Sunday morning in Fort Worth, John attended church at First Baptist, home of Entzminger and Norris. In fact, Norris's eldest son stood in the narthex, greeting visitors. He met John and bought him a cup of coffee and a doughnut in a little café there. John went to his Sunday school class, and over the course of the next few weeks, the two men became good friends. J. Frank Norris himself had just gotten back from the Middle East and was preaching that Sunday afternoon at Will Rogers's coliseum. John caught a bus and went to the meeting.

In December 1939, John surrendered to go to Africa as a missionary at about three a.m. from his rooming house in Fort Worth. The next morning,

---

10   Dr. Mike Zachary, *Remembering the Old-Fashioned Sunday School* (North Valley Publications: June 2004).

he told Mrs. Rawlings about the experience. "Strange as it may seem to some of my friends," he tells the story, "God never wanted me to go to Africa as a missionary. He wanted me to be willing to go to someplace or anyplace He might lead me."

John was considered Norris's prize pupil. Norris had a great impact upon young John, who was quick and eager to learn. Norris once told him, "I know you're going to be a leader, and you're probably sharper than a lot of the professors. You need to go ahead and become a pastor."

Shortly after John arrived at the Bible Institute, a fellow by the name of Jackson, a teacher whom Norris had fired, began watching John and was impressed. He called and asked him to take over his class. Even though he didn't have a car, John took the man up on his offer to teach the class and doubled the attendance in just a few short weeks.

Looking back on the time he spent learning from Dr. Norris and others at the seminary, John said that the school exceeded his highest expectations in every way. John's study of Scripture began at the beginning of the book with Genesis 1:1 and continued throughout the whole Bible. "We spent two weeks studying the first two chapters of Genesis," John remembered. "There we found the origin of many of the great doctrines of the Scriptures, such as the doctrine of God, the doctrine of creation, the doctrine of inspiration, the doctrine of the Holy Spirit, and the doctrine of man." Studying Scripture book-by-book, chapter-by-chapter, and verse-by-verse proved to be the most profitable of all methods of study. Norris told him, "If you memorize that book, your ministry will be much more effective." And John memorized it in a year and a half. He drove himself relentlessly, eating and sleeping only when he had to. He buried God's Word in his heart because he knew he would need it when he became busy "out yonder" in ministry.

From Norris, John learned the art of attracting a crowd. One method included always fighting and standing up for truth. Another profitable line of study John pursued in school was character study. He and his classmates were required to memorize Scripture having to do with the lives of the heroes of the faith, such as Abraham, Isaac, Jacob, Joseph, David, Paul, Peter, and, most importantly, the life of Christ. The students at seminary also scrutinized prophetic Scriptures. John believed the wonderful thing about this was that their study was not limited to future events so much as to the evangelistic side of the Word.

The unity of the students at the Bible Institute was an inspiration to John, who cherished the memories of kneeling with his entire class in prayer to thank the Lord for what He had done for them and what He had taught them as they sought wisdom and knowledge. One moment that touched John deeply was a prayer service just before Dr. Norris was about to leave Fort Worth for the first time after his return from Europe. With the responsibility of two churches upon him as well as so many other things, the students' prayer moved him as they all knelt together during the service. This man whom God was using in such a mighty way poured out his soul to God, and it seemed that they were in the very presence of God in that moment. It reminded John of when King Solomon prayed for wisdom to lead the people of Israel.

John learned to mirror Norris's unusual style of preaching. Norris, an avid scholar of both biblical and world history, was able to speak extemporaneously for the length of a sermon, a skill that is extremely rare from the pulpit. As Jesus taught using parables, Norris used stories in his sermons as illustrations, which John also found effective.

Much of what John learned during the time he spent under Norris's leadership proved useful in his ministry throughout his life, such as Bible study techniques. A thorough knowledge of Scripture was foundational to both Norris's and John's preaching styles. However, realizing that reciting Scripture in its entirety was too difficult, Dr. Norris taught John to memorize verses based on people, places, and events. For example, memorizing entire chapters, John would write and memorize a word outline of each chapter in each book of the Bible and learn to recall the stories told in individual chapters. As a young pastor in Tyler, Texas, he preached and spoke as many as eighteen to twenty-two times a week. As there was not enough time to prepare for each individual sermon, John simply delivered them on the spot as his thorough knowledge of Scripture allowed.

Outside of his classes, John used every opportunity to perfect his preaching skills, speaking whenever and wherever he could, even on street corners. He spoke at the Fort Worth courthouse with fellow student John Birch every Saturday night. Norris had brought a sound truck down to Fort Worth from Detroit, knowing that John was a responsible young man who had gained experience. With the sound truck, John held services on the street and worked specifically with young people to build up the youth department at Norris's church.

On occasion, John traveled from Fort Worth back to the river country in Arkansas to hold revival meetings. Two of the churches he visited included his own childhood churches Mount View Missionary Baptist Church and

Cedar Grove Baptist Church. The revival meetings were so successful that John reconsidered his life calling. Had the Lord called him to be an evangelist rather than a pastor with a home church? After some time off to be alone and reflect in prayer along the tranquil waters of the Mississippi, John communed with God and felt his call to pastor reconfirmed. To prepare for this calling, John returned to seminary at Bible Institute to train as a soul-winning pastor.

While attending seminary, John began preaching in Euless, Texas. The little independent church there had nearly died because its founder left shortly after starting the church. During John's first service there, five people were present, three of them family members. But in two short months, he was running about 150 in attendance. He would "thumb his way out," or hitchhike, to the church and back to seminary because he didn't have a car. On Saturdays, he would visit members of the community, recruiting new members. He would get up before daylight and stand by the road and catch a ride with cowboys or ranchers. Then he would stay in Euless until everybody went to bed. For food, he would "feed off the ranch." While out visiting, John would walk into people's homes and ask, "Hmm, that smells good! Are you baking a cake?" It worked every time. His hosts kept him fed physically, and he kept them fed spiritually through prayer, Bible reading, and conversation.

Soon a big meeting was held at the church in Euless; they were going to call a pastor during their large dinner. John didn't stay for the meeting. He borrowed a car from his school friend, Mr. Hughes from Illinois, and waited to go out until after the business meeting.

A man by the name of Bell was called as pastor even after John had increased it after just a couple months. It shook him, but despite his complaints to the Lord, God didn't seem to be paying attention. John soon sobered up and focused on getting his heart right before God. "If that's the way you want it, Lord, that's good," he finally admitted, and so he dismissed it. John learned not to dwell on things that didn't work out but rather put them out of his mind and waited for God to open another door.

9

Miracle in Springfield

*As for that in the good soil, they are those who, hearing
the word, hold it fast in an honest and good heart, and
bear fruit with patience.*

—LUKE 8:15

John's Graduation from Seminary (left)
and the Rawlings Family in 1940 (above)

In May 1940, John's first year at seminary was drawing to a close, and soon the Bible Institute saw its first graduating class. After the Sunday service, Dr. Entzminger approached John and asked about how he would be spending his summer. "What are you going to do now?"

"Well, I'm going back to Arkansas where I came from because I don't have anything to do here, and I want to do some preaching if I can back in that country during the summer."

"I'm going to Springfield, Missouri, to reorganize High Street Fundamental Baptist's Sunday school," answered Dr. Entzminger. "I need some help. I can't pay you anything, but I think the members will provide food and a place to stay, and you can help me. It will be a good experience for you."

John was more than happy to have this chance to work with Dr. Entzminger. The next day, he caught a train in Hardy, Arkansas, and made his way to Springfield. Entzminger covered his travel expenses, which was something in those days. John headed to the church of High Street to conduct a religious survey with Dr. Entzminger, and they had about fifty-seven hundred prospects.

While in Springfield, John stayed with the Montgomery family. Bill Mactier, who was pastoring a church in a small town of about 118, and John became friends. John also worked with a young man named Charlie Pringle in the reorganizing, a typist who had just graduated from high school and nephew of the church's pastor, Charlie Dyer. They worked with the list of prospects, organizing them into categories. John was there for about a week and a half, and during their time there, they doubled the Sunday school attendance. John extended his time for another week, and Dr. Entzminger fished down at the lake while John did his work for him.

John did learn a great deal from Entzminger, who empowered him to think for himself and get work done. Entzminger said in a class on prayer one day, "There will be days when you pray and it just seems everything opens and you know beyond any doubt that God has answered prayer; it's so evident; it's there. But you'll pray prayers and there's not anything that happens. But our heavenly Father has a way of handling us; sometimes He'll say, 'Wait awhile,'" Entzminger said. "When you have prayed and there's no concrete evidence God has answered that prayer about that matter, use your best judgment and make a decision and go ahead and do it. And if it's not the right one, God will turn you in the right direction He wants you to go." John learned to operate by this premise, and even though he made a few mistakes along the way, he turned them into stepping-stones.

As Entzminger wisely taught, we cannot always know God's will expressly, but we must act according to His principles and allow Him to govern our steps as we walk forward boldly and obediently. John was hoping to get the pastorate at High Street and thought he would get it, for he believed he preached well when he spoke there. But he didn't get called and, in fact, didn't even know if he even got one affirmative vote. Mactier didn't receive the pastorate there either; a man named Dowell was called, and he and John became friends shortly after that.

After learning through his experience in reorganizing High Street Fundamentalist's Sunday School and then the disappointment of not receiving the pastorate, John headed back to Cave City, Arkansas, without anywhere else to go and wondering what God was doing. After drinking from a fire hydrant at seminary and now that the miracle in Springfield was over, suddenly all doors shut with a bang, leaving John very discouraged. What was he to do now? After those times of everybody wanting to hear him—the cowboys he preached to at the wagon yard, moments God wonderfully blessed—now not a single door would open. John had lived in the fast lane but now even just a few short days passed painfully slowly. In despair, John spent the night out on a rock pile by himself. He told the Lord as daylight was coming, "If you don't open up something, I'm going to California and am getting out of the ministry because if I'm going to try to serve somebody and every door is closed, I'm not going to do this."

Daylight came and with it John's brother-in-law Webster Cordell for a visit. John had led Webster, his mother's brother and his favorite uncle, to Christ in 1937. "John, let's go down to your uncle's," Webster suggested, referring to Uncle Daniel James, who lived about seven miles from there.

John and Webster rode down on horseback to his uncle's. From there, Uncle Daniel wanted to take John in his Model T Ford touring car down to the 104 District near the Black River. "You know you might get that building there to hold a revival." It had been about fifteen years since a man named Barry Wilson had tried to hold a revival, or "protracted meeting," there, and the river rats or "wild boys" had come and broken up the meeting. From the summit of the high hill behind the church, the men had thrown rocks during the service. The stones pelted the tin roof, and the loud noise frightened the congregants. Meanwhile, the men cut the stirrups from the horses' saddles in front of the building and removed the wheel nuts from the churchgoers' wagons so the wheels fell off when the families headed home. Since that day, no one had tried to hold a protracted meeting again.

John and his companions got in the car and drove down to Sam Lyle's five-hundred-acre farm along the creek. John had known Sam, whose father had been a friend of John's father, although Sam was much older than John. He had seven boys and a daughter and was chairman of the school board. When they pulled up to Sam's in their Model T, he was baling hay in his cowboy hat, puffing on a crooked-stemmed pipe.

Uncle Daniel said, "Sam, John is trying to make a preacher." (That's how they worded it in those days.) "He'd like to have a place to preach, and I thought maybe he could get the 104 school building." In those days, they held school and church services in the same building. At the time, John's second cousin Phillip James was teaching at the one-room schoolhouse; Phillip later wrote six textbooks that were used by Harvard, Yale, and other eastern schools.

Old Sam Lyle carefully filled his pipe with Prince Albert tobacco, pulled off his hat, puffed on his pipe, and looked up into the sky. "Well, I'm just ignorant. My boys are growin' up heathens. I'm sorry to say, but my boys have never heared a sermon. It could be that God Almighty has sent you here so my boys can hear a sermon."

"Well, Sam, what do I have to do to get the building?"

"John William, I'm chairman of the board. They do what I say." You could already feel the Spirit of God as the farmer turned to John and said, "John William, you can have the building. My boys might get religion. I'm a sinner, so I don't guess there's any hope for me."

"Well, we'll go on over and see two other board members just to make it easier," John said.

"You don't have to because you can have the building, but you can if you want. When do you want to start?"

"Wednesday night at eight o'clock."

The family climbed back into the Model T and drove down to the 104 school and church building.

"John, it's nice to have you!" John's cousin Phillip said. John asked him if he could announce the revival to the "youngsters," and Phillip was happy to comply.

As planned, John started his meeting on Wednesday night. He had a single songbook and no piano, but he managed to lead the mere seventeen people in attendance, all women and children, in singing "We'll Work Till Jesus Comes." He sang the same verse three times as he tried to get them to sing on key with three kerosene lamps and a lantern the only sources of light in the little room. On the second night, there was a young chap in attendance, Charlie Lewallen's youngest boy and a distant relative of John's. He had a country band back in Jonesboro, Arkansas, that produced live shows on the station in Jonesboro. He said, "John, do you have anybody leading the singing? Would you like me to try? I'll help you."

"Okay," John agreed. "Anything's better than what I'm doing. You lead the singing, and I'll do the preaching."

Instead of religious songs, most of them were western.

John preached from that Sunday evening through the following Sunday morning, without one single soul coming to a saving knowledge of Jesus Christ. By the third night, however, the building was packed to the gills, with people spilling out the door and standing outside. Still, no men would come in, for that was the culture in that area. The women and girls stayed inside and the men out, while John stood in the door to preach to them all.

Soon, word reached the "wild boys" in the river country that John was bringing a revival to the area. They made plans to tar and feather John and run him off. But a rancher in those parts by the name of Oliver Rider, a man from a well-to-do family, came by the third day of the revival when John happened to be out visiting (he would walk over fifteen miles a day to visit the ranchers and farmers in the area). Oliver Rider had once shot a man down in the Delta country; John's dad and Uncle John James had witnessed the event. Oliver pulled out his .38 and pulled the trigger on the man, who was kneeling on his knees begging Oliver not to kill him. They had fought over a woman.

That day of the revival, Oliver came to John because he knew his family. "John, I hear that they're going to try to run you off." He knew the river rats, the "wild boys," had it in for John and were planning to tar and feather him.

"Yeah, the rumors are they're gonna break up my meeting!" said John.

"Son," Rider answered. "I'll be here at church tonight, not to hear you. But there won't be anybody botherin' you."

John preached for another week, and still not one soul came to Christ to be saved. On Sunday, the last day of the meeting, Oliver Rider stood in the back of the church. John begged him to come to the altar and get saved. He was as white as a sheet of paper as he looked John in the face and answered, "John, I told God to leave me alone a long time ago, and I'm going to hell when I die. I like your preaching, but don't bother me."

Despite the fact the meeting did not appear successful, John had sown many seeds that later came to fruition. His wife's cousin Earl Lewallen preached at the same church the next year and saw seventeen grown men and a good many teenagers saved. All of Sam Lyle's boys got saved, the youngest of which later became a preacher and took a pastorate in California. Even Sam himself was saved!

It turned out to be a miracle after all. It simply took some time for the seeds that John had sown to take root and flourish.

10

Back to Seminary

A crowd won't remember what you said unless you couch it in language and in personality for them to remember!

—DR. JOHN W. RAWLINGS

That summer, John preached another revival at the Church of Christ outside of Tuckerman, Arkansas. The building was large for those days, seating about five hundred people. John preached two weeks there, but at one point, a riot occurred, and John was nearly thrown out. Nonetheless, several people were saved, but the whole ordeal left the county shaken for a time.

John himself was shaken in his health; he weighed only 137 pounds and felt as if he were bleeding from the inside. August was passing, but John had several revival meetings opening up as far away as Memphis, Tennessee, as word was spreading about the young preacher. Despite his apparent success, he was troubled. He told Mrs. Rawlings, "Honey, I've got to get alone. Something's got to happen."

He borrowed a nice saddle horse from his friend who owned a cotton farm nearby and took his .22 rifle with him into the old sloughs, or swamp-like region, of the Delta country where turtles and snakes were in abundance. He rode his horse about three miles to one of the sloughs, shot snakes for a while, and prayed. He didn't eat anything; he only spent time with the Lord. He told the Lord he would cancel all the meetings and go back to seminary in Fort Worth because that was the burden that weighed so heavily on his heart. This was one of the great turning points in John's life. Though he was only twenty-five years old, he felt sixty years old in experience.

When he came back home, he told his wife, "We're going back to Fort Worth." Being the good wife that she was, she trusted her husband and didn't argue. In less than ten days, John loaded his wife, Herb, Harold, Carrol, and all their meager belongings into a borrowed 1932 Ford pickup. A trip that should have taken only eight or nine hours ended up taking thirty-four hours! John and the two oldest boys sat in back with furniture piled all around and over them while his wife and nursing son rode in the cab with the driver, Mrs. Rawlings's brother Clark Mobley. To protect the belongings in the truck bed and those who took turns riding there, they fashioned a tarpaulin.

Six times during the 650-mile journey, the truck broke down and had to be repaired. Three tires had gone flat during the memorable journey, and at one point the engine had actually caught on fire. By the time they arrived in Dallas, the brakes were no longer working, so they drove the final miles to Fort Worth without them. Mrs. Rawlings was so exhausted from the ride and thankful when it was over that she proclaimed she just wanted to lie flat on the ground.

The Rawlings family moved into a little one-room apartment on Fifth Street in the Mexican district of Fort Worth. They were, of course, very poor at the time. One day, a secret benefactor left a twenty-five-pound sack of peanuts on their front porch, which the family survived on for the ensuing weeks. Also left on the porch that day were tiny toy trucks for the two oldest boys, Herb and Harold.

During those days at seminary, John witnessed to all he met at school, at home, and in Tyler when he became the pastor of a little church while still a student in seminary. "How well I remember the old drunkard, gambler, and murderer down in East Texas that I led to Christ," Dr. John would begin telling a story:

> His oldest son was a 'lifer' at the Atlanta prison. His next son committed suicide, and I conducted his funeral. On his old man's dying bed in the Mother Francis Hospital in Tyler, Texas, he told

.a friend of mine, 'You tell Dr. John that when he leaves this world, just inside the gates, I'm gonna be there to welcome him because he cared for me when no one else cared.

Every day on his way to seminary, John would pass that gambler, drunkard, and bootlegger's home as he left for the old bus station. Then, on Saturday night about two or three o'clock in the morning, he would walk by again and see cars there. On occasion, he would speak to the man for a moment. God didn't save this man because he was a murderer, Dr. John believed, although it was said he had seven notches on his gun because he killed seven men. John went to visit him one last time before leaving Tyler; he remembered: "I'll never forget as he put that old skinny arm around my shoulder, face as pale as death—he had cancer then—and he thanked me and said, 'You're the only man that has shown any concern for me.' You talk about a preacher enjoying heaven ... [I look forward to] when I get there and look upon those redeemed souls that I had a little part in winning." John had prayed, talked, and worked with that man for ten and a half years. After he left town, John heard the man got saved. John had planted the seeds!

The Rawlings family lived in a house without hot water and John didn't have a car. Mrs. Rawlings made him sandwiches, put them in a shoebox in his little old cardboard suitcase to see him off each morning, and then washed the children's clothes on a scrub board while he was at school trying to get his education. The Rawlings family later relocated to Gladys Dockstader's attic apartment on Summit Street. Gladys had thrown out the previous tenant so the Rawlings family could room there. One unusual time when John came home from school, Gladys came into John's room in a sheer negligee and approached him. When he refused her by telling her he loved his Lord, wife, and children, she responded, "You S-O-B, I knew you wouldn't do it!" Years later, the same woman and her husband attended a revival John was preaching at First Baptist Church, and they made decisions for Christ. He remembered the night they were "gloriously saved." How disastrous it would have been to both John's ministry and family and how differently things would have turned out had he succumbed to temptation.

Shortly after returning to Fort Worth for his second year at seminary, John was walking down Fourth Street and Throckmorton when he met Louis Entzminger. "John, I've been worried about you. Where have you been?"

"Dr. Entzminger, I've been preaching revivals, but I've been led to go back to school and finish my education. I told the Lord if he'd open up a church for me, I would pastor."

Dr. Entzminger had just the news John needed to hear. The weekend before, he had visited Tyler, Texas, where a little church called Fundamentalist Baptist had recently split. He asked John if he would be interested in visiting the church. When John said he would, Dr. Entzminger answered with a nod. "I'll send a telegram," he said, and he made arrangements for John to preach at Fundamentalist Baptist.

John preached that weekend at Fundamentalist Baptist Church. He rode the train from Fort Worth to Tyler, and two women picked him up at the train station and took him to the hotel. One of these ladies was Mildred Aven, one of the organizers of Fundamentalist Baptist Church, along with two other families from the Tyler area. Mrs. Aven had been converted under John R. Rice during a three-month-long citywide tent meeting in Wichita Falls, Texas. The very first night, Mrs. Aven went forward and accepted Jesus Christ as her personal Lord and Savior. In an article by her daughter, Katherine Aven Goldman, from the *Baptist Bible Tribune* of May 2009, Katherine wrote that her mother attended every night for those three months and became a committed and zealous soul winner.

Mrs. Aven's husband, Matt, had been working in the oil fields of West Texas known as the Permian Basin before moving his family to Smith County in East Texas. They and two other families bought a six-room frame house, took the partitions out to create a small auditorium, and Fundamentalist Baptist Church was founded. This occurred in the late 1930s during J. Frank Norris's pastorate at the First Baptist Church in Fort Worth, Texas. Mrs. Aven and her friends had formed a relationship with Norris's new seminary in Fort Worth through Dr. Entzminger.

The church in Tyler had been in existence for two to three years and, during that time, had been pastored by a Reverend Curtis and later by a Scotsman named Don Frazier. Under Pastor Don and his brother Dr. Bill Frazier, the church split over an alcohol issue, as the Fraziers were wine drinkers. This was not acceptable at Fundamentalist Baptist Church, so the Frazier brothers started a new church two blocks up the street. Mrs. Aven's desire was to see the small congregation of Fundamentalist Baptist led by a full-time pastor, but she realized it needed to grow enough in order to support one. "She drove to Fort Worth to the First Baptist Church and talked to Dr. Louis Entzminger, head of the Fundamental Baptist Bible Institute. He recommended a young student named John W. Rawlings."[11] Dr. Entzminger believed that John had the ability to build a successful Sunday school.

John was to preach at their church that weekend, but after picking him up at the train station that day, they asked him, "Brother Rawlings, we've got a sick call we'd like you to make. We don't have a pastor." On that one visit, John led two people to Christ. They joined the church the next day and got another new couple to join also. And so, in October 1940, at Dr. Entzminger's recommendation, John was called to the Fundamentalist Baptist Church in Tyler, Texas, as Sunday school superintendent. In addition to his duties, he also preached on Sunday morning. A man by the name of Morgan preached on Sunday nights. Although he could preach, he could not pastor.

The Rawlings family lived in a three-room apartment with no hot water and a "two-holder" out back. They lived close to the dangerous area of town where they would hear of a killing nearly every Saturday night.

John commuted back and forth from Tyler to Fort Worth by bus for $4.34 because he didn't own a car. He was paid a "hefty salary" of $17.50 per week. From Monday through Friday, he attended seminary, except one week out of each month when he had a Monday off, at which times he would stay in Tyler. Normally, after his last class on Friday, John would take the bus to Tyler, where he arrived early Saturday morning at 1:45 a.m. In those short four months, John built the tiny Sunday school of Fundamentalist Baptist Church from 37 to 144, all while commuting. During John's time at seminary, he and other independent Baptists were known as a "Norris-ites" by the Baptists affiliated with the Southern Baptist Convention.

On Saturdays, John would knock on doors from morning until evening. When he went home at night to the small, three-room apartment, Mrs. Rawlings would have supper ready. After eating, they would visit until the lights were turned out. It was often the responsibility of their oldest son, eight-year-old Herb, to take care of Harold and Carrol. On Sunday afternoons, John and Mrs. Rawlings would go visiting again. Then early Monday morning, John would catch a bus and travel back to Fort Worth.

In addition to his studies and responsibilities at Fundamentalist Baptist, John followed Dr. Entzminger all over the States and into Canada, organizing and reorganizing Sunday schools. He also worked in the evangelistic campaigns

---

11   Katherine Aven Goldman, "How one woman made a big difference," *Baptist Bible Tribune* 9, no.59 (May 2009), 13.

of Mordecai Ham and B. B. Crimm. Training under personalities like Crimm and Ham inevitably shaped John's persona as well as his preaching style. In fact, he later described himself as Ham's "fair-haired boy," or favorite.

Originally named Birdie Bridges Crimm, later shortened to simply B. B., the six-foot-two cowboy evangelist "gratefully accepted the sobriquet 'Cowboy Crimm.' The nickname probably was acquired during his careers as a rodeo performer and a cattle rustler before he lit out down the Sawdust Trail."[12] But this six-gun totin' cowboy of Indian blood was also a college graduate who dressed meticulously in tailor-made suits and was fond of wearing a thin bolo necktie. One night during a tent meeting, this simple necktie played a pivotal role in an event that greatly impacted John's dramatic preaching style.

About five thousand people were present the night Crimm looked at John and said, "Now, John, I want to show you how to hold this audience."

The music portion of the service over, and it was time for Crimm to take the small, two-by-eight makeshift pulpit. As the audience waited expectantly, Crimm took the microphone. After a pause, he cleared his throat. He reached up and, very dramatically, began to untie his necktie. You could have heard a mouse walking on cotton.

Crimm said not a word. He just stared at the audience, adjusting his tie. Finally, he broke the awkward silence. "If you got what you deserve tonight, every one of you should be in hell!" He then turned around and sat down. Drama at its best! He had the audience's attention.

John learned a timeless lesson that night. "A crowd won't remember what you said unless you couch it in language and in personality for them to remember."

---

12   Gene Owens, "Cowboy Crimm and Dixie Exactitudes," *USA Deep South*: *http://usads. ms11.net/gowens5.html* (February 21, 2013).

11

Awakening

Awake up, my glory; awake[!]

—PSALM 57:8A

Fundamentalist Baptist Church was very small when John arrived in Tyler. Faithful church member R. L. "Bob" Jacobs recalls as a young man seeing John for the first time.

Bob lived about a mile away from the church on North Normandy Street. He had formerly been a teacher of Morris telegraph in Tyler Commercial College. As he walked to church by himself one morning, he saw a young man coming from the other direction wearing a green-striped, single-breasted suit and carrying a great big Bible tucked under his arm. "I will never forget it," Bob says.

This young man coming toward Bob was John. They met right at the church steps. John stuck out his hand. "Howdy, my name is John Rawlings." He gazed up at the little church building and said, "How I would love to build a great New Testament church." The church was small, with only eleven pews—five on one side and six on the other—and without a bathroom, just a commode by the door (around which John later put up sheets for privacy).

That Sunday, there were thirty-seven people in attendance. "Church started," Bob recalls, "and it was a good spirit. Brother Rawlings got up to preach, and I never will forget this either—he was chewing gum." The title of John's first sermon was "The Four *S*'s of Scripture: Satan, Sin, Salvation, and Service." By service he meant soul winning. Bob observed John's preaching style was "a lot like Dr. Norris's: pointed and straightforward."

"Folks," John said to his new congregation, "I'll never forget the first soul I led to Christ. I was sitting on top of the world." His words moved young Bob deeply. "That fired me up as a seventeen-year-old boy and made me want to win souls."

One of the first things John did when he arrived in Tyler was take a religious census. He gathered a group of people early on a Sunday afternoon, fed them, and sent them out across the city. When they finished that weekend, five thousand prospects were reportedly signed up.

During that time, in the piney woods of East Texas, Tyler was a quiet, sleepy town and was recognized as the "Rose Capital of the Nation." There were numerous large nurseries growing roses where they were grafted and then shipped all over the United States. Also known for the Azalea Trail and the annual Texas Rose Festival, "approximately one-fifth of all commercial rose bushes produced in the United States are grown in Smith County, while over one-half of the nation's rose bushes are packaged and shipped from this area."[13] This was after the Roaring Twenties had come to an end and after the bank crash of '29. They were emerging from the primitive agricultural condition into the manufacturing period, when suddenly a terrible drought came upon the country. The decade of the thirties was extremely difficult on the country financially, educationally, culturally, and especially spiritually. However, a lot of wealth had come into the city not only because of the rose industry, but also because of the surrounding oil fields to the east in Kilgore and to the west in Van.

> Tyler experienced a huge economic boom in the 1930s, when the East Texas oilfield was discovered. Numerous oil companies and field developers established offices in Tyler, and the city emerged as an important regional center for the oil and gas industry. Tyler's population mushroomed to 28,279 by 1940.[14]

---

13 "Our Finish Line Area!" *The Tyler Rose: Marathon, Half Marathon, 5K*: http://www.tylermarathon.com (February 21, 2013).

14 "Tyler History." *City of Tyler: A Natural Beauty*: http://www.cityoftyler.org/Vistors/TylerHistory.aspx (February 21, 2013).

Tyler was far enough away for its citizens to avoid the social problems of Kilgore, which was a lot like the Wild West, but close enough to enjoy the wealth. Kilgore was a dirty town and at the time was the center of the largest oil discovery in the world. Nineteen oil derricks stood on one city square block, and every month, hundreds more sprang up in other locations.

Smith County, where Tyler was located, had passed an ordinance stating that no oil or gas well would be allowed there, so many families who had made their fortunes in oil brought their money to banks in Tyler. Large estates sprang up as families relocated there, so Tyler and Dallas became the favorite places for the wealthy to live. Tyler's economy was thriving.

However, according to Dr. Don Walker, there had not really been any strong religious presence in the community for a long time. John initiated the first weekly church visitation programs in Tyler and began a Bible study on Friday nights. Brother J. E. Herrin was one of John's first faithful members, joining him regularly on his visitations. He was a great encouragement to John as they worked together.

About a fourth of Tyler's population was black. Segregation was still prevalent in the community. Blacks were still riding in the back of buses, and restrooms, water fountains, and restaurants were still segregated. Even though blacks attended separate churches from the whites, John was nonetheless invited to preach for many black churches because of his enthusiastic style. Many from the black community were faithful listeners of his radio broadcast when it began about four months later.

In the early 1940s, Dr. James Ulhmer approached John and informed him that a renowned black choir was coming to town. However, they were not yet booked and therefore available for a Sunday morning service. As a promoter and, more importantly, a proponent of spiritual equality and the brotherhood of believers, John said eagerly, "I'll take 'em!" He had only one week to prepare and wondered what reaction this would prompt, given the segregation of the community. One of his deacons demanded to know in a quite profane manner how John could allow this choir to appear in their church.

"They're going to be here this Sunday morning," John reiterated.

"Well, I'm not going to be here then!"

John thought and then said, "Well, they won't be here Sunday night. So why don't you come Sunday night, and you can bring your tithe with you then."

Sunday morning of the performance was standing-room only, and a special area in the front of the church was roped off for the choir members. According to those who witnessed the choir's performance, they "tore the place up." It was a holy revival!

When he first became the new pastor of Fundamentalist Baptist Church, John preached on Sunday mornings and Robert Morgan, a man who worked for the Missouri Pacific Railroad as a telegraph operator, preached on Sunday and Wednesday nights. John, however, could see at the time that although Morgan could preach, he was not a pastor. He and John had their disagreements; for example, Morgan was preaching *against* tithing while John was preaching *for* it.

During his early leadership at Fundamentalist Baptist, John also installed new Sunday school teachers and gave young Bob Jacobs and Jack Bridges their first Sunday school classes. Bob was only eighteen years old when he started teaching junior boys. Jack, at age seventeen, began teaching the primaries. They grew up together under John's ministry, and later, they both surrendered to the ministry. Jack pastored for many years in Houston, Texas, and his younger brother, Jerry, became a successful Christian writer, publishing two bestsellers, *The Pursuit of Holiness* and *The Discipline of Grace*. All three of these men were greatly influenced by the ministry of John Rawlings.

In four months, from October 8, 1940, to February 2, 1941, John built the tiny Sunday school from 37 to 144, all while commuting by bus from Tyler to the seminary in Fort Worth where he was still a student. John was paid

JOHN W. RAWLINGS
TEACHER OF THE LARGEST ADULT
BIBLE CLASS IN TYLER, TEXAS
SUNDAY MORNING 10 O'CLOCK
Central Baptist Church

seventeen dollars a week while supporting a wife and three small children. Fundamentalist Baptist had begun in a little white frame house with less than fifty people but suddenly began to grow. By 1945, John was named "Teacher of the Largest Adult Bible Class in Tyler, Texas."

John spent many Saturdays walking to the "Wagon Yard" just east of downtown Tyler to preach to shoppers and farmers who had brought their produce to town in horse-drawn wagons to sell. The city jail was a stone's throw away, and from John's preaching spot in the Yard, prisoners were clearly visible as they peered out the windows with their arms hanging through the iron bars. In the afternoon, John would head to Lindale, Texas, just three miles north to preach on the street. His efforts there led to the formation of a church that remains successful to this day.

John also went from house to house, seeking new members and witnessing to the unchurched. Since he had no automobile, he walked for miles on both weekdays and Saturdays to speak to people face-to-face about the Savior.

Though the church was growing, First Baptist Church in Tyler was "the big church" and looked down on Fundamentalist Baptist because it was young and independent from other Baptist churches. The pastor of First Baptist called the congregation of Fundamentalist Baptist "the overalls and apron crowd." However, Robert and Stella Welch, members of First Baptist, who were originally members of J. Frank Norris's First Baptist Church in Fort Worth, decided to move their church membership to Fundamentalist Baptist because it was a product of J. Frank Norris's ministry. The pastor of First Baptist was not happy with their decision and tried to call the couple back, but to no avail. Robert and Stella Welch personally bought John his new automobile, a 1946 Plymouth, and they remained faithful members of Fundamentalist Baptist until their deaths.

Prior to the Sunday he was called as pastor, John traveled to Tyler, knowing he would have to take action and be willing to fight for leadership. He knew he had better implement a plan, so he lined up two men, one to make a motion to call him as pastor and the other to second it. He always thought ahead.

John had been called as Sunday school superintendent with a contingency: If the church grew, they would call a full-time pastor. At the Sunday morning church business meeting moderated by Emmitt Bridges, John's two men, Perry McDonald and George Norsworthy, were ready for a motion and a second, assuming the church leaders would honor their word to call a pastor if the church grew.

Emmitt Bridges, the church clerk, stood up and said, "I was authorized by the church to take action [when in fact he was authorized by John], so I must recognize Brother Rawlings as pastor. Someone else second the motion."

Morgan stood up. "Everything is going well. I don't see why we should change." John informed him later that there were changes that needed to be made, and that Morgan would no longer be speaking on Sunday and Wednesday evenings much to his disappointment.

John was voted in with a slight majority, but twenty-seven of those who voted no walked out, resulting in another church split. John went on to preach, and Brother Morgan led the singing.

John moved his family to Tyler shortly after he was called as superintendent and continued commuting to the seminary in Fort Worth to complete his studies.

Under John's new pastorate, the church family quickly outgrew the existing building and was ready to construct a new one. One morning, John gathered "a goodly number" of church members to accompany him before the city council at the city hall to try to obtain a building permit.

The majority of council members did not want to give the permit, but one among them, a Catholic man, spoke out. "I see no reason why these people can't have a permit to build themselves a church." The other council members relented and granted the permit, so construction began.

During construction, a building inspector questioned a building practice and informed John he must halt construction. Dr. John picked up a two-by-four wood plank and chased him off. "Look," he said, "we're trying to build a church; you stay away from here. If you come back, I'll use this on you!" He had a church to build, and he was going to get it done. However, he was often in trouble with inspectors for what they determined to be failure to apply for building permits or not precisely following city and county requirements. John cared more about people than protocol.

In 1941, the auditorium, built near the north side of the previous small auditorium, was completed. The small auditorium was originally a dwelling house, but the original founders of Fundamentalist Baptist purchased it and converted it into a church. This was where Bob Jacobs was saved as a sixteen-year-old boy back in 1939.

The original auditorium was divided into Sunday school rooms, which were separated by drawn sheets. Later on, the little building was bought by Miller Gregory, one of John's "preacher boys," who moved it and converted it back into a dwelling house. The building still stands to this day at 1414 East Houston Street.

On October 8, 1941, the new two-story, fifty-by-eighty foot, cream-colored brick building was dedicated. John remembered the specific numbers: "The contract was turn-key $15,387. We owed the Citizen Bank $800 for chairs and the contractor $1,000 or so. The offerings were averaging $1.34 [per person]."

An ad in the April 17, 1943, *Tyler Morning Telegraph* described Central as a church adhering to "old-fashioned, independent, missionary Baptist faith." In July 1944, Fundamentalist Baptist became Central Baptist Church and adopted a new slogan: "The Heart of Tyler—In the Heart of East Texas."

The founding of Central Baptist Church was a lasting legacy of Mrs. Mildred Aven. Her foresight coupled with the dynamic leadership and evangelism of John W. Rawlings led to a continuing revival in the east Texas town of Tyler, and many souls were claimed for Christ. Dr. Don Walker, friend of the family, testifies, "I think John Rawlings's presence … brought about a Christian awakening."

12

Upside Down

You have been the greatest Baptist preacher in the state of Texas.

—DR. BALES

During John's eleven and a half years as pastor of Central Baptist, the church grew into the largest congregation in all of East Texas, with attendance reaching a high of over three thousand people. Through Central's influence, three auditoriums were outgrown and dozens of new churches were planted in the East Texas area. In the religious history of Tyler, no church had ever made such an impact on the city. Not only was the church growing, but John's family was growing as well. A fourth son, George Robert, was born to the Rawlings family during John's pastorate at Central.

John had a desire to begin a daily radio broadcast, so he went to the radio station KGKB in Tyler to speak with Dr. James Ulhmer, the station owner and graduate of Princeton University.

Dr. Ulhmer looked at John with a little skepticism. "It takes a lot of skill to be able to fill a daily time slot like you are asking for, but I'll think about it."

John left, but the more he thought about Dr. Ulhmer's statement, the more annoyed he became. He went back to the station a week later to meet with Dr.

Ulhmer a second time, only to receive a similar reply. "You need to have a lot of knowledge of the Bible to be able to fill a daily time slot!"

With a nod and a mischievous smile, John replied by quoting Dr. Ulhmer a complete outline of the fifty chapters of Genesis. Then he began with the book of Isaiah. When he had finished, he said, "Would you like me to give you an outline of the New Testament?"

Dr. Ulhmer, dumbfounded, answered, "That's not necessary. What time slot do you want?"

So John got the daily fifteen-minute slot he wanted. He also began an hour-long broadcast of the Sunday evening service, and the *Central Baptist Hour* had its beginning, which ushered in a successful radio ministry that spanned almost fifty years.

Dr. Don Walker remembers, "You could walk down the street on Sunday evening, and people who were not at church would be listening to the *Central Baptist Hour* [from 8:00 p.m.to 9:00 p.m.]. You would hear John's preaching from house to house through the open windows. This was before the days of television [and air conditioners]."

Beginning in 1942, John began preaching in the town square of Tyler and also Brownsboro and Lindale through a borrowed public address system he had connected to his car for amplification. During his time at Central, John preached controversial sermons, so people either really liked him or disliked him.

Bob Jacobs described John as "a fighter ... [not] afraid of anybody." John was no stranger to confrontation. Reverend Fred Harris describes one such conflict. "I saw Brother Rawlings coming down the stairs from his office, and a man who was mad at him was standing at the foot of the stairs. Brother Rawlings stopped a few steps above, and the man really told him off. He didn't like how Brother Rawlings had been preaching."

John waited for the man to finish and then said, "If I wasn't a Baptist preacher, I'd kick you down these stairs."

The man, defeated, went on his way.

Bill Aven remarks, laughing, "Everything happened to Dr. John that could ever happen to a man because he was involved in so many things. No matter what he did or said, there was always a reaction to it. That's what is so unusual about him. He turns adversity around and uses it."

John would often preach on topics of interest and current events. For example, there were two movie theaters in town, and should "a risqué movie come to town," Don Walker remembers, "Brother Rawlings would get on the radio and have something to say about that."

Johnnie Stewart says, "Brother Rawlings was a very colorful character. If things got slow, he'd cook something up." He recalls the town newspaper called the *Tyler Morning Telegraph*, owned and operated by Hugh Vaughn. An article once appeared "giving Brother Rawlings a hard time," Johnnie laughs. "Half the church was ready to get ahold of Hugh Vaughn and whoop him."

However, it turned out that John had "cooked it up" himself to create controversy and "get people talking." His aim was to draw a crowd, and he was quite successful. John thrived on controversy. "I don't care what they're saying as long as they're saying something," he said. He turned the small East Texas town of Tyler upside down.

One such controversy was a sermon John delivered on Acts 2:38, a passage that some consider vital to their belief in baptismal regeneration. However, John contradicted that belief in his sermon, explaining that salvation is not obtained through baptism but by a belief in Jesus Christ alone. The Church of Christ, which believes baptism is a requirement of salvation, was very strong in Tyler. For this reason, John would deliberately advertise his Acts 2:38 sermon and create the kind of controversy for which he became known.

"Any way you look at it," Bill Aven says, "he was always doing something new. If something wasn't happening, he made it happen. He'd come up with a way to make it happen."

Bill and many others described Dr. John's ministry in Tyler, Texas, as a very colorful one. He vividly portrayed biblical truths in unforgettable ways.

In late December 1949 during a radio broadcast, John announced that he would be preaching a funeral the next Sunday evening during the Watch Night service on New Year's Eve. He told them it was going to be *their* funeral. Because Watch Night services lasted until midnight, several other pastors would speak during the service as well, including Pastor Fred Harris.

Dr. John asked Johnnie Stewart, who was working part-time at Thorndike Funeral Home while attending high school, to find a coffin and bring it to the church. Johnnie enthusiastically agreed to help. He had grown up with John's eldest sons, Herb and Harold, and later became a well-known funeral director and part owner of the Lloyd-James funeral home in Tyler.

At that time, people were very superstitious, and John's announcement piqued their curiosity. "That night ... we had a house full of people," Johnnie says. "They'd come from far and wide to see it. Brother Rawlings had built it up pretty good," as people were curious about witnessing "their" funeral. Johnnie was ushering that night, but the task became difficult, as extra chairs had to be brought in and the aisles were congested with people. It was a full house.

"Way down in the front was a lady right on the end of the pew," Johnnie recalls with a smile. "I took a couple down there, where there were two spaces right beside her. I touched her shoulder to let them in to sit." Johnnie could only guess what the woman might be anticipating, for when he touched her shoulder, she "jumped and hollered."

The service began as a funeral would, and at the appropriate time, Johnnie and others rolled the coffin out from its hiding place behind the choir loft. Then Pastor Harris delivered the "eulogy."

"It was pretty effective," Johnnie says. "Lots of people responded to the invitation."

Even as a six-year-old boy, Lynn McClellan, nephew of Bob Jacobs, was awed by "the sight of a casket at a service that was *not* a funeral." His aunt Gwan Jacobs recalls it stirred quite a controversy, as others in the church thought their pastor had gone too far.

John's creativity in evangelism was innovative and motivated people into action. He taught his congregation the art of promotion and evangelism. Every Saturday morning, the youth would accompany several adults by bus and canvass the Tyler area, leaving sermon pamphlets on house doorknobs. The young people would sing songs and preach from the loudspeaker while riding on the bus.

Through his ministry at Central Baptist, John certainly left his mark on life in Tyler as well as on many other towns in East Texas. The many churches he planted in towns like Athens, Lindale, Sulfur Springs, and Center, Texas, was one of his lasting legacies. As of 2009, Lindale remains a large church, and the church in Sulfur Springs averages about seven hundred in attendance.

"He started churches all over East Texas, which is really unusual," Bill Aven comments. "He didn't just send money; he went out. The men and women from Central would build church buildings in a day. The innovation ... was just phenomenal."

When there was no time to build a new church, Dr. John was busy holding tent and open-air meetings to reach other neighborhoods in and outside of Tyler. He would also visit surrounding towns and preach on the streets.

There was never a dull moment during Dr. John's ministry. Often after preaching in a tent meeting, he would drive home that night and go about his pastoral duties the next day, including his daily radio broadcast.

At the close of revivals and tent meetings, Dr. John would work with the people who had been saved along with the leaders in the community to help organize new, Bible-believing churches.

13

How to Handle Busybodies

*Let no corrupt communication proceed out of your
mouth, but that which is good to the use of edifying,
that it may minister grace unto the hearers.*

—EPHESIANS 4:29

John astonished many audiences during his time in Tyler; he was known for
doing unexpected and controversial things. David Murrow, in his book *Why
Men Hate Going to Church,* discusses how men have stopped attending church
because many pastors have failed to address the problems and issues men face
in today's culture, and that there is a lack of strong leadership. Many preachers
now lack the passion and enthusiasm John expressed from the pulpit. He was
"zealous of good works" (Titus 2:14).

In one of his early sermons at Central Baptist Church, "The Horrors of
Hell That Have Never Been Told," John presented a vivid picture of hell. That
sermon greatly impacted many in the church, such as young seven-year-old
Leland Kennedy, whose mother had been instrumental in the founding of the
church. "It was so vivid, I could smell the smoke and feel the flame," Leland
comments, recalling the story of his salvation. "I wanted to be saved so badly …
as I left, it was so vivid and so strong. It was more than just the fear of going to
hell, although I did fear it. It was the understanding that we're sinners without

Christ. And Brother Rawlings did a very wonderful job in presenting Christ and the need for people to be saved.

"I lay awake after I went to bed ... I couldn't sleep. And about two o'clock in the morning, I felt a great conviction and stirring of my soul. I awakened my mother and said, 'Mother, if I die, I'll go to hell. I really need to be saved!' She got the Bible and led me to the Lord. And I remember the peace that came in."

Many others besides young Leland were affected by John's dramatic presentation of hell. Sometimes he even frightened his own children. One evening around Christmastime, Dr. John had just preached on hell. Suddenly, during the night, there was a scream from eight-year-old Harold.

"Mama! Mama!" he cried. "It's dark as hell in here!"

John preached "The Horrors of Hell That Have Never Been Told" more than once. On Sunday, August 31, 1947, he conducted a revival under what the ad described as a "big blue tent" in the six-hundred-block of West Erwin. Another instance was on the first Sunday morning of 1950, the day following the infamous Watch Night "funeral" service. Despite the strong medicine of that Sunday morning service, John offered an antidote in his sermon "The Glories of Heaven That Have Already Been Revealed" in that evening's service.

John does not claim perfection in his knowledge of matters of heaven and hell; rather, he admits, "There are many things about life I don't know or understand ... I have learned a long time ago not to expend all of my energy trying to figure out the degrees or temperature in hell. I just know it is hot. They are thirsty. They have memory, and they are tormented. They don't like it. They wish they could get out of there, and they can't. That is enough to cause me not to want to go there. I don't know a whole a lot about heaven. I just know that it is a place of beauty. They have singing there. It is a place that is very colorful. It is a place of peace. They say there are no tears there. So if that is it, I would like to go there.

"One fellow was talking about hell and [flippantly] said, 'All of my friends are there,'" Dr. John related. "They are not very friendly in hell. You don't find one verse in Scripture that talks about congeniality in hell. Instead, there is gnashing of teeth! ... Hell is no joke. It is a serious matter!"

Because of his unashamed stance on such issues, John sometimes faced opposition and resistance that did not always come from people outside the church, but occasionally from within. Johnnie Stewart and Don Walker both remember a time when several people at Central Baptist had just about had enough of it and were gossiping about John.

Johnnie recalls sitting in church on a Sunday morning and watching John stride down the long aisle. He took two steps up to the platform and looked out over the congregation. "He was an impressive-looking fellow," Johnnie remembers.

"There are some people in this church," John began, "whose tongues are so long they can stand in the living room and lick the skillet in the kitchen. And they've been talking about me and giving me hell."

Startled, Johnnie sat up a little straighter; he'd never heard a preacher use that kind of language before.

"If you don't come pick up your letter [to transfer your membership] this afternoon by two o'clock," John warned, "I will announce your name on the radio tonight."

The story goes that six or seven people went and picked up their church letters that afternoon.

John knew how to handle such gossips and busybodies. Church member Mary Kennedy, mother of Leland Kennedy, had her own predicament with a church busybody and came to John with her problem.

Leland recalls all that his mother had to endure. One such matter was frequent visits from a woman who Leland describes as "a gossip and complainer and faultfinder and busybody." He remembers the woman coming to visit his mother every Monday morning after his father left. "She'd come by the house and just unload on everybody and everything, including my own dad … the whole works," Leland says. "My mother was so burdened by it."

When Mrs. Kennedy called Dr. John and asked him what she should do, he answered, "Now, Mary, will you do what I tell you?"

"Yes, I will, Preacher," she said.

"You're going to do *exactly* as I tell you?"

"Yes, I will, Preacher."

"Well, now," John answered, "what I want you to do is this: When she comes, you let her in, but before she gets started, you say, 'Now before we visit, we need to have a little Bible study.' You start reading, and you read, and you read, and you read.

"Then after awhile, say, 'Before we continue reading, let's have a prayer.' So you get down on your knees, and make sure she gets on hers, and you pray, and you pray for everything that you can think of—every member by name, all the missionaries, you pray all around the world, and when you get around, start all over again. You keep her on her knees, and you pray, and you pray, and you pray.

"When you finally stop praying, say, 'Now let's get back to the Bible and do some more study.'"

Mrs. Kennedy kept her word and did exactly as her pastor suggested. When she finished praying and said they should read further, the gossip interrupted quickly, "You know what—it's getting kind of late. I think I need to leave."

And she never came back.

14

In Trouble with the Preacher

My son, despise not the chastening of the LORD; neither be weary of his correction: for whom the LORD loveth he correcteth; even as a father the son in whom he delighteth. Happy is the man that findeth wisdom, and the man that getteth understanding.

—PROVERBS 3:11–13

"You are looking at a man who believes in law and order! I have never been ashamed of it [because] God is a God of law and order," Dr. John once proclaimed.

All of his children and grandchildren knew well this philosophy. He was not one to spare the rod of correction. He was a firm believer in the biblical definition of discipline and, as a father, applied it enthusiastically.

During a sermon on August 21, 1977, John addressed such chastening and correction and gave as an example his three oldest sons. "The two oldest ones [Herb and Harold] were doing something they ought not to do, so I was giving them a pretty good flame (spanking). They were screaming like I was killing them, Harold especially. I think that is what is wrong with his voice [today]. He could scream in a high tenor voice like you've never heard. 'Daddy, you're killing me!' I hadn't even hit him, and he thought I was killing him.

This particular day, Carrol [the third son] was really enjoying this. He was younger, of course, than those two. I passed pretty close to where he was, and I ... whooped him about four or five times. He started screaming, 'What have I done?' I said, 'Not anything, just general principles. It is not what you have done; it is what you are getting ready to do.' I mean, you could whip a boy nearly anytime, and it's applicable ... If you have ever raised four boys, you know what I'm talking about."

John recognized the importance of biblical discipline, for "afterward it yieldeth the peaceable fruit of righteousness unto them which are exercised thereby" (Hebrews 12:11). John preached: "We ought to thank God for the rod of correction. Oh, how peaceable and wonderful it is! We need to be corrected! ... If we are a good son and good daughter, God is going to reward us for that ... God is not going to ignore your faithfulness, your obedience to Him! He is going to see to it that you will be rewarded for that."

Over the years, John's disciplinary methods became the topic of humor among close friends and family, although the children did not always find it so funny.

One night when Harold was eight years old, John was preaching a sermon at Central Baptist Church in Tyler, Texas. He and his boyhood friend, Delma House, were sitting near the front row during the service and struck up a long and lively conversation during the sermon, unaware of John's watchful eye. Suddenly, John stopped preaching and silence followed for about ten seconds. Herb, watching from the choir loft, saw Delma slowly slouch down in the pew as a crimson flush crept up his neck to the tips of his ears.

Then John's shrill voice rang, "William Harold, I'll see you at home tonight about this talking in church!"

Harold and Delma went very still and began to pray for the Lord's return before the service ended. John's open reproach took the boys' joy out of the rest of the sermon.

During the drive home, Harold earnestly told his dad what a good preacher he was and how much he enjoyed the service. Unfortunately, his attempt at distracting his father failed, and Harold got the punishment he deserved.

John's children and grandchildren recall times when they came under his firm hand. Carrol recalls an incident with the famous Mexican quirt, a braided leather, forked-type of stock whip with two fall on the end, John's chosen "rod of correction," which he had received during a preaching trip earlier in his ministry as a gift from one of the church members who had visited Mexico. John used this quirt to discipline his sons "several times," Carrol recalls.

Once, when John was away preaching at a revival, Carrol and George conspired to find the Mexican quirt and get rid of it. They found it in the closet and buried it out in the field. When John returned from his meeting, one of the first things he noticed was the missing quirt, but nothing more was said until almost sixty years later when the boys finally confessed. George claims he could find the very spot where he and Carrol buried the "weapon."

Such were some of the ongoing incidents in the Rawlings's household as John's sons grew up. They were never far from adventure or, more likely, trouble.

Johnnie Stewart was one of the Rawlings boys' good friends in Tyler. He recalls spending time with them one day when Herb and Harold were supposed to be mowing the family lawn. Johnnie did not realize this, and they continued playing during the afternoon until around five o'clock when John drove up.

"I thought I told you boys to mow this yard," Johnnie heard him reprimand his sons, who had forgotten as boys often will. "I tell you what," John warned. "If you haven't got this yard mowed by sundown, I'll whoop all three of you." Perhaps it is for reasons such as this that Mrs. Rawlings's maid, Josephine, a half-black, half-American Indian woman who loved Mrs. Rawlings and the boys, called John "that mean old preacher."

On many occasions John's "righteous indignation" was warranted, such as the time Herb and Johnnie switched the church restroom signs during a fellowship meeting and several visitors into Herb and Johnnie's trap. The boys heard John "holler" from all the way upstairs when he found out. "Herb! Johnnie! Get yourselves up here!"

Recalling the story, Johnnie says, "We were in trouble with the preacher."

They found themselves "in *real* trouble with the preacher" yet again one Saturday morning. Herb and Johnnie, along with their friend Silas Moore, set out on the old church bus to inform people about the revival that was in progress, driving through the neighborhoods and advertising over the loudspeaker. But as time wore on, boredom set in, and they "got to hollering on that thing," Johnnie describes. "We started announcing that floodwaters were rising and telling people to leave their homes immediately."

Of course, John uncovered this plot—after the police called his office.

"He always found out," Johnnie jokes to his friends with a laugh.

Good thing the Mexican quirt was buried and gone.

15

Innovations and Escapades

I believe in being an innovator.

—WALT DISNEY

"Here in Tyler in the mid forties," Bill Aven says, "we had the innovation of a bus ministry, tent meetings, music, great evangelists, and more."

During the time John lived in Tyler, most people did not own automobiles, so the bus ministry at Central was vital. For many who lived on the outskirts of the city, it was their only way to attend services. Even in a small city like Tyler, Central Baptist enjoyed success with its free charter bus service with eight charter buses bringing an average of 295 people to Sunday school. A church publication dated Sunday, January 1, 1950, announced that 29,011 passengers had ridden Central Baptist charter buses in the past three years.

"Central Baptist Church was built on music as well as preaching," Bill says. Choir director Verle Ackerman and his wife, Lucille, the pianist, were both excellent musicians. Verle built a tremendous choir, and Dr. John would often invite popular Gospel quartets to visit the church.

The church also had its own quartets. Harold with his friends Bill Aven, twins Delma and Thelma House, and Sammy Baron formed a group Dr. John labeled "The Onion Blade Quartet" (even though there were five members).

Bill, at age twelve, was the oldest member of the group. Their most requested song was "On the Jericho Road."

John's sons Herb and Harold sang in their own quartets. Some years later, Herb, Joe House, Bill Aven, and Herman Johnston formed "The Young Men's Quartet." People loved to hear these two groups perform because at that time it was a "big deal" for young kids to be involved in church music programs.

John not only invited many well-known singing groups to Central but well-known and popular evangelists and pastors as well. Once he invited evangelist Mordecai Ham to speak in a special Easter service at the high school auditorium in Tyler in 1946, almost a year after World War II had ended. There were thirty-five hundred people in attendance that day, yet only one person, an eleven-year-old girl, came forward for salvation. Ham told John he didn't find it easy to preach on Easter because people had their minds on other things, such as their newly purchased Easter clothes.

Ham, a native of Scottsville, Kentucky, was a personal friend of John's as well as one of his mentors. Ham was the evangelist under whom the world-renowned Billy Graham was saved during a revival in 1934. At present, Dr. John recalls Ham saying that was one of the most Satan-fought revivals that he had ever preached. John also remembered well one of the sayings of the famous evangelist, "Young men and young ladies, always listen to people. God may be speaking." That comment later inspired one of John's sermons.

Central Baptist celebrated their seventh anniversary during another special service at the Tyler High School auditorium, this time on October 12, 1947. A full, double-page ad entitled "What Central Baptist Believes" in the Tyler newspaper promoted the service and included a list of nine points. The first and ninth points stated, consecutively, "We believe the whole Bible from Genesis 1:1 to Revelation 22:21 is the verbally inspired and infallible Word of God" and "The only mission of the church is not to reform the world but to preach and teach the Gospel of salvation to the individual soul." The ad also listed Central's average Sunday school attendance, showing an increase of 60 in 1940 to 960 in 1947. Since John first became pastor of Central, 1,765 people joined the church and 1,430 radio programs were consecutively broadcast.

John's innovation of his radio and bus ministries coupled with inviting singing groups and speakers to Central Baptist helped reach thousands of people in East Texas. Central was growing in the early 1940s during World War II. Many soldiers also attended Central Baptist, as Camp Fannin, a large military installation, had been built on the Gladewater highway just northeast of town, which, in addition to the growth of the oil industry, contributed to Tyler's economic boost. Forty thousand soldiers occupied the camp during the war and trained soldiers in infantry skills.

John and others were able to minister to many apprehensive young servicemen, some of whom never returned to their homeland. Bob Jacobs met many of these soldiers as a Morse telegraph operator in Tyler Commercial College, which contracted with the government to train twenty-two hundred or more soldiers to be radio operators. Because of Bob's skill and speed in sending and receiving messages, he was chosen to train other soldiers. He made many friends among them and, best of all, was able to invite them to Central Baptist Church. One young man from Georgia was saved and upon being shipped out to the Pacific war theater, wrote Bob, stating that he had begun teaching a Bible class on one of the Pacific islands.

One of the most dramatic conversions under John's ministry in Tyler was that of "Big Jack" McGaughey, a bootlegger, gambler, and alcoholic. He was a man well known to the sheriff's office, as he was in and out of jail many times. Big Jack had also been a personal buddy of the southwest outlaw Pretty Boy Floyd, who owned a successful dry-cleaning business in town.

John led Big Jack to the Lord in his home, and after his conversion, Big Jack poured all his whiskey down the drain of the kitchen sink. Afterward, John immediately put Big Jack to work with Mrs. Rawlings in the junior department of the Sunday school with eight-, nine-, and ten-year-olds. John realized that this would help Big Jack grow in his faith and keep him on the right track. In fact, John's third son, Carrol, was saved under Big Jack's ministry in Sunday school.

Bill Aven says, "When people got saved, Brother Rawlings would put them to work immediately. He felt they'd be better off if he could tie them on than to wander astray."

Dr. Don Walker remembers meeting the six-foot-four, three-hundred-pound fellow for the first time shortly after Big Jack's conversion. Big Jack made a fist and held it out toward Don. "You know what all those scars on my knuckles are?" he said. "Those are men's teeth [marks] when I used to fight."

Of course, old habits die hard. Don Walker remembers an incident involving Big Jack a couple years after he had become a Christian. When he asked Big Jack how he was doing, he answered, "You know, I'm not doing too good. My brother-in-law Heath Lamb made a profession of faith and said he became a Christian. Here the other day, he just went out and got dog drunk.

I took him here in the back of this cleaner and just whipped his ass and told him, 'Christians aren't supposed to drink.'" He added, "I don't think he'll be drinking anymore." Through God's grace and Big Jack's whipping, Big Jack's brother-in-law Heath later became a Sunday school teacher and was very faithful in attending church visitation programs. Bob Jacobs recalls that Heath always brought a flashlight so house numbers could be easily seen.

Big Jack had more success in ending his drinking habit than in cleaning up his language. Even so, he grew in his walk with the Lord and later began his own ministry and pastored a church for over thirty years in Overton, Texas. Big Jack was one of the people who was really touched and changed by John, and they became lifelong friends.

"If you're going to talk to a Methodist," John said, "you need a bodyguard. You know how I know? I married a Methodist." Big Jack was, as John said, "my bodyguard."

John took Big Jack on a camping trip once along with some other men from the church. Though several of them stayed up late talking, Big Jack grew tired and lay down on his cot. After he went to sleep, the men very quietly and carefully lifted his cot and set it over the hot coals of the fire. You know you are a good friend of John's when he sets you atop a bed of red-hot coals.

John and Big Jack had many interesting experiences, and stories abound of their exploits. Carrol recalls the time his father began driving a brand-new Chrysler. Big Jack and John were driving one day when suddenly another driver forced them off the road.

Big Jack, spotting a big tree ahead, panicked and cried out, "Oh, please, God, don't let us hit that p--s elm!"

The car rolled completely over and then fell back onto its wheels. Big Jack had fallen on top of John. They righted themselves and John was able to drive the damaged vehicle home in its battered condition, as Chryslers were well built in those days.

When Mrs. Rawlings greeted him as he arrived, "Daddy, what have you done to our new car?!" She never asked about his or Big Jack's physical condition.

In facing such perils and escapades, Big Jack developed a keen sense of humor similar to John's. At one time, he was asked to preach a revival for an inner-city mission in downtown Cincinnati, Ohio. While he was at the podium, a huge sewer rat ran across the floor right in front of the platform. Big Jack's immediate response was, "One of you ushers get that mouse out of here!" After all, Big Jack was of a Texas mind-set. Everything is bigger in Texas.

16

The Voice of God

Always listen to people. God may be speaking.
—DR. MORDECAI HAM

Attendance at Central in 1948 had reached its peak of just over three thousand, of which the equivalent today John estimates would be about nine thousand, considering the size of the city. John was sitting in his office on Tuesday morning, July 20, 1948, waiting to begin his daily 12:15 p.m. radio broadcast when he heard a gentle knock on the door. When he looked up, he saw Mother Mills, wife of Tom Mills and mother of four children, two girls, and two boys. Her sons lived in Shelby County about ten miles southeast of Tyler, while Mother Mills only lived two blocks up the street from the church. Her husband had been in an accident while working for a railroad company and ended up with an artificial limb, and her youngest son had been killed in World War II. Standing with her hands wrapped in her apron and tears on her cheeks, she said, "Pastor, pardon me, but ... could I talk to you?"

John answered with a smile, "Mother Mills, you can talk to me anytime." He walked over to her and put his arm around her.

"Pastor, I don't want to bother you, but I was praying and became so burdened. God spoke to my heart. I had to come see you. Would you please consider preaching a revival meeting in Shelby County? I've been praying for years someone would hold a revival in Center, Texas, and that my two older children would get saved." B. B. Crimm, the "Cowboy Evangelist," had once held a meeting there, but the men of the town had broken up the meeting and had a "knock-down, drag-out fight." As a result, there hadn't been a meeting there of any consequence for over ten years. It was pretty Western and not very civilized back then!

John hugged her. "Mother Mills, I will."

They prayed together, and John always remembered her radiant smile and shining eyes. She believed in her young pastor.

When Mother Mills had gone, John called Mrs. Rawlings and told her he was leaving for Center. He then called his associate Jack Bridges and told him the same, asking him to preach at 12:15 on the radio in his stead. "I'm going to Center, Texas, in Shelby County to see about a tent campaign."

John gathered some literature and material and headed to Center, one hundred miles from his church. In about ninety minutes, he arrived in the town square in Center. When he pulled in, somebody yelled, "Hey, preacher!"

John saw Byford Robertson crossing the street.

"What are you doing here?" the young man asked.

"What are *you* doing here?" John asked. Byford and his wife, Joyce, had been saved under John's preaching in Tyler when they had gone to a beauty shop training school there.

"Didn't anyone tell you? Joyce and I moved back to Center three weeks ago. What are you doing here?"

"Nobody told me. I'm down here to see about doing a city-wide tent campaign."

"Glory to God!" the young man exclaimed. "Joyce and I were just praying this morning the Lord would put it on your heart to come down here to Shelby County to hold a meeting."

"Well, get in the car, and let's look around," John said. "I want to locate a place."

The young man considered for a moment. "Preacher, I know two blocks [off the town] square that is a beautiful place. But you can't get it. Others have tried to get that lot for a meeting, and the woman won't let them have it." The acre and a half of land was located on the corner of Church and College Streets, but it was overgrown with weeds.

"Where does this woman live?" John asked.

The young man told him that she lived south of town and was very wealthy. "She's a widow, and I think she's a Methodist."

"Well, where's she live?" asked John again.

"You can't get that property," the young man said again.

John insisted on knowing where the woman lived, so finally, the young man gave in and agreed to show him.

The widow, Mrs. Vinyard, lived in a beautiful home with an indoor swimming pool, which was quite unusual in those days. John rang the doorbell and waited until the housekeeper, an African American woman, opened the door. He asked for the lady of the house

The housekeeper hesitated. "Do you has an appointment?"

"Yes," he answered confidently. "The Lord told me to come. My name is John Rawlings, and I'm a Baptist preacher."

"You a reverend?"

"Yeah, not much of one, but I am!"

"Well, if the Lord done tol' you, lemme talk to her!"

It turned out that Mrs. Vinyard was standing in the shadows and had heard everything John said. "I know what he wants! He wants my lot to hold a tent meeting on, but he can't have it! I'm not going to rent it!"

According to his raising, John pushed the door open and went into the house.

He walked over to Mrs. Vinyard and said, "You misread my intent." He put his arm around her shoulders. "I married a Methodist girl several years ago. And that's the meanest woman I've ever lived with." Of course, he had never tried to live with any other.

"Well," she blustered. "We're not all that way!"

"I don't want to rent your property," John said. "You're going to let me put my tent on that property, and you're going to write the check for the first week's expenses. So just go on into your office and write out the check."

"You sure are pushy!" she said.

John grinned. "You haven't seen anything yet. No, this is God's business. You're interested in God's business, and I am, too. So go in your office and write the check."

Mrs. Vinyard had nothing more to say, and John received both the check and the use of her lot. Then the housekeeper, Mrs. Vinyard, and John prayed together, and the housekeeper was already rejoicing!

From there, John drove down to the office where they published the weekly newspaper and went inside to speak with the owner, Mr. Anderson. "I'm going to preach a revival meeting starting Wednesday night here in Center, and I want to put an ad in the paper."

The owner hesitated. "Well, Reverend, I've already got all the material together, and we can't put it in the paper for this week."

"Mr. Anderson, I've studied journalism," John insisted. "I know that you're the man, and that you own it. You've got a lot of fillers in there that don't amount to anything, so you can pull something out. I'll help you. You can put the ad in the paper, and it will come out Thursday. You can also print me seven thousand handbills."

"I think I can do that," Mr. Anderson said, and John helped him set up everything. Then he drove to the radio station in town that his friend James Ulhmer had built with his own hands but had recently turned over to a new manager. John headed upstairs to the study and said to the young redheaded receptionist, "I want to see the manager."

"That's him, sir," she answered. "Just coming in."

John introduced himself to the gentleman. "My name is John Rawlings. I'm starting a crusade in town on Wednesday at eight o'clock, and I want a radio broadcast."

In return, the man posed several negative questions.

"Look," said John. "I've been listening to the station on my way here. You can pull that country-and-western music, and I'll take fifteen minutes."

"Sir, we already have spots."

"That's okay. I'll take thirty minutes. You can go ahead and put the spots in, and I'll make my first broadcast." The manager hurled profane language at him, but John said, "That's okay, I used to cuss mules in the cotton fields anyway; maybe somebody needs cussing."

John talked his way into studio A and made a thirty-minute broadcast. He even read the advertising spots on behalf of advertisers and told listeners to go places, buy products, etc. John told the manager he would be back the next day for his second broadcast.

John arranged for members from Central Baptist, Big Jack, Brother R. L. "Bob" Jacobs, and Curtis "Goldie" Goldman to meet the Boy Scouts and their troop leaders the next morning. They would head to Center to prepare the property and the community for the impending revival. John put his sons Herb and Harold and their friend Silas Moore in charge of clearing the weeds and brush. Their job also included guarding the tent at night. Bob, Goldie, and the

Boy Scouts also set to work. John's associate in Tyler, Mr. Shockey, had already brought the blue tent, poles, and lumber for building 150 benches. Bob built all the benches between Saturday morning and Wednesday afternoon, finishing the very day of the revival. A crew of men from Central put up the tent.

Bob and Goldie drove around advertising the revival in Curtis's old '41 Chevrolet with a loudspeaker on top of it. They went into every business place on the square and invited people. Meanwhile, the team of Boy Scouts took approximately thirty-five hundred circulars and "sowed" them throughout Center, house to house and on the courthouse square. This was Saturday, and each night until the following Wednesday, Curtis and Bob slept on a couple of fold-up army cots in the tent on Mrs. Vinyard's property. They had to wear citronella mosquito repellant in order to get a little sleep at night. The very hot summer weather didn't make them smell any better than the mosquito repellant did!

John went to one of Center's several sawmills and had sawdust shavings hauled to and spread under the tent, reminiscent of Billy Sunday's sawdust trail in the early 1900s. In addition to the physical preparation, extensive planning and prayer preceded the revival in Center, as were all of John's past and future meetings and revivals.

Everything was ready by 4:00 p.m. on Wednesday, July 28. The fifty benches had been nailed together, the grass and weeds cut, and the loudspeakers set up. That night, about forty curiosity seekers came for the first service. John introduced the little crowd to Curtis and Bob.

Bob, who had just graduated from seminary in Fort Worth, kept an accurate record of everything and worked with the youth every night for about thirty minutes. Curtis and his wife, Katherine, were in charge of the music. This was a special time for Bob because his future wife attended the meeting and was led to the Lord by John one night after the services. Her sister was also saved that night.

The first night of the revival, a dead spirit seemed to prevail. No one responded to the invitation that evening. But this indifferent attitude did not last long, as the crowds began to grow rapidly night after night. However, on Thursday, Friday, and Saturday evenings, there was still no response to the invitation. Finally, on Sunday night, August 1, the tent was practically full, and a new, more positive atmosphere prevailed. John preached and gave the invitation. After two or three verses of the invitation song, John stopped the singing and shocked everyone.

"What is the matter with you folks?" he cried out. "I've never seen such a hard-hearted bunch of Christians as some of you are! Don't you have a friend or loved one here that is lost? If so, why don't you go to them and ask them to come forward and get saved?"

As his words pierced the hearts of the audience, utter silence settled over the tent until several saved attendees began to step out. Weaving among the crowd, they searched for friends and relatives and asked them to go forward and receive Christ. The very first person to step out was a young man, Gene Richards. His wife, being a Christian, leaned over to him and spoke about going forward and getting saved. He responded instantly. Not long after his conversion, Gene was fatally electrocuted while working on a line for the Texas Power and Light Company.

After Gene stepped out that night, other Christians began pouring down the aisle, bringing lost people down to the altar. It was then that the revival spirit really burst to life.

The revival was only supposed to run two weeks, but because it was such a tremendous spiritual awakening for Center, it ran for thirty-nine nights, attracting people from surrounding towns, such as Tenaha, Joaquin, Timpson, and Carthage, Texas, every night. Some came from Lufkin, Texas, and Logansport, Louisiana, fifty miles away.

For seven weeks, John drove back and forth daily from Tyler to Center, preaching and broadcasting on the radio. At the time, John's friend, Coke R. Stevenson, was thirty-fifth governor of Texas and filed for US Senate. He was pitted against US Representative Lyndon B. Johnson of Austin who came to Center and, knowing John's current tent revival was drawing large crowds, tried persuading John to participate in a political rally on the square.

"You're nuts!" John answered. "I'm having four thousand people in my meeting, and I'm not going to dismiss a revival for a political rally."

Johnson never liked John after that, and only seven people showed up for his senatorial rally while John had the rest of them down at the tent! In the hotly contested senatorial runoff, Johnson won by only 87 votes out of the 988,295 votes that were cast. Later, after becoming the thirty-seventh vice president of the United States, Johnson served as president from 1968 to 1973 after the assassination of President John F. Kennedy.

The night John preached his sermon "Living Too Close to Hell," twenty-four people walked to the altar, most of them for salvation, one old man in particular by the name of Clement. Clement lived in Carthage whose niece and her husband were members of Central Baptist Church in Tyler. She had convinced her uncle Clement to go to the revival in Center. He didn't want to go—in fact, he was belligerent—but she talked him into it.

One night, Bob Jacobs was at the altar leading someone to the Lord when, all of a sudden, he heard a commotion. At first, he thought a fight had broken out. John had spoken to Clement the night before about getting saved, but the man had refused. But on this night, when John went down the aisle to speak to a few people Clement stepped out and stopped him.

"Preacher," the man said. "I ought to be saved. Preacher, I *want* to be saved."

Clement followed John down the aisle to the altar, and when both men were on their knees on the sawdust-covered ground, John led Clement to the Lord. When the old man got saved, he jumped up and started shouting. That was the commotion Bob heard.

Clement called to his wife, "Gurdy, come down here! You've got a saved husband!" Bob remembers after that Clement became "one of the best Christians I've [ever known]."

Bob himself took the sermon that John preached that night, "Living Too Close to Hell," with him on a visit to the Philippines. He shared the outline with Pastor Matta, who, Bob discovered from a letter years later, preached the same sermon and ninety-two people were saved. Even then, John's legacy was beginning to reach around the world.

During the time of the tent revival in Center, there was an impending election over whether Smith County, Texas, would remain "dry" or allow the sale of alcohol. On a Sunday evening one week prior to the election, John scheduled an open-air meeting at Central Baptist in Tyler and invited several former alcoholics and bootleggers, such as Big Jack, to share their testimonies. Another former alcoholic and bootlegger who spoke was a barber nicknamed "Talkin' Tapp." Johnnie Stewart recalls Talkin' Tapp's good sense of humor and testimony. "I'll be a Christian until I turn my toes up this way," Talkin' Tapp said, speaking of his body in his future coffin.

Another guest speaker was Pastor Cecil Simmons, an evangelist from Gadsden, Alabama, and former bootlegger. Bill Aven recalls him arriving in his big, black Buick. "He parked that thing outside the church," Bill says, "and had everybody go out and look at it." And Pastor Simmons told the wide-eyed children, "There are eighteen bullet holes in this car I got from running liquor."

The meeting place was packed with curious seekers as well as most of the members of Central. There were perhaps a dozen or more well-known people who shared their testimonies. They told how God's miraculous healing power through John's ministry had helped them overcome the desire to drink or sell alcohol. It was a very captivating and moving meeting. John had set this up specifically to fight the "liquor crowd."

The first night Pastor Simmons spoke during the tent revival, the Lord laid it on Bob's heart to buy fifteen minutes of airtime on the local station in Tyler, KGKB, to advertise the revival. "Cost me five dollars," he remembered. The next day, John and Cecil Simmons went to the radio station at four o'clock. John introduced Pastor Simmons, who was sitting at the table by the mic. The "on" light flashed, and he began, "Good afternoon, radio friends. This is your country preacher Cecil Simmons from Akron, Ohio, bringing the old-fashioned Gospel heaven-high, hell-deep, worldwide, and gun-barrel straight." Folks in Tyler had never heard anything like that before, but almost everyone listened to the radio. Listeners called in and asked, "Who is that preacher?" Pastor Simmons was a dynamic speaker and had a unique sense of humor.

Bob Jacobs became the catalyst for the new radio broadcast borne from that first five-dollar, fifteen-minute spot. The last night of the revival in Center, Central Baptist Church of Tyler went on the air full-time on Sunday nights from 8:00 p.m. to 9:00 p.m. John also had a daytime program Monday through Friday for fifteen minutes each day. Many people were saved through the new radio ministry.

Meanwhile, election time came for the citizens of Smith County to vote on the "wet or dry ticket," whether or not to legalize the sale of alcohol. John had some wood benches around Tyler painted with the church's name and a message to vote no to liquor sales. All of his efforts proved successful, as Election Day brought victory for the dry ticket, which turned out to be a lasting achievement. Smith County in Texas has remained a dry county for almost seventy years. "They whipped that thing to the ground," Bob remembers with a smile. "It was a victory all because Brother Rawlings fought it so hard."

Obviously, this victory did not please everyone. Because the people of Smith County would often drive to Kilgore, Texas, to buy their alcohol, some of the townspeople in Tyler thought John was "in cahoots" with "the Kilgore liquor men," supposing that he was attempting to drive business from Tyler to Kilgore.

The stories of different people saved during the tent meeting in Center are countless. On August 15, 1948, John baptized fifty-nine converts in Adams Lake on Arcadia Road just outside the small town of Center in a baptismal serviced called "Baptized Just Like Jesus Was Baptized." The people present at the baptism included John, Bob Jacobs, Curtis Goldman, and Katherine (Aven) Goldman. Curtis led the song services, and Katherine played the piano.

A man named Bud Lowell attended the revival as a lost man and finally got saved. He confided in Bob, "You know, that night that Brother Rawlings preached, I think I told him I'd pay him twenty-five dollars if he'd preach that sermon again." When Bud received the Lord, "he went all out," according to Bob, and became a church officer. Later, Bob's first funeral service was for Bud Lowell's son, who was killed in the war.

The wife of Eddie Mahan, a paint contractor known as Slim, received the Lord during the revival, but it made her husband very angry, and he accused John of having an affair with her. One night, he got drunk and decided to break up the revival. Slim owned a cookie delivery truck with a straight exhaust, and he went around and around the block with the old muffler rumbling. The third time he went around, John paused in the middle of his sermon to say, "Let's pray for God to either kill this man or save him."

Someone told Slim what John had said. Later that night in bed, after Slim had sobered up, he told his wife, "Are you asleep? That preacher prayed for God to kill me. I need help. Do you know how to pray?"

"I don't know too much," she answered. "But I'll try."

He asked her to pray that he would last another day, so she prayed for God to let him live until the night. Slim lived. That night, about halfway down the center aisle, he sat in church for John's revival "as sober as a judge." During the invitation, he came down to the altar and asked John to help him "get religion," a phrase commonly used in those days. Slim fell to his knees, John led him in prayer to receive Christ, and he was saved.

A former rig builder in the oil fields, known by the name of Stub because several of his fingers had been cut off, had a niece who was a member of John's church in Tyler. She brought her uncle Stub, who didn't believe in religion, to John's revival in Center. The first Sunday night he attended, he said publicly, "I don't believe a d--n word of what that preacher is saying!" Nonetheless, his niece persisted in bringing him to the revival, and he relented for three or four nights. The night John preached on hell, Stub realized he was on the brink of burning in the lake of fire. He stood up in the middle of the tent and said in a raucous voice, "Preacher, you tell me God would save a man like me, wicked as I've been?"

"Yes, come on down. Tell Him how sorry you've been."

Stubs went down the aisle, stood at the altar, and said in a loud voice, "God, this reverend told me You'd save me if I asked You. So I'm gonna ask You, Would You please save me? I don't want to go to hell!" Afterward, he let out a loud cry, for he didn't know how to say hallelujah because he had never been in church. But he was rejoicing because he had gotten saved. Years later, on his deathbed, he told his wife, "You tell Brother John, when he gets up there, I'll be waiting at the gate. Tell him how much I love him because he's the one man who told me how to stay out of hell and to go to heaven."

Three other new converts at the Center revival included eleven-year-old Bob Hughes and his grandparents, who each came forward one night and accepted Jesus Christ as their personal Lord and Savior. His grandparents were well-to-do people but had never been to church; Bob's family was nonreligious, even antireligion.

After receiving Christ, Bob's story had worldwide impact. He went on to graduate from high school and as a teenager joined the air force. He was shipped to the Philippines, where he met missionary Joe Vella, a former sergeant from Michigan, who was stationed in the Philippines during the World War II. Bob became convicted to rededicate his life under Vella's ministry, and God called him to be a missionary. He graduated with honors from Baptist Bible College in Springfield, Missouri, where for a time he was chaplain of the student body. He then went to Cebu City, one of the largest cities in the Philippines, where he founded the Bible Baptist Church, which became the largest Baptist church in the Philippines, having reached a high attendance of around fifteen thousand.

John and Central Baptist sponsored Bob Hughes's radio broadcast that covered much of the Philippines during Bob's ministry. One of his sermons, "I Sat Where They Sat," became so sought-after that it was placed on a record album and was purchased by thousands of individuals. Bob Hughes was one of the greatest missionaries of the time.

Under Bob's ministry, a medical doctor, Dr. Armie Jesaluva, was converted, who, after Hughes's untimely death from cancer, was called as pastor. In 2005, Dr. Jesaluva created a program in Cebu City that inspired hundreds of Christian laypeople to begin evangelizing throughout the city, house to house, on college campuses, and at various businesses. By 2007, approximately 390,000 people had been saved. Through His sovereign plan, the Lord accepted John's loaves and fishes in the small town of Center, Texas, and multiplied them to feed the world.

Before the new congregation formed from the revival in Center, Texas, could be organized into a church, there was a battle to be fought. The president of the bank didn't want to give a loan to start the church because he attended a different church and wasn't too excited about the prospect of another Baptist church being built in Center.

John would not be hindered and went to the see the man, accompanied by Bob Jacobs. John asked the banker, "I want to know why it is that we have a man in this new church who will stand good for this loan [and you] won't … give it to us."

"I got to go to lunch," the banker said.

John face was red as fire. He leaned into the man's face and pointed his index finger. "You're not going anywhere until I get done talking to you!"

Bob thought if the banker had stood up, John would have knocked him down. "I thought he was going to jerk that guy out of his chair and give him a whooping!" says Bob.

John would not let anything get in the way of the Lord's work. He was determined to see God's will accomplished and would use pressure if necessary. So the banker sat back down, trembling all over, and reluctantly gave them the loan.

On the evening of August 9, 1948, John organized the new church in Center with thirteen charter members, and Bob became its first pastor. By Saturday, September 4, there were about 141 members. The following morning, Bob organized the Sunday school with 133 present in the first actual service of the fledgling church.

Most of the 141 members in the new Central Baptist Church were recent converts. In the late summer, Bob baptized fourteen more converts who were saved during the tent revival. One of them was eighteen-year-old Edward Welch whom Bob had led to Christ one afternoon on the square in Center in front of Perry Brothers store. Bob pastored the new church in Center for fifteen months before returning to Fort Worth.

The revival in Center was truly miraculous, its effects far-reaching and turning the town upside down. The revival actually began in the heart of Mother Mills, who heard the voice of God and went to see her preacher. The preacher also heard the voice of God, and sixty years later, the name of the Lord continues to be glorified because one woman did what God wanted her to do.

17

Defining Moment

I walked out and looked up at the stars that night. I said, "O God, you've spoken to my heart. I've not done enough for my blessed Lord."

—DR. JOHN W. RAWLINGS

The death of John's father during the same year as the Center, Texas, revival thrust John into a new level of ministry. While the death of his mother prompted him to recommit his life to serving Christ, his father's dying admission helped raise his ministry to a higher degree of intensity. However, even before the death of his father, the passing of his uncle Porter James had a profound impact upon him.

When Porter James contracted cancer and was on the threshold of death, John visited him. With deep emotion, his uncle said, "John William, I want to commend you for staying in the ministry and being strong in what you're doing. God called me when I was a young man, and I was disobedient. You can look at me today and see the result. I'm saved, and I'm going to meet the Lord in a few days, but I've lived a fruitless life." He began to weep and died later that evening.

Uncle Porter's admission prompted John to purpose in his heart to live a fruitful life by abiding in Christ. John 15:7–8 says, "If ye abide in Me, and

My words abide in you, ye shall ask what ye will, and it shall be done unto you. Herein is My Father glorified, that ye bear much fruit; so shall ye be my disciples." By daily walking with God through prayer and meditation of God's Word, the believer bears much fruit. John walked closely with the Lord, and the fruit of revival was borne. Thus, John discipled many who, like him, bore fruit for the glory of God the Father.

In 1946, John transported his seventy-three-year-old father from Arkansas to Texas, where he was admitted into the hospital for the last time. He had contracted cancer and had undergone several surgeries. In Mother Francis Hospital in Jacksonville on the north side of Tyler, Texas, John kneeled and prayed for his dying father. "I just can't stand it," he confided in his Lord. "I'm a grown man, but I don't think I can stand to give up my daddy. My mother is gone, and I just can't stand to be an orphan." He could not tell how long he prayed, but when he rose from his knees, peace washed over him. "Oh, Lord," he breathed, "if it could be Your will, take Dad home and get him out of his suffering." He felt an echo of peace and victory in his heart. That night, he slept like a babe in his grandmother's arms.

His father asked him later, "Son, take me to the house. I'd like to spend one more night at home." He was released from the hospital and allowed to go home with John, where he lay on a hospital bed. The next day at noon, John and his family sat beside him. "I don't want to die," he said.

John kissed him on the brow with the cold sweat of death upon it and placed his hand under his father's head. His eyes were already set when he repeated, "I don't want to die."

"Papa, Mama is in heaven. You're old, and you can't live. And you're saved."

"Son, I'm saved, but I don't want to die."

"Tell me why," John pleaded.

"Son, I've not done enough for my blessed Lord." His mouth closed, and those were the last words he spoke in this life. His regret was that he had wasted his life. John would never forget that day.

That night, John walked outside and looked up at the stars. "O God," he prayed. "You've spoken to my heart. I've not done enough for my blessed Lord."

The following Wednesday night, John preached at his church. He and Mrs. Rawlings had already gone to see the body that Dr. John later described as "so precious to me." After preaching his sermon, John got in his car and drove nearly six hundred miles back to Arkansas to the McGee Funeral Home in Cave City, Arkansas. The funeral home had sent an ambulance to Tyler to pick up the body of John's father and transport it to Arkansas for burial in the old family cemetery. On Saturday, John preached the funeral for his father at the James Family Cemetery near Cedar Grove Church.

On Sunday, when John preached in the First Baptist Church in his hometown where he went to high school, the building was standing room only; some people even stood outside. Standing in the back vestibule was a man by the name of Guy Taylor, whose own father had died without knowing the Lord. In fact, he had been a wicked man; yet he and John's father had been friends and had freighted together with teams and wagons.

When John presented the invitation that morning, many people walked to the altar to receive Christ. John worked his way down the aisle back to the vestibule where Guy was standing. "Guy," John said, "my daddy prayed for you."

According to Dr. John, Guy was "as pale as a corpse." Shaking like a leaf, he put his arm around John and said, "I can't stand it any longer. Your dad was a daddy to me when no one else cared."

John supported him as they walked back down the aisle together. Guy was broken to pieces but at the same time was walking on air, for he had accepted Christ as his personal Lord and Savior. Filled with joy, he was hugging, shouting, and kissing everyone within his reach all because "an old hillbilly man" by the name of George Rawlings prayed for a young boy whose father was lost.

For John as a young preacher, his father's death coupled with Guy's resulting conversion was a defining moment in his life. Standing beside his dying father, John determined that, with God's help, he would not come to the end of his life making the same admission, "I haven't done enough for my blessed Lord."

18

Sulphur Springs

*He takes advantage of a situation. He turns it around
and draws crowds.*

—BILL AVEN

After the tremendous revival in Center the previous year, John's work had
only just begun. He intended to preach a citywide meeting in Sulphur Springs,
about sixty-five miles north of Tyler but was prompted to cancel the proposed
meeting when his father became seriously ill. In June 1949, a woman who lived
in Sulphur Springs and listened to John every Sunday night on the radio, called
him. "Brother Rawlings, I'm praying that you'll come to Sulphur Springs for a
tent crusade. I've got a daughter and son-in-law who are unsaved, and maybe
we can get them saved."

A few days later, John went to Sulphur Springs and found a beautiful piece
of land across from the city park that was ideal for a tent meeting. On Saturday
morning before daylight, John had an eighteen-wheeler loaded with his tent
and seats sitting on that lot, ready to go. By daylight, he had about forty men
working, and in less than an hour, the tent was up. Several police cars were
driving around, watching, but nobody stopped John and his men.

The meeting was to set to start the following Wednesday. Despite the
ordinance in Sulphur Springs that prohibited handing out religious literature,

John sent Curtis Goldman and Fred Harris to pass out pamphlets and preach on the streets to gear up for the revival. John booked a radio program so he could get the news out over the airwaves and made arrangements to have an ad placed in the city newspaper. After all this hard work, everything was in order by Wednesday night.

Before the meeting began, John received a strange call from Curtis at his home in Tyler. He had just taken a shower, and it was about five o'clock in evening when the phone rang. "Preacher, the chief of police just hit me and had his hand on his gun." Curtis had gone to see him about the meeting. The chief realized he had overstepped his bounds when Curtis, who had been a glider pilot in World War II, turned his other cheek toward him and said, "I've only got two cheeks. When you hit this one, it's going to be different."

Now in those days, phone calls meant telephone operators. John was well known in his hometown of Tyler, and the girls at the telephone company liked to listen in on his conversations because they were often pretty "salty." The story of Curtis being struck by the police chief soon began to spread. One of John's church members, who was also a telephone operator, spread the news to the other girls, and they got on their phones and began spreading the word.

Meanwhile, John put on his clothes and told his wife, "Honey, if the chief puts me in jail, don't worry."

His wife, the practical woman she was and just as tough as her husband, simply answered, "Okay," and watched him drive off.

John took West Bole Street and headed for Sulphur Springs. On the way, he stopped at a service station for a fill-up. Two of his friends happened to be there: a member of the Hughes clan, who held a rifle, and Big Jack McGaughey who had a .44 pistol on his belt. In those days, Texas still held the reputation of being part of the "wild wild West."

"What in the world you fellas doing?" asked John.

"Going to Sulphur Springs. We hear they're gonna have church tonight." They'd already heard the news from the telephone!

That night in Sulphur Springs, sixty-five miles from Tyler, there were 237 members from John's church in Tyler on the grounds where the tent was located. Many of the men had shotguns, some of them just back from World War II. They said, "This is our country; we can have church anywhere, anytime. That's what we fought for—liberty!"

Seventeen police and sheriffs' cars were parked near the tent. Tension was high. John didn't know what was going to happen, but he told his people, "We're not going to have a riot unless the law enforcement under direction of the chief of police takes action. If they abuse me, we'll take over the city." He asked his pianist to play a congregational song, and the congregation sang two verses. John's plan was to then go to the platform to pray and begin preaching.

His first sermon was titled "Who Is the Devil in Sulphur Springs?" Of course, most of the townspeople assumed he was referring to the police chief, so interest was building. The police chief himself even came to see what John would say about him. John's sermon was really about the Devil of the Bible, not the chief of police, but he knew how to take advantage of a situation, turn it around, and draw a crowd to lead people to Christ.

The first night of the meeting, about seven people were saved during the service, including a young mother and her three teenage daughters, but the Devil continued to fight the meeting as it continued. And it seemed that nothing was happening. The lull in the meeting continued through Sunday night and all the next week. Crowds were slim, and tension was high.

On Saturday of the second week, a Boy Scout jamboree was to take place in the city park, where about fifteen to twenty Boy Scout troops were camped out. John had rented a big-frame house for his staff to stay in while in Sulpher Springs, which was just down the street from the park, when he had an idea. He had his picture printed on posters and sent one of his preachers to the store to get masking tape. On Friday night after church, he and his friends taped posters and handbills all over about twenty cars, giving them something to look at when they were finished. The next morning was the Boy Scouts parade. John worked it out so that those cars were interspersed among the Boy Scout troupes. When the first troupe came by playing trumpets, it was followed by one of the advertising cars. Then came the next troupe, next car, next troupe, next car, and so on. It was something!

One of John's men, Fred Harris, was an innovator himself. He had gone in front of the parade, picked up a ladder, and climbed up on a building next to the courthouse square near the entrance of the street where the parade had commenced. The chief of police was directing traffic, standing at the entrance of the street. And who was driving the first car in the parade but Goldie, the man the chief had attacked. Fred called out in a loud voice, "Hey, Goldie, ain't that the chief of police that whipped you?"

The chief was standing within five feet of Goldie, and they both became very nervous. Harris continued for several minutes, and then the chief started directing traffic again. Soon, John heard what sounded like a riot about 150 feet from where he was. Fred Harris had gone up the street and recruited a bunch of Sulphur Springs natives and told them about the chief "whipping" Goldie. Those men would have started a riot and maybe even tried to hang the chief had John not intervened!

After all the advertising during the parade, the tent was packed with people that night with the audience spilling outside. After that night, the tent meeting lasted about seven and a half more weeks, and hundreds of people were saved.

Out of curiosity, John asked a native of Sulphur Springs who owned the land where he was holding his revival and was told two "old maid" sisters. He then asked if he could be taken to their home, which was only about a half mile or so from the lot. John knocked on the door until he heard a woman's voice answer sweetly, "Just a minute!"

She answered the door in her nightgown. "What do you want?"

John introduced himself, "I'm the preacher, and I need to talk to you about using your lot."

"I heard you already had a meeting on our property!" she answered.

"I hear you and your sister are Methodist, and that you love Jesus."

"Yes, we're Christians."

John began to unfold his plan. "The Lord told me that you are to sell those lots to this new baby church."

"We've never thought about that."

"Well you can't take it to heaven with you," he said strategically. "And your dad and mom in heaven would like that. They may even talk to Jesus about it. So tell me, how much you want for them?"

The woman hesitated. "We would have to talk to our brother."

There wasn't a moment to lose. John told her and her sister to get dressed and get in his car. He would take them to go talk to their brother.

The sisters dutifully obeyed, and the three arrived at the brother's farm at about ten o'clock that night. John persisted in his desire for a price on the property. The brother and sisters discussed it and offered him a sum. It was too much.

"I'll give you twenty-four hundred dollars," John offered.

That looked like pretty big stuff, so they finally agreed. They would close on the deal the next day.

So there he was, having taken a leap of faith in saying he would close the deal for twenty-four hundred dollars but without the funds. *Either stupidity or faith or maybe both,* he thought. He took the sisters back home and returned to his own home in Tyler. He slept for a mere two hours before going visiting the next morning as usual.

John drove around the west side of town to where one of his friends owned a used car lot. This man had previously made his living as a bootlegger. "Well, preacher," his friend said. "How's the meeting going?"

"It's coming along," answered John.

"Good. We've been praying. You need anything?"

"Yessir," he answered. "I've got a business deal. We're buying the property where the tents are set up, but I've got no money."

"How much are you paying for it?" the man asked.

"Twenty-four hundred dollars cash. I'm supposed to be at the courthouse at 1:00 p.m. today."

The man fell silent for a moment and then responded, "Would you answer my phone here while I'm gone? I'll be back in a little while."

John said yes but was in a bit of a stupor. He didn't know what was going on, but God did.

His friend came back twenty-five minutes later and handed him an envelope. Inside were twenty-four one hundred dollar bills!

"Brother, I don't have a note," John said, overwhelmed. You can imagine how happy he was!

"Brother John, I was lost and on my way to hell, and you cared about my soul. The least I can do is make these funds available. Your word is as good as your bond. I know you'll pay me back when you get the money. No hurry."

Talk about God taking over! John drove back to the house, put his "preacher clothes" on, and told his wife, "Honey, I'm going to Sulphur Springs to make a transaction. I won't be back until after the meeting tonight." He drove to Sulphur Springs and was at the courthouse by one o'clock. The transaction was completed, the deed signed, and the new church born from the tent meeting now owned the property!

During the meeting that night, John told the congregation that a friend had loaned money to purchase the property and that they needed to take up money. "I want everybody that doesn't have a hundred dollars to start praying for it," he said, and before that meeting was over, he had twenty-four hundred dollars. The baby church had paid for its property!

Curtis Goldman's father, who was a builder, laid the foundation for a new forty-by-sixty foot church building. Later that week, on a Saturday morning, a large group of men from Central Baptist took buses to Sulphur Springs and began constructing the church building, starting with nothing but a cement foundation. John's son Carrol remembers seeing nearly one hundred men working on the new building; they looked to him like a "swarm of bees." A number of women also came to prepare food and assist in ways men don't necessarily excel. When time came for the evening service, the walls were up, the roof was on, the windows and doors were installed, and the temporary lighting was ready. Although the building probably did not meet all of today's strict building codes, the church body at that time met in this structure until the permanent building was completed.

On the last Saturday of the meeting in Sulphur Springs, John supervised a crew of seventy-four volunteer workers from Central Baptist to build the new building in a single day. He went to Sam R. Hill Lumber Company and explained what supplies they needed to Sam, the owner, who was a Methodist who attended Marvin Methodist in Tyler.

"But I don't have any money," John told him.

"That's alright, John. You're an honest man."

John got his materials, but he realized he had forgotten about electricity. Previously, he had led a beautiful young lady to Christ whose husband was an electrician in Tyler, the one who had boldly said he'd "whip the hell out of John" for "trying to have an affair with his wife." When he asked who was the best electrician in town, it turned out to be this lady's husband. So John contacted Jack Bridges, who drove him down to the electrician's house. Forty minutes later, they pulled into the driveway, and a pickup truck pulled in behind them. Out climbed the electrician. John got out to meet him. "I've heard that you want to whip me," he said, "but I've got one problem."

"What the hell is it?" the man demanded.

"I've got to have an electrician, and they told me you're the best in this county. I want you to wire up my building for me."

"You want me to *what*?"

"I want you to wire this building. Jack here has the money, so you and he go downtown, buy all the electrical equipment you need, and fix up my building. I've got some helpers here for you too. You're the boss. I want this building wired, so I can preach in it tonight."

The electrician shook his head in disbelief, but he gave in. Jack went downtown with him to make the necessary purchases. When they came back,

John sent about six helpers to the property to wire the new building, telling them, "Joe here is the boss. When he tells you jump, you jump."

At six o'clock that evening, they finished the job, and Joe turned the lights on. John said, "Joe, there's unfinished business between us. Now I don't know whether you have a good smeller or not, but I'm sweaty, and I haven't had a bath in two days … been too busy. I haven't slept. So if you don't mind, let's put this business off until tomorrow so I can get a bath and preach tonight."

Joe took John by the hand and said, "Reverend, you're alright." Joe got saved, became an officer in that church, and he and John became good friends. God blessed and anointed the experience.

The new church was named Central Baptist Church after John's back in Tyler and was officially organized June 14, 1949, with twenty-six charter members and pastored by F. R. Sudduth. Seventy-two workers built the first church building, a one-story frame structure, in just one day on Saturday, June 25, 1949!

19

The Search for Souls in East Texas

John began preaching on the streets of Brownsboro, Texas, a small town located between Athens and Tyler, but after preaching there a couple of times, he met with opposition. On a hot August day with the temperature hovering around one hundred degrees even in the shade, John received a letter from some of the citizens saying that the next time he showed up, they would tar and feather him and ride him out of town on a rail. Brownsboro was a "wicked" town situated at the edge of the oil field, and their intention was to stop him from preaching altogether. For protection the next time he headed into Brownsboro, John thought, *I had better get me some fellas to take with me.*

But with a great deal on his mind and an entire week having gone by, he neglected to make the necessary calls for his companions. When Saturday morning came, Jack Bridges, the leader of the church's youth group who usually traveled with John, was unable to accompany him. John began to have second thoughts about taking his wife and baby boy. A man was considered a sissy if those Texans "saw [him] under a petticoat," and they wouldn't have had any respect for him. John was scared for his life, but he wound up driving from Tyler to Brownsboro by himself. He put his public address system on the top of his vehicle and drove to an abandoned gas station about a hundred yards south of town where he usually stopped to look over the situation.

Looking "up yonder," John saw about four hundred people milling about the town square, presumably waiting for his impending arrival, but the number looked more like four hundred *thousand* to the anxious preacher.

John played a recording of Dr. Charles Fuller's Old Fashioned Revival Hour Quartet singing, "Having a Little Talk with Jesus Makes It Right." That week John had tried praying, but the Lord "was somewhere, not paying any attention to me, it didn't seem like." He had tried studying his Bible, but it felt as dry as the Sahara Desert. He was now ready to preach a sermon on the street, but he didn't know what he was going to say. He felt absolutely devastated. Out of fear, he opened the Book and said, "Now, Lord," and a breeze gently touched him from another world. He read these words, "The wicked flee when no man pursueth, but the righteous are as bold as a lion" (Proverbs 28:1). Goosebumps stood on him "as big as goose eggs." He said, "Thank you, Lord." He put the Book on the front seat, restarted the song, and drove into the middle of town. The people parted on each side like the waters of the Red Sea, but nonetheless, he could feel the spirit of the angry mob.

John got out—"one lone little hillbilly redneck preacher"—turned the microphone on, and said, "You sorry so-and-sos who wrote me this letter, you don't have enough guts to digest a hamburger!" With the Bible in his hand and the verse God had shown him, he preached to them. It was by the grace of the Lord sustaining him that he didn't suffer from heatstroke. Because of the heat and adverse conditions, his vision clouded, but he kept preaching anyway, the power of the Holy Spirit sustaining him physically and spiritually.

The crowd stood there without any movement. Suddenly, a couple standing to the side—a man wearing an old, floppy cowboy hat and boots and a woman wearing an apron, "who looked liked a nail keg with a band around her"— came toward John. The man took off his hat and said, "Reverend, me and my wife are sinners, and I'd appreciate it if you'd tell us how to be saved." John led them to Jesus, and the old man turned and told the people, "You know me and what a sinner I've been!" He made evident the change in his heart, and the floodgates opened.

John then began leading others to Christ. There was a tall Texan with a cowboy hat who stood up on the bumper of John's car and said, "This little preacher's got more courage than all the men in this county. We've never given him anything, but we're going to take up an offering!" Deep down within himself, John thought, *AMEN!*

Afterward, the cowboy came up to John and asked, "What do you want me to do with the money?" John told him to put it in his car, and the cowboy dumped it in the front seat.

John had been so intoxicated with the Spirit of God that he hadn't noticed the crowd had dispersed. While he was preaching, he had noticed a well-dressed man leaning against a white column of the bank building. Now that man walked toward John until he stood towering over him.

"Brother John," he said, putting his arm around John's shoulders, "let's go over here into the drugstore. It's the only place in town with air conditioning. You need something cold to drink."

"Let me get my money," John said.

"Oh, it'll be alright."

They walked across the street, and the man asked the person behind the counter to get John a glass of water. The big, old, tall Texan put his hand over John's. "Preacher, I'm president of the bank. There was a crowd of us who had already got together, and we weren't going to let anybody hurt you."

Why in the name of God didn't you tell me that before? I was scared to death! John thought.

Out of those meetings, a Baptist church was organized, began to grow, and exists to this day.

John faced many similar situations and challenges as well as exciting and unique opportunities. During a tent revival in Longview, Texas, producers of an upcoming film starring Rock Hudson contacted John to request that the people who came to the tent revival be extras, or background performers. John met with Rock Hudson over a meal to discuss the idea, and John agreed to the proposal because it served as a great promotion for the revival. This was very early during Rock Hudson's film career; he continued to work as an American film and television actor, recognized during the 1950s and 60s as a heartthrob and leading male actor. Rock Hudson sent his right-hand man to get John's crowd to come up and pack the streets the next day. Over their meal together at a restaurant in Longview, John tried to win Hudson to the Lord, but to no avail. He did not express any interest in what John had to say in sharing the Gospel. Rock Hudson died of AIDS on October 2, 1985. Though John did see many salvation decisions during his ministry as a pastor, not all who heard the Word of the Lord chose to be saved.

20

Baptist Bible Fellowship

When you look at these characters, these personalities, that were really the founding fathers of this movement, you're looking at men who were missionaries, educators, soldiers, leaders ... these men had it! They were not intellectual pygmies, they were giants. Doctrinal footing and foundation keeps us together ... that alone. And it's based upon this Book.

—DR. JOHN W. RAWLINGS

In 1950, John met with a group of approximately 150 Baptist ministers at the Texas Hotel in Fort Worth, Texas, to help organize the Baptist Bible Fellowship (BBF). A split had divided the independent Baptist ranks. The old guard was led by J. Frank Norris; the new group in Springfield was led by G. Beauchamp (G. B.) Vick, the youth director at First Baptist Church in Fort Worth in the late 1920s before becoming the Sunday school superintendent and music director under Norris at Temple Baptist Church in Detroit, Michigan, in 1935. After the split, he was voted in as pastor of the congregation. Vick was joined by John W. Rawlings, Noel Smith, W. E. Dowell, Fred Donnelson, R. O. Woodworth, Wendell Zimmerman, and Loys Vess in founding the BBF.

That same year, they published and began circulating a weekly newspaper, *Baptist Bible Tribune*, and Baptist Bible College was also started in Springfield, Missouri. Because of the rift that developed between Vick and Norris over the operation of Bible Baptist Seminary in Fort Worth, Vick and his colleagues determined to establish a new Bible college in Springfield, Missouri, separate from Norris's school. Thus, John contributed to the establishment of the Baptist Bible College in Springfield, Missouri.

The split was due to the financial condition of the Fort Worth seminary. At the time of the split, Norris was in his seventies and was facing a real leadership crisis with the board of the seminary and the younger pastors. He felt he was no longer in charge and was fighting for his life. Norris didn't have anyone capable of directing financial support at the school. Vick, who followed in Norris's footsteps as pastor of Temple Baptist Church in Detroit, Michigan, was singled out for the job because he was so gifted with finances. In 1948, John met with Vick and discussed his assuming the presidency of Bible Baptist Seminary in Fort Worth. At first, Vick wasn't interested because on Friday nights he taught an adult Bible class at Temple Baptist that was broadcast live on the radio to over sixty stations. He was known for his expository teaching and didn't desire the position of president because of time constraints and the additional work. He felt he would need to relinquish his radio ministry to become president. Vick and John remained as close as brothers during this time.

Vick and Norris both possessed very strong personalities; neither was afraid to contradict the other. Norris saw some leadership problems arising and anticipated that he would have to take his hand off the main throttle sooner or later. Much of this activity developed between 1948 and 1950.

Norris made accusations against Vick, and then Vick rebutted them and felt forced to resign. Norris fired the trustees and most of the staff and at a meeting on a Tuesday morning set up a "kangaroo court" with a new Board of Trustees to "clean house." Bill Dowell, pastor of High Street Baptist Church in Springfield, Missouri, had the courage to stand up during the meeting and challenge Norris. For the first time in his ministry, Norris was confronted by a group of young men who were not afraid of controversy. That was how the BBF movement was born.

The controversy continued, however, when Norris took Vick out to lunch following the morning session of a business meeting and attempted to brainwash him. John later said he thought Norris did a good job at that. Norris allowed Vick to take the platform when they reconvened, not knowing he had talked

Vick into starting a school in Springfield and working with him. Norris was going to cut off one person at a time. John found Vick in a small room off the auditorium, sitting with his head in his hands. The split was harder on him than anyone else. John took him by the arm and said, "Beauchamp, get up. [Someone] said you sold us down the river."

"John, I haven't sold you fellas down the river."

"You didn't compromise with Norris?" John asked.

He hesitated. "Let's get out of here and tell the pastors."

Reg Woodsworth had told Norris, "You can't control these young men. They're going to split. You've got a make a concession; it's not going to hurt you." He did his best to make Norris see it and to retract what he had done, but Norris wouldn't do it. He said, "I don't think they'll split. You talk to them." Norris said those who split could be easily replaced but Reg kept saying, "They'll quit." Reg later became the business manager and Vick's right hand man at BBC. He made many favorable contributions to the BBF. He was a people person and did so much for young preachers and their wives.

Early on Monday, as people were driving in for the election of a president for the seminary, Norris pulled a quick one and elected his own presidential candidate. John and others were concerned Norris was trying to destroy them.

Noel Smith was the first to walk out of the meeting. As he left, he posed the searching question, "Isn't there any honor left among men?"

Others left the meeting and agreed to convene at the Texas Hotel ballroom in downtown Fort Worth. This was destined to be the place for the formation of the new fellowship, an independent, autonomous church movement without any denominational or hierarchal control, making it unique to other movements and organizations. It was not organized according to a top-down, command-and-control hierarchy, but built from the ground up with its members held together by common interest. Other groups founded by one man became cultic in some cases, but the BBF movement never came to a titular head and did not require one, as it was a living, breathing movement founded upon zeal for Christ and His kingdom.

The ballroom began to fill with young pastors and college students who had been expelled for opposing Norris. Loys Vess, a young pastor from Denton, Texas, played a vital role because he was responsible for helping to organize the meeting. At noon, a vote was taken to elect Vick as the new president of the college. John was elected vice president and Bill Dowell was elected president of the new Baptist Bible Fellowship (BBF). Noel Smith was appointed as editor of the paper *Baptist Bible Tribune,* and the paper was in circulation within about ten days.

One hundred and four pastors were present at the meeting. The whole movement was born on a Wednesday afternoon in 1950, including the missions organization and the Bible college. This was a happy time for many as the Texas meeting moved up to Denton and the joyful celebration continued on into the evening. Fred Donnellson summed it up this way, "I feel like I've been cleansed!" It was as if a yoke had been thrown off.

But Norris was not giving up; he still felt he could hold the Texas pastors together. Soon after the split, he began slandering the character of many of the pastors who rebelled against him. He sent his sister-in-law Miss Britain to try to split John's young church in Tyler, though Norris didn't attack John personally.

After that portion of the controversy was over, Vess never did get the honor that was due him. He didn't have a formal education, but he was a powerful evangelist. He took beating after beating, as did L. T. Grantham. Mrs. Vick and her family also went through a great deal of stress from Norris's attacks, which were in the paper and on the radio, as well as from the Fraser brothers from Fort Worth who had once pastored John's church in Tyler, Texas. A few weeks after the controversy, one of John's men said to him, "John, Bill Fraser was in town yesterday trying to dig up some dirt on you."

"Really?" he said.

"Yeah, he went to old man Miller's and was trying to find out if there's anything financially or morally they could use against you."

Another fellow told about two other people Bill had talked to. John knew Bill very well. That night driving home, John told his wife, "Honey, I'm going to Fort Worth in the morning."

"You have a meeting?"

"Yeah, a business meeting."

Early the next morning, John drove 140 miles to Fort Worth. At about a quarter to eight, Bill Fraser would show up at First Baptist Church and head upstairs to Norris's staff meeting.

John waited in his car and watched Bill waddle up the street. "Good morning, Reverend Fraser."

"Huh? Um ... huh? John, what brings you to Fort Worth so early in the morning?"

"I have a meeting," John answered.

"Oh, really?"

"Yeah, I have a meeting with *you*." John invited him to breakfast at the café nearby on Fourth Street.

"Hmmm, well … hmm … okay."

John led him to the restaurant.

The waitress brought two glasses of water and two menus, and John said, "We're not going to eat anything. Bring him a cup of tea and me a cup of coffee.

"Reverend Fraser, I understand you were in Tyler Saturday trying to dig up some things for Dr. Norris on my character."

"Huh-uh, no, John, I, just, uh, I was just down there visiting some friends!"

"Yeah, I know they're your friends, but some of them are my enemies. Reverend Fraser, look at me." John reached into his holster, pulled out his .38 revolver, and laid it on the table. "You have to understand where a man comes from. My family just will not tolerate things like this. I come from a different breed. I'm not G. B. Vick; I'm not L. T. Grantham. I'm John Rawlings." He broke down the revolver and asked, "You see that bullet in that barrel? That has your name on it. You see this other one? It has Dr. Norris's name on it. Norris shot Chipps and never spent a day in jail. I'll get both of you, and I'll get a medal of honor from the state of Texas. Now, Reverend, don't ever let my name come across the headlines of *The Fundamentalist*. You understand?"

Reverend Fraser turned white with a sheen of sweat on his brow and beads of sweat dripping off his face on that hot Texas morning, as restaurants in those days existed without the luxury of air conditioning.

"Don't do it, because the day you do and that paper comes out, you and Dr. Norris have had it." John was raised to handle his problems adeptly, quickly, and cleanly. "Do you understand?" he repeated.

"Yes, I understand."

"Do you *really* understand?"

"Yes, I *really* understand!"

John put his gun back, picked up the ticket, left a tip, paid for the coffee and tea, said, "I'll see ya." He then left the restaurant, got into his car, and drove back home.

And his name never did appear in *The Fundamentalist,* and that put a capstone on the controversy. John jokes, "I don't know what the Lord will do to me when I get to heaven. I've prayed about it; it's in His hands. I did what I thought was right at the time."

Baptists also broke away from the Northern Baptist Convention. The BBF movement was birthed through Norris's clash with the convention. John was friends of many great leaders of other Baptist movements that broke away from the Northern Baptist Convention, such as Robert Ketchum, head of the General Association of Regular Baptists (GARB); Dr. Jackson; Dr. David Jeremiah's father, Dr. James Jeremiah; W. B. Riley; and T. T. Shields, who was considered the Charles Spurgeon of Canada. These men were a great influence on the conservative Baptist movement of the twentieth century.

Because of John's preaching in the South, he knew of Noel Smith, but he was not close to him while he edited Norris's paper. But after the split, he and John became friends. Noel came to class one morning at Baptist Bible College, and his luggage had gotten lost. He was grunting and grumbling about it, saying, "I suppose when I die, they'll try to ship me to Knoxville, but they'll lose the body." His words were prophetic; when he died, the funeral was held at BBC in Springfield. The next day as the body was to arrive in Knoxville for a graveside service, to the surprise of all, it wound up in Miami, Florida.

Fred Donnelson and John traveled together. Fred was a "one-track man," a missionary, who never did anything but missions. He lived it, breathed it, slept it; he did it day and night. He was a giant in the faith. Mission was the right arm of the BBF movement. The late Wendell Zimmerman, a pastor from Kansas City, was not a great preacher when it came to evangelism, but he was the best expositor in the movement. George Hodges of Jacksonville, Florida, was a friend of John's and was the hardest working pastor he ever knew. He played a large role, as did Dennis Brown who pastored in Greely, Colorado, at the time.

United States Senator Earle Bradford Mayfield from Texas was a personal friend of John's as well governor Coke R. Stevenson, the thirty-fifth governor of Texas from 1941 to 1947. Norris believed that John had some influence in Austin, so he asked him to set up a meeting with the board of education, and he, Entzminger, and John would go to the board in Austin to get credentials for the seminary. John spoke to the board and accreditation was given to the school. John enjoyed the political facet of ministry.

John met G. B. Vick in 1939. Vick was a "hillbilly redneck" from down in the hills of Kentucky. If you wronged him, he had extreme difficulty getting over it. But if you were his friend, he couldn't see your faults. John used to kid him a lot, telling him he named a bull calf Beauchamp after Vick.

Vick couldn't sing, but he knew how to get a crowd to sing.

When Vick went to Temple Baptist at Norris's request, the church grew over fifteen hundred members in one year under his leadership. God was really in Vick's move to Temple, Michigan.

John preached at Temple for the first time in 1942 or 1943. He had never flown in a plane before, and he flew into Michigan in a "little puddle-jumper." He thought he was going to die that day. He got into Detroit at 11:25 p.m., emotionally exhausted and scared to death. But a great crowd of young people from Temple met him at the airport and made him feel so welcome. He never forgot that wonderful experience. John loved going to Detroit because they would tell him, "You're the best preacher we've ever heard." The preachers were foolish enough to believe it! Dr. Vick was greatly loved and respected by his congregation at Temple Baptist.

The Baptist Bible College once went through a deep recession due to a number of reasons, but some of it was attached to the times through which the country was passing. But the college has been the bedrock and foundation for the growth of the movement. Pastors and missionaries received their training, doctrine was instilled in the hearts and minds of the students, and young men and women went out throughout the country representing a common cause.

Suddenly, men began surfacing across the country, and fellowship meetings were held to unite them. Doctrinal footing and foundation held the BBF together. The meetings were essential to the growth, development, and vision of the movement, for it was at these meetings that visions were caught and young men rededicated their lives to their callings. John likens it to a prairie fire that once started begins to spread, and it has been blazing ever since. The number of churches grew from one hundred to four thousand by the early 1990s.

When John became president of the BBF, he recognized a growing negative spirit. He knew the mission of the movement needed to be retooled. A split was avoided, bringing about a swing of growth for the mission movement and the college. "You cannot put a harness on a real Baptist or a real Baptist church and survive. It is necessary to have an organization that keeps people headed in the right direction." As Vick said, "The difference between a mob and an army is organization."

Landmark Baptist Temple
Site of September, 1974 Annual Baptist
Bible Fellowship business meeting in Cincinnati, Ohio.

John Rawlings
1975 President, Baptist Bible Fellowship

Bill Bright of Campus Crusade for Christ once called to ask John, who was president of the BBF at the time, to head a national affairs committee. "Bill, you know I'm a Baptist and one of the founders of Baptist Bible College and Baptist Bible Fellowship. If I were to take this position, a number of my young preacher friends would misread it and not understand. I want to thank you for your consideration of me." John had led to Christ and baptized one of Bill's right-hand men at Landmark Baptist Temple. Dr. Bright said, "Brother John, deep down in my heart, I believe just like you believe. But because of my position, I can't be as outspoken about it like you are."

BBC started classes at High Street Baptist Church at the corner of High and Prospect with 107 students. By the mid-1970s, enrollment hit a high of two thousand students.

In about 1972, the Fellowship was near splitting. In places like Illinois, Indiana, Kansas, Texas, and others, there was great dissention. At a meeting in Cincinnati, John was elected president. He appointed Wendell Zimmerman as the chairman of the revision committee. Alvis Edmondson also was a real help. Pastors and missionaries were brought in to "air their grievances." They felt it should be restructured.

In the Denver meeting two years later, the Fellowship voted for the current structure. Neither could Texas tell Oklahoma what to do, nor the other way around; a structure existed with liberty. A church could not join the Fellowship but had to become a part of it, if they were comfortable with the doctrine. The BBFI stands head and shoulders above all, including the Southern Baptist Convention, because churches, pastors, and missionaries can have great fellowship, liberty, and unity in doctrinal beliefs, all without fear of intimidation.

21

Baptist Bible College

Herb Rawlings, Bill Aven, and his future wife, Phyllis, were first-year students at BBC in 1950 with 107 students. Harold Rawlings attended a year later, and Jerry Falwell enrolled the next year. During the time Herb spent with Jerry Falwell at the Baptist Bible College, they were roommates with Julius Blaz, who had a girlfriend in Lynchburg, Virginia, named Macel Pate. Herb recalls that Jerry "stole" Macel away from Julius, although no hurt feelings resulted. Subsequently, Macel became Mrs. Falwell, and she and Jerry later had three children. Their daughter Jeannie became a surgeon; their son Jonathan a senior pastor of Thomas Road Baptist Church in Virginia; and their eldest son, Jerry Jr., chancellor of Liberty University.

While studying at the Baptist Bible College, Jerry's goal was to build the largest twelve-year-old class in the intermediate department of Sunday school at High Street Baptist Church in Springfield, Missouri. He succeeded in doing so his very first year.

John "put the wheels on the plans for securing the campus," according to Leland Kennedy, future president of the college, "and many of the major decisions made in the early days came from his heart." When John became vice president of the college, he started traveling to promote the BBF and BBC. Also around this time, in 1958, John was presented with an honorary doctorate from Bob Jones University in Greenville, South Carolina, and became widely known as Dr. John W. Rawlings or just Dr. John. He devoted one week of the month to promoting the Fellowship and the college, but he often traveled and promoted the school almost weekly. Nearly every Monday, he caught a flight out of Cincinnati and returned on Tuesday night. Countless times, he caught a plane in Los Angeles, flew all night, and was back in Cincinnati the next morning at eight o'clock.

Youth camps became the lifeline of the BBC. By 1965, the institution was comprised of about twelve hundred students. By the mid-1970s, Baptist Bible College had become one of the leading institutions in training pastors, evangelists, and missionaries.

Dr. John served as vice president of the school from its inception until 1975 alongside President G. B. Vick, who served from 1950 until his death in 1975. The second president was W.E. Dowell from 1975 to 1983, followed by A.V. Henderson from 1983 to 1986. Leland R. Kennedy served from 1986 to 2002. Kennedy notes that, as organizers of the BBF and BBC, "Dr. John and Vick made a good team." As the catalyst for building the BBF, Dr. John "was a motivator, and Vick was an organizer. Vick wouldn't have had as much to organize if Dr. John had not cast the vision." After Kennedy resigned as president of the college, Mike Randall followed.

Dr. John was later elected president of the BBF, which was later renamed BBF International. Twice he served as president of BBF International, from 1952 to 1954 and 1974 to 1977. By 1975, the missions program was supported by approximately four thousand pastors and churches. At one point, the organization ranked the third largest Baptist group in the United States, surpassed only by the Southern Baptist Convention and the American Baptist Churches.

A branch campus of Baptist Bible College was founded at Shrub Oak, New York, as Baptist Bible College East in 1976 by Dr. John and A. V. Henderson. The school moved to Boston, Massachusetts, in 1981. In 2002, the name of the college was changed from Baptist Bible College East to Boston Baptist College. Since its founding in 1976, the school has been equipping and training men and women for service and ministry in the United States and around the world.

Later, Dr. John aided in the development of the International Baptist Network, an organization involving many independent Baptist churches. According to the organization's website, "The iBaptist Network is a national and international network of Baptists, linked together by common doctrine and a desire to effectively carry out the Great Commission."[15]

---

15   "About iBaptist.net." *International Baptist Network:* http://ibaptistnet.blogspot.com
      (February 22, 2013).

Dr. John's work with the other founders of the BBF was not limited to business matters only. They also enjoyed camaraderie and often played practical jokes on one another.

Leaders of the BBF were constantly on the move, traveling throughout the States to get the movement started. Once, Fred Donnelson and John were traveling together in Fred's Buick Roadmaster from Florida to Richmond, Virginia, to attend a Fellowship meeting. They drove through northern Georgia through all the police traps. But Dr. John said he only "pays taxes" in the fast lane, so he took the wheel and Donnelson was "all prayed up" by the time they reached Richmond. Vick flew from Detroit to Richmond for the Fellowship meeting.

John and Vick attended the meeting together on Tuesday afternoon after lunch. They sat on the second row from the front, listening to "the preacher, God love him," whose sermon was "pretty dry." Having just eaten, Dr. John and the other preachers were feeling drowsy. "You would get so doggone sleepy you just nearly die!" Dr. John remembers.

Vick lapsed into a deep sleep and began to snore loudly, and Dr. John was scratching his head and picking his nose, anything to stay awake. *What in the world am I going to do?* Dr. John was thinking. Vick's snoring was making it even harder for him to stay awake. But then the Spirit of the Lord moved Dr. John to open a hymnal and tap Vick's arm. As Dr. John held out the open book to Vick, Dr. John rose just a little from the pew, as if he was about to stand and join the congregation in song. Vick awoke immediately, startled, and shot straight up to his feet to sing, only to find he was standing alone. Embarrassed, he quickly sat back down and turned to Dr. John. "I could kill you," he whispered.

Dry sermons were not the only inducement to put Vick to sleep. He had a fondness for fiction books about cowboys, Indians, and the Old West—especially books by Zane Grey—and reading these before bedtime often lulled him to sleep. One night while rooming together during their travels, Dr. John fell asleep as soon as his head hit the pillow. However, he awoke a little while later, only to find the lights in the room still on, and Vick propped up in bed, "snoring up a storm." Dr. John decided he would have a little fun. He got out of his bed, jumped on top of Vick's, and screamed, "Fire! Fire!"

Vick shot up, knocking Dr. John backward. "Where?" he cried.

Sharing the story, Dr. John remarked, "It was a little bit wild."

Just like the Wild Wild West.

22

City Life in Cincinnati

*For whither thou goest, I will go; and where thou
lodgest, I will lodge: thy people shall be my people, and
thy God my God.*

—RUTH 1:16B

In late February after the Fellowship was established, Dr. John and Dr. Vick
were traveling by train through the mountains of Virginia. Snow blanketed
the ground outside and dusted the boughs of the evergreens. They met one
morning in the breakfast car and talked as the train clickity-clicked through
the beautiful Blue Ridge Mountains.

Having preached at churches all throughout Texas and spending about
twenty-three to twenty-four weeks out of the year on the road, Dr. John was
very troubled at the time. He wondered if perhaps God had finished with
him in Texas, for during invitations at Central Baptist nothing seemed to be
happening. He had been in radio ever since he began pastoring, the church was
out of debt, and they had saturated the city of Tyler, Texas. Every door had been
knocked on many times over. Church attendance was hitting three thousand on
special days and was over thirty-three hundred at the most-attended service—an
astounding feat given the population of the relatively small town. Dr. John
simply felt limited by his present circumstances.

That morning in the train, he shared these concerns with Dr. Vick, who listened with empathy. "John, it may be that one of these days God's going to move you."

For now, the matter was dropped. Dr. John didn't let the feeling disturb him, but he was very concerned. It was during this span of time he was involved in a large meeting at High Street Baptist Church in Springfield, Missouri, where Dowell pastored. Over one hundred people were saved during the Sunday morning service and another one hundred that evening, including some prominent people from the city.

In the spring, Dr. Vick received a call from the chairman of the deacons at First Baptist Church in Lockland, Ohio, a church technically under the American Baptist Convention. They had lost their former pastor and wanted Dr. Vick to recommend a preacher from the number of southern Baptist preachers that had been interviewed. Dr. Vick said, "I know of all the men you're talking about, but there's a man in Texas that you really need. Now the church really has some problems, but of all the preachers I know, Dr. Rawlings can solve those problems for you."

"We've heard of him," said the deacon on the other end of the line. "But we've never heard him preach. If you can, get him to come and preach."

The following Sunday, Bill Dowell traveled from Springfield to preach at First Baptist in Lockland. They interviewed him as well, but he said, "If you can get John Rawlings, do it!"

John received a phone call from Dowell who spoke with him about the position at Lockland. "Bill, look," John answered. "I've just started a thirty-day tent revival in Tyler." The tent seated five thousand, and John was preaching.

"John, you need to pray about this."

John was fighting this call, but God had already begun a work in his heart. Bill Dowell was very persuasive, and John ended up traveling to Lockland that weekend. There had been a hailstorm the previous week, and the smell coming from the fertilizer plant permeated the air. It was such a stench, "you could take a biscuit and sop it up!" John exclaimed.

On Sunday morning, John sat in the chair set aside for him as the congregation sang the doxology, feeling as out of place "as a groundhog at a wedding." When he preached, seven people came forward, some to join the church. That night, John was asked to march in with the choir and sit on the platform, but he declined, saying, "No, no, I'll sit in the congregation with the sinners. When you finish, call me to the platform, and I'll come up to preach."

That night, the treasurer of the church drove John to the train station where he would depart on the 11:30 p.m. train. John was thinking, *This fella is so quiet, I think I've handled this. I won't have to come back here.*

On Thursday night, John received a phone call from the chairman of the deacons and learned the church had called him as pastor. It came as quite a shock, "like you just got married and your mother-in-law calls you up to say, 'I'm coming to live with you!'"

John knew God was working in his heart. His teenage sons gathered around and said, "Daddy, daddy, accept the church! That's where the Cincinnati Reds play!" They truly felt that it *must* be the Lord's will!

"Are you going to accept it?" Mrs. Rawlings asked.

"I told them I'd wait until tomorrow night to tell them." He called the following night and gave his answer. "I'll be up in thirty days."

In the summer of 1951, Dr. John turned in his resignation at Central Baptist Church after pastoring there from 1940 to 1951. It was a difficult transition period for the Rawlings family and the congregation of Central Baptist, but John accepted the pastorate in Lockland, Ohio, a suburb on the northern side of Cincinnati. Charlie Dyer was called as pastor of Central after John left Tyler.

The Rawlings Family in 1951

John and his family had visited Cincinnati, Ohio, before. While pastoring in Tyler in July 1949, John had planned a trip to Detroit, Michigan, to speak at the famous Temple Baptist Church pastored by Dr. Beauchamp Vick (known as G. B. Vick). John also wanted to take his family to Niagara Falls in Canada. The family stopped in Arkansas along the way to pick up his nephew Howard Brewer, so seven of them were packed into the 1948 Chrysler. They drove through Cincinnati, Ohio, a great industrial center at that time. Companies such as Proctor & Gamble, Nu-Maid Margarine, Kahn's meats, and many distilleries lined the valley. Dark smokestacks and towering factories stood against the gray sky. Despite the billowing smoke and what people would now label as pollution, people considered the businesses a great thing because they consistently created jobs.

The family passed the fertilizer plant, Darling & Company of Lockland, where horse carcasses were processed to make glue. After leaving the city, the adventure became a joke among the family. "We sure hope the good Lord never calls us to that place," they would laugh. "You could take a slice of bread, hold it up, and you had it already anointed. It was really rancid."

"Of all the places we've ever been," said Mrs. Rawlings, "that is one place I will never live."

But in a matter of a few months, the Lord changed their minds, or as Dr. John puts it, their "want to." Transitioning from the quiet, peaceful town of Tyler, Texas, to the bustling, industrial city of Cincinnati was difficult at first for John and his family. The stark contrast between the beautiful, green East Texas town and the gray, smoky skyline of Cincinnati was vast. But slowly, they became accustomed to the foreign atmosphere and the new sights, smells, and sounds surrounding them.

The New York Central mainline railroad was directly behind Lockland Baptist Church, John's new pastorate. There was a roundhouse rail station located in Sharonville, just north of the church, so there was a great deal of rail traffic—noise all hours of the day and night. At that time, the homes burned coal as did the trains. No matter how often a car was washed, it always seemed to be coated in a layer of soot.

A certain tenement house between where the Rawlings family moved and the railroad tracks still had an outhouse standing in its yard, or an "outside crapper," as John labeled it.

Darling and Company was just northeast of the property and put out a terrible stench. It was so bad that people were relieved when the wind blew the smell in the opposite direction. Also, the Hirschberg Steel Company, which collected scrap metal and other recyclables, adjoined the property at the back of the church. It was noisy, very dirty, and known for its many stray cats. Cincinnati had earlier been known as "Porkopolis," as it had been a leader in pork processing and packing. But later, as one of the largest cities in the country, it was more glamorously referred to as the "Queen City of the West," a major thoroughfare for people traveling west.

Around the 1920s, the Cincinnati area was known as "the graveyard of evangelists." The population was in large part German and had Roman Catholic and Lutheran heritages. It was a heavy beer-drinking town, as there were more than twenty breweries and distilleries in the city and in Northern Kentucky. Popular brand names included Burger, Schoenling, Hudepohl, Bavarian, and Wiedemann.

Billy Sunday visited the Cincinnati area in 1921 to challenge sinners to hit the "sawdust trail." On his revival tours, he would often erect a wooden tabernacle for the services with sawdust spread on the ground. In the revival meetings John had conducted throughout East Texas, he used tents as Billy Sunday did and often covered the ground with sawdust as well. Although Billy Sunday's meetings in the 1920s were well attended and received a great deal of publicity, Billy Graham didn't come to the area until much later, as the area was not viewed as a hospitable area for Gospel preaching.

Cincinnati was a very important center of American commerce during the Second World War, producing products like engines, guns and weapons systems, ammunition, uniforms, and medals. A Landmark member, Esther Vittitoe, described how part of her work was sewing buttons on officers uniforms. She was one of the best at what she did and spoke proudly that she had personal requests for her services.

Although Cincinnati was considered a conservative town with a strong German heritage, entertainment seekers could go across the river to the city of Newport, where gambling and prostitution were rampant but cleverly disguised behind seemingly legitimate businesses, restaurants, and nightclubs. "Otherwise legal businesses ... now became 'speakeasies,' or in Kentucky parlance 'tiger blinds.'"[16] This drew thousands to Newport every weekend. Until 1961, gambling was open in the city.[17]

---

16   Matthew DeMichele and Gary Potter, "Sin City Revisited: A Case Study of the Official Sanctioning of Organized Crime in an 'Open City.'" *Newport Gambling: http://www. rootsweb.ancestry.com/~kycampbe/newportgambling.htm* (November 4, 2010).

17   Calvin Trillin, "Across the River," U.S. *Journal: The New Yorker* (March 1976): 114.

George Ratterman, a reform candidate running for sheriff of Campbell County, Kentucky, just across the river from Cincinnati, ran on a pledge to clean up vice and gambling due to the reign of the Mafia, or the Syndicate, in Newport. Ratterman, a well-known former quarterback for Notre Dame's 1946 national championship team and for the Cleveland Browns, drew national attention when he was framed for arrest. A local attorney and a nightclub operator drugged Ratterman "in an attempt to force him to withdraw from the sheriff's race."[18] They were later convicted for violating his civil rights. "Ratterman had been given a knockout drug and had been taken to a [Newport] hotel room while virtually unconscious in what was evidently a setup."[19] They posed a stripper by the name of April Flowers in the bed with him, and a photographer took pictures to document "the incident," as it later came to be called. However, the FBI uncovered the plot and after a thorough investigation cleared Ratterman of all charges. This was the beginning of the end for the Mafia in Newport. Many of the men involved in the corruption there relocated to Las Vegas and were founders of the gambling industry. Today, there is a restaurant in Newport named The Syndicate as a memorial to that notorious era.

Popular TV shows produced in Cincinnati at the time were the *50-50 Club* with Ruth Lyons, including the Cliff Lash Orchestra and popular singers Bonnie Lou, Marian Spellman, Ruby Wright, and Betty Clooney. The broadcast could be seen all over the Midwest. Another show was the *Midwestern Hayride*, formerly known as the *Boone County Jamboree*. Peter Grant was the premier TV newsman in Cincinnati at the time on WLWT. He was succeeded by Al Schottlekotte on WCPO Channel 9, who became the top television anchor in 1960.

Cincinnati had a large influx of southerners, especially from central and southern Kentucky, in the 1930s and 1940s as Cincinnati grew into an industrialized area and jobs became plentiful. John later would joke about the large segment of the future Landmark church membership that hailed from Pulaski County and the city of Somerset, Kentucky. He would kid them about their Friday afternoon/evening commute "down home" and give

18   Richard Goldstein, "George Ratterman, Football Star and Sherriff, Dies at 80." November 10, 2007. *The New York Times: http://www.nytimes.com/2007/11/10/sports/ football/10ratterman.html* (November 4, 2010).

19   Richard Goldstein, "George Ratterman, Football Star and Sherriff, Dies at 80." November 10, 2007. *The New York Times: http://www.nytimes.com/2007/11/10/sports/ football/10ratterman.html* (November 4, 2010).

them grief for constantly traveling back and forth and frequently missing church services. People moved to the Cincinnati area from eastern and central Kentucky, Tennessee, and North Carolina to work for prominent businesses, such as Proctor & Gamble, General Electric, General Motors, and Ford Motor Company.

Some of these congregants from Kentucky had colorful and sometimes rough backgrounds. Stories abounded from members who drove south on the weekends to their Kentucky homes. Mrs. Elizabeth Downey, who later ran the Landmark Baptist Temple bookstore, told stories of visiting her family in Hazard, Kentucky, where they found entertainment by sitting on a porch watching boys have their Sunday afternoon fights along the main street in town.

The Rawlings family's move from Tyler, Texas, to Cincinnati, Ohio, was clearly the work of the Lord; only for Him would John's family leave their beautiful home in East Texas for what might as well have been another world. John's steadfast loyalty to the Lord was inspiring to many, including those faithful people who, over the years, followed the Rawlings family to Cincinnati from Texas. These loyal friends included family members Earl and Amy James; Silas Moore; Bill and Phyllis Aven; the Kennedy family; Jimmie Kilpatrick (who became John's pianist and financial secretary), and others.

As Ruth of the Old Testament followed Naomi to a new land, John was willing to follow the Lord anywhere, including to unfamiliar surroundings, unknown faces, and a different culture, all for new opportunities to spread the Gospel.

23

Tucker's Station

I have got a lot of critics in this town because I burn every ounce of energy I have to try to reach people with the Gospel. I plead guilty. I make no apology for it.
— DR. JOHN W. RAWLINGS

Historical Marker in Cincinnati, Ohio

John's arrival as the new Lockland minister was announced in the *Cincinnati Post* on Wednesday, July 4, 1951, in an article entitled "Texan Is New Lockland Pastor."

When he arrived in Cincinnati, Dr. John set out to see the city and stopped in a J. C. Penny store at Sixth and Race. He walked into the store and approached the assistant store manager, who looked him up and down. John was wearing his wide-brimmed, tan cowboy hat, dark cowboy boots, and a wide, eager smile on his face. He later was nicknamed "Tex" by those he befriended in his new surroundings. In an article written in 1976 on the front page of the *Cincinnati Post,* reporter James L. Adams described him as a man with "a square face that could have been chiseled off Mount Rushmore, a raspy Arkansas accent, a down-home sense of humor, and a warm handshake. He's easy to like."[20]

"I just arrived in Cincinnati!" John declared to the curious manager. "You're the first man I've shaken hands with."

The man's name was Ralph Aust, who later often visited John's church services. He and his wife, Betty, were easily recognizable to John from the pulpit. Later in life, Mr. Aust became a deacon at Highland Hills Baptist Church in Fort Thomas, Kentucky, where John's future first grandchild, Steve Rawlings, was also ordained as a deacon. Even later, when Mrs. Aust was near death, Mr. Aust would play her favorite album to comfort her. The album was called, "'Til the Storm Passes By," which was sung by the combined choirs of Lockland Baptist Church and Grace Baptist Church with John's son Herb as the soloist. This choir was an integral part of services at Landmark Baptist Temple, formerly Lockland Baptist Church. As the church in Lockland grew, it became necessary to relocate in 1963, and the name was changed.

Lockland Baptist Church was originally instituted in 1798 and enjoyed a long and rich history for over two hundred years. The city of Lockland was named thus because the Miami Erie Canal, which joined the Ohio River in Cincinnati, Ohio, with Lake Erie in Rochester, New York, ran through the heart of the city and connected with the locks located there. Slaves moved horse- and ox-drawn barges of freight through the waterways from Kentucky to the northern states. Currently, Interstate 75 follows most of the old canal route.

At its beginning, Lockland Baptist met at Tucker's Station, or "Old Fort Tucker," built in 1792. Located on the west side of Wayne Avenue just south of Marion Avenue, Tucker's Station was adjoined with Tucker's Cemetery, a

---

20   James L. Adams, "Landmark Baptist Temple: Plan it big, keep it simple," *The Cincinnati Post*, (August 21, 1976): 1, 31.

burying ground at the crest of a hill in what was later Woodlawn, Ohio. Tucker's Station, named in honor of Henry Tucker who came to the Mill Creek Valley in 1778, was fortified as a camp to protect against Indian raids. Henry and Mary Tucker were two of the earliest settlers in Ohio, and today, a historical marker commemorating them is located at the back entrance of the current Landmark Baptist property in Glendale, Ohio. The inscription reads in part:

> In the year 1792, Henry Tucker started clearing land and erecting a Station House on the old Indian Trace in what is now the Village of Woodlawn. He had purchased the land from John Cleves Symmes for two dollars per acre. Fear of Indian attack drove the pioneers back to Columbia where they remained until General Anthony Wayne started his march north to engage the Indians in battle.   Henry and Mary Tucker returned to this farm in 1794. The Station House was completed and was to be used as a fort in case of Indian attack. Worship services were conducted in the Station House and later in neighboring cabins. The result was the organization of The Springfield Baptist Church in 1798.[21]

Church members would come by ox wagon, horseback, and even on foot for Saturday services. These handfuls of Christian people would stay in the compound, which served as protection from Indians raids. After Sunday morning service, they would return home.

Springfield Baptist Church moved to Lockland, Ohio, and became known as the Lockland Baptist Church in 1840. After meeting for several years at the church in Springfield, a dispute erupted between two factions in the church: the pro-missionary group, and the anti-missionary group. These two belief systems had traveled to America with the immigrants from England, Scotland, and Ireland, and the controversy divided American Baptists throughout the country. The larger of the two factions at Springfield, the pro-missionary group, or independents, began meeting on Lockland property, while the anti-missionary faction, or hard-shell/Primitive Baptists, split off but eventually disbanded. The Primitive Baptists are still alive primarily in the southeastern United States.

The independents from Springfield founded First Baptist Church of Lockland and incorporated in the State of Ohio on October 9, 1925. An old

---

21 Glendale's Historical Markers: Tucker's Station. *The Village of Glendale, Ohio: http:// www.glendaleohio.org/markers.html* (February 22, 2013).

church bulletin from Lockland Baptist announces a centennial celebration and describes the very first church structure as a crude frame building about one mile northwest of Lockland in Springfield Township.

G. B. Vick and W. E. Dowell recommended John as pastor to the pulpit committee of Lockland Baptist after the church had suffered a horrendous fight and split. Prior to this, since the beginning of his pastorate in 1934, Pastor B. H. Hillard had built the church into a large congregation, what would now be described as a megachurch for its time, as they averaged around fifteen hundred for Sunday services. In 1950, Pastor Hillard became very ill and was unable to appear at the church for a time, and dissension began to build among the members during this void of leadership. Uncertainties grew about the pastor and many felt alienated while some believed the assistant pastor, Russell Singleton, should become the senior pastor. The resulting church split greatly affected many members for several years afterward. In a slashing article in the *Cincinnati Post* on January 9, 1951, entitled "Leadership Battle Splits Lockland Church Congregation: Parishioners Take Sides in Fight against Pastor's Aide as Suit Follows 'Near Riot,'" bold text and photographs of J. Frank Norris, B. H. Hillard in his sickbed with his wife at his side, and his assistant Russell Singleton headlined the controversial article:

> A heated controversy over leadership has split the huge congregation of the Lockland Baptist Church, 326 Mill Street, Lockland. Members of the congregation of over 4000 have taken sides, either supporting Reb. B. H. Hillard, pastor for the last 17 years, of his assistant, 27-year-old Russell Singleton. News of the factional dispute became public Monday when a congregational committee sought a court injunction to prevent the Rev. Mr. Hillard from continuing as pastor. The 61-year-old pastor who suffered a heart attack three months ago was near tears Tuesday as he spoke of the church quarrel. "It is one of the most shameful things that can happen to a church, to be dragged into the courts this way," he said. "I can only look on it as one of God's tests." ... While the regular pastor is incapacitated, he has asked Rev. J. Frank Norris, pastor of the Baptist church of Ft. Worth, [TX], to take over his pulpit. The Rev. Mr. Norris, a crusader against vice, race horse gambling, liquor, smoking by women, and other "modernistic" trends, was acquitted in 1936 of a murder charge

filed after a fatal shooting in his study in Fr. Worth. It was while the Rev. Mr. Norris was addressing the congregation Sunday that a "near riot" occurred among 1500 in the congregation as friends of the Rev. Mr. Morris reportedly attacked the Rev. Mr. Singleton. Friends of the latter quelled the trouble before any damage could be done. However, the Rev. Mr. Singleton filed assault and battery charges against three who took part in the physical quarrel. The Texas minister, according to one report, refused to leave the pulpit, although requested to by an overwhelming majority of the members present. At a prayer meeting Monday, more than 350 heard the Rev. Mr. Singleton speak, although attempts reportedly were made by the Hillard-Norris faction to persuade congregation members that the meeting had been canceled. The Rev. Mr. Singleton described the controversy as "the accumulation of several years of dictatorial action on the part of the pastor. If anyone opposes or shows any opposition to the Rev. Mr. Hillard, he is sent a letter asking him to leave the congregation," said the assistant pastor. "I believe that a majority of the members of the congregation support me." I was discharged by the Rev. Mr. Hillard two weeks before Christmas," he said. "The trustees and deacons and the church congregation were not consulted."[22]

Dr. John later tells that J. Frank Norris actually had a hand in the splitting of Lockland Baptist Church. When Norris was invited to speak there, Dr. John said he "pulled an Entzminger" by requesting Pastor Hillard be brought from the hospital to the church on a stretcher. To evoke sympathy, Hillard was rolled down the center aisle on a gurney from the back of the church so the congregants could see their pastor was yet alive and be reminded of his great leadership. From the pulpit, Norris defended former Pastor Hillard in the hope that this reminder would dissuade the members from leaving Lockland and encourage them to remain faithful to the church.

Norris, from whom John derived his firebrand style of preaching, did not have a longstanding reputation as a peacemaker, but rather as a feather-ruffler. His words at Lockland that day, criticizing some of the members and their

---

22   "Leadership Battle Splits Lockland Church Congregation: Parishioners Take Sides in Fight against Pastor's Aide as Suit Follows 'Near Riot,'" *The Cincinnati Post* vol 69, issue 308 (January 1951): 1:2.

actions, stirred up the hornet's nest. A woman leapt from her pew during his sermon, exclaiming, "J. Frank Norris, we didn't invite you to come, and as far as we are concerned, you can go back to Texas where you came from!" A melee ensued that lasted the duration of the service. People began standing up and shouting others down; one lady hit someone's head with her purse. The incident was so controversial that it made the local papers and was featured on the front page of the *Cincinnati Enquirer* and the *Cincinnati Post*. At the following service, Lockland police officers gathered outside the building to maintain the peace. The tension in the church did not totally dissipate for a while thereafter and, consequently, the court appointed preachers over the next six months through the man who headed the local YMCA.

About seven hundred members left Lockland, leaving about seven hundred people behind. The militant-minded congregants who remained were still in war mode for a while afterward. As for Pastor Hillard, he was more ill than he thought and died about a year after the onset of his illness.

The members who left Lockland began meeting in a theater in Saint Bernard, Ohio, near Proctor & Gamble's Ivorydale plant. Later, this church called a seventeen-year-old man named Lasserre Bradley as pastor, who, because of his young age, was highlighted in *Time* magazine. Bradley's sermons were still broadcast on the radio in 2011.

When G. B. Vick and W. E. Dowell suggested John Rawlings to the pulpit committee, he was invited to preach a trial sermon. Not many days afterward, the church extended a call to John to be their pastor. When John accepted this call in 1951 to pastor Lockland Baptist, he was thirty-seven years old.

24

The Viper's Nest

It's wonderful that I've got a pastor that tells me what I need to do!
— MEMBER OF LOCKLAND BAPTIST CHURCH

After John arrived in Cincinnati on Saturday, he preached at Lockland on Sunday morning and evening and left by train Sunday night at 11:35 p.m. for Enid, Oklahoma, to preach there. A Reverend Bales had been asked to fill in for him at Lockland that Wednesday night. The deacons were not sure what to make of this. Since the recent split, they had penned new bylaws, one of which required the senior pastor to never be absent from the pulpit more than two Sundays a year, one for vacation and one for speaking at another church. Before even his second Sunday at Lockland, John failed to abide by this newly enacted rule, and the trustees' feathers were ruffled. One of men was elected to confront John.

He stuttered nervously as he reminded the new pastor of the newly enacted bylaws, to which John answered, "Am I to answer to the church bylaws or to the Lord?"

The trustee paused, and then said, "What if the bylaws are from the Lord?"

On the Wednesday that John was in Oklahoma, the men held a business meeting to vote on the new preacher and gave him a 93 percent vote. Though

132

they had not yet met John's wife or sons, John told the deacons, "You don't need to meet my wife. I'm satisfied with you, so you don't have to go to bed with her. I do! And you don't have to discipline my boys; I do that. So you're calling *me* if you call me. I'm the preacher! I'm the leader!" They actually liked that, and they called him to preach.

The opposition did not end there, however. From spring until the end of August, business meetings were conducted frequently. Dr. John soon discovered the church was divided about everything, "even the color of the toilet paper." Dr. John was insistent that the church support missions and had already been giving money to the home missionary the church was supporting. He had the church vote to give the tenth Sunday's offering to missions, but some men in the church opposed it. He made them a proposition. "You who oppose it, just hold your tithe the tenth Sunday and give it the next week." It was then an issue no longer, and they could no longer fight; that is how Dr. John would say he "whooped them on that one, you see." Offerings on the first tenth Sunday was bigger than other Sundays, and so God put his approval on the new system. There was just a small group who was against everything.

The conflicts Dr. John had faced in Tyler had equipped him for difficult situations in this church. After a brief power struggle for leadership between John and the finance committee, who actually controlled the proceedings of the church, a business meeting was held during which the opposing church officers were ousted by the vote of the church. Even though the event created such controversy as to be reported in the local newspapers, John undauntedly proceeded to build the church, win souls, and effectively reach the entire Cincinnati area. In four months, he baptized four hundred people there. But it wasn't all "honey and peaches and cream." No, there was a war going on. A great deal of immortality had seeped into the church, prompting John to fire the choir director, Sunday school superintendent, and organist. "We'll either dismiss them and I'll stay," was Dr. John's warning, "or you keep them and I'll leave."

During his early days at Lockland, five women's classes voted not to cooperate with him on a certain matter. Publicly from the platform he referred to these women as "the viper's nest," as Jesus in Matthew 23:33 describes the Pharisees as a "generation of vipers" for their hypocrisy and iniquity.

Just as John lacked the support of these women for a season, the trustees never came to the auditorium to hear him preach; they merely transacted business and discussed monetary affairs. On Sunday nights, they counted the money and discussed business matters in the downstairs office rather than attend the service upstairs. Their leader was trained as a lawyer and also practiced real estate.

"Now you talk about opposition?" Dr. John leans forward. "I threatened to kill one of the ushers. He thought I meant it, and I think I did. He left and didn't come back. I knocked them off one at a time." Of course, the church had already split right down the middle before John had arrived. The divisiveness and immorality that had infiltrated the church became apparent to John almost as soon as he arrived at Lockland.

Dr. John said he was criticized and "called everything that you could call a man" during his time in Cincinnati. After becoming the pastor of Lockland, he walked down the streets of the city and people were spitting at him even though he had only been there a short time. Never before had he endured such a tongue lashing as he did from some of the citizens in Lockland, and he didn't even know them. "I didn't even try to find out who they were," he said.

"I remember when we were trying to get this church straightened out we had to dismiss some people. Those people who were angry—a sizable number of them—would get up and walk out while I was giving the invitation during the services. Many of these people were surprisingly mean-spirited and had checkered backgrounds."

John even faced conflict over the smallest of things, even air-conditioning. He arrived in Cincinnati and became pastor of Lockland during the dawn of air-conditioning. When it was proposed the church make use of this new technology, a "full-blooded hillbilly" and an agitated deacon headed the opposition. During a deacon's meeting, he announced, "I would like to say a word." When John permitted him to speak, the deacon went on to say there was no air-conditioning where he came from, and it was not an item that the church really needed.

"That's nice," said John. "Would you put that in the form of a motion and then a second?"

"Well, yeah. I'd be glad to."

John answered, "I'd like to add to it." He paused for effect. "I imagine where my brother here grew up is like where I grew up. We didn't have indoor toilets. So I suggest that we remove all of the toilets in our buildings. And toilet paper is expensive, so we'll abandon that since we didn't have toilet paper in my day either." On and on, he went through "the whole gambit," He suggested having the electricity cut off and having congregants bring kerosene lamps instead.

"We had a potbellied stove," he added, referring to his childhood. "Coal is expensive, so we'll take out the boiler so we won't have to buy coal. We'll just have the men go down and cut wood in Kentucky and bring it in." He paused again.

After a long moment or two, the deacon broke the awkward silence. "B-b-but I didn't mean that."

"Yeah, you did, too," John countered. "We didn't have air-conditioning where I grew up either."

By now, the rest of the deacons and trustees were all snickering.

John smiled. "Now, we're open for discussion and a motion and second."

One of the fellows grinned and said, "Brother John, I think we ought to just table this."

The offended deacon never liked John much after that.

The opposition went a step further when one man from the church—a "tall hillbilly," as Dr. John described—traveled all the way to Tyler, Texas, to investigate John's background in an effort to "dig up dirt."

Near the end of a business meeting on a Wednesday evening, during the time set aside for members to raise important issues of their choosing, the "tall hillbilly" strode to the platform to say a word. John met him and poked a finger in his ribs, saying, "I've got a .38 pointed just inches from your heart, and if you tell one lie about me, you're dead."

"I-I-I d-d-don't have anything to s-s-say about you, Brother Rawlings."

"Good, take a seat then."

Another business meeting was planned for a Wednesday evening, and the sanctuary was full. During recent building programs, it had been expanded with wings built on each side. A group of dissidents sat together on the left side. John was prepared; he anticipated trouble and had already spoken with the man running sound before the service began.

The spokesman for the dissidents stepped up to the microphone, but as previously arranged, his volume was on low.

A deacon called out, "We can't hear you!"

The soundman cranked the volume up to high, and when the spokesman uttered a few words, a loud screech sounded across the sanctuary, echoed by earsplitting feedback.

The spokesman leapt back in alarm, but John nudged him forward to the mic again as if to say, "Go ahead. Try again!"

When the same thing happened, another deacon yelled out, "You're too loud!"

By now flustered and outwardly trembling, he tried to speak a third time but gave up completely, muttering, "Never mind, I don't have anything to say." And he took his seat at John's command.

As for busybodies and gossips, John had dealt with such things before. When two women at Lockland began to spread rumors and gossip, John knew how to take care of things from his experience at Central Baptist. According to John's experience, when you have an older woman who gossips, she'll always select a younger one to go along with her. After awhile, John had put up with the gossip at Lockland long enough. He informed the older woman he needed to talk with her. On Monday morning, she came into his office, and he told her not to sit down.

"Every time I go for a meeting and come back," John said, "you and your friend have been gossiping." He slowly stood up and, to her astonishment, began to unbuckle his belt.

With the belt in one hand and the other hand on her arm, he continued, "I'm going to whoop you so that you'll stop this gossiping."

She could tell he meant what he said, that he was "about to lay it on her." As she began to cry, she put her arms around him and wept, "My husband is so henpecked, and he never contradicts me. It's wonderful that I've got a pastor who tells me what I need to do. Would you forgive me? I promise you, I'll never again gossip."

John hugged her and prayed for her, and she became one of his best friends. He later called the other gossip in and used the same technique on her. This solved the gossip problem at Lockland, and the need for a church-wide meeting was vanquished.

Events like these were part of the necessary purge in order to shepherd the Lockland congregation back to a solid biblical foundation. At one point, a court case resulted from the expulsion of one individual from the church, initiating a dark period for the church for a time. But thanks to the friendship of a local newspaperman and his positive coverage of the church, this darkness came to an end, heralding a new, brighter period for Dr. John and his new congregation.

25

To Draw a Crowd

*I don't want a little consecrated church or a big worldly
church. I want a big consecrated church!*
—DR. JOHN W. RAWLINGS

John's skills with dealing with busybodies were not his only talents that he
brought to Lockland from Central. He continued to excel as a great promoter
at his new pastorate as he had in Texas. During a sermon preached on January
15, 1978, John addressed this topic:

> Since I have been in Cincinnati, one of the criticisms of the
> religious and professional community has been this: "Rawlings
> will do anything to draw a crowd." I have got a lot of critics in this
> town because I burn every ounce of energy I have to try to reach
> people with the Gospel. I plead guilty. I make no apology for it.
> I was on a program with a fellow down in Knoxville, Tennessee.
> He ... spent a long period of time telling how he didn't want a
> big worldly church; he wanted a small, consecrated church. He
> said, "I believe in quality." I had to preach next, and I said, "I don't
> want a little consecrated church or a big worldly church. I want
> a big consecrated church!"

Music was always an integral part of the services. Dr. John organized a quartet at Lockland with his sons Herb and Carrol, which also included Hoy Burton, Carl Noe, and pianist Jimmie Kilpatrick. After the move to Landmark, a ministry to the deaf developed with the help of faithful friends, such as Bill and Betty Hillard, Ed and Jean Hemplemen, and Sonny and Linda Snell. The ministry began when a Brother Hennessey came from Middletown, Ohio, to teach an American Sign Language class, for which about fifty people enthusiastically signed up. This initial first step propelled the new ministry into a powerful, unique outreach in the community.

On one occasion, another man involved in the ministry said to John, "We have a problem. I have these two young black girls in our deaf ministry, and they want to get baptized." This was well before the Civil Rights Act of 1964, and though segregation was not practiced openly, it still lurked beneath the surface of Cincinnati.

Never one to procrastinate for any reason, John said, "Well, get up there, get everything ready, and baptize them! When you bring them out, tell the experience and explain [to the congregation]."

When the time came, the two young ladies were ready for the baptism, and Mrs. Rawlings accompanied the two young ladies to the baptistery to prepare and help them into their white robes. When they stepped into the baptismal pool, members of the congregation below exchanged confused glances. They were unaccustomed to seeing blacks in the church.

After the pastor baptized the girls, John took the podium to soothe any uneasiness and said, "Isn't it great these girls got baptized? Isn't it a great thing that when these young [deaf] ladies go to heaven in their new bodies, they will hear for the first time?"

Under John's ministry, the church thrived and at its peak attendance surpassed three thousand. With the congregation quickly outgrowing its current capacity, the need for additional buildings quickly became apparent and thus also the need to borrow funds. However, Lockland was still a part of the Northern Baptist Convention, and a reversionary clause in the church deed stated if the church ceased to be a regular Baptist church, it would revert back to the convention. Even though the church had contributed to the convention, the convention had never given to the church, so it had a stranglehold on Lockland Baptist. When Lockland needed to borrow money for building funds, they had to obtain it from the Hamilton County Baptist Association. Since becoming pastor of Lockland Baptist, John had never been invited to the convention meetings, which he assumed was because of his reputation. The amount of offerings had dropped substantially and during the six months prior to his arrival totaled just twenty-six thousand dollars.

John took his dilemma to one of the leading men of the convention. "You and I are Baptists, and you know it's unscriptural to have that clause in our deed, that we have to go to the association in order to borrow money. I tell you what I'm going to do. I'm going to be kind and nice and try to work this out. But if you guys don't take that reversionary clause out of our deed, I'm going to sue you, and that will wreck the association."

The man's son was chair of the committee and also an attorney. John threatened to file suit if something wasn't done but thought of a way to give them an out in an uncompromising way. "I'll give you a sum of money—I know you want to build a church on the northwest side of town—and I'll put it in the form of missions money."

Even though they were now between a rock and a hard place, the convention leaders liked John's idea. On behalf of his church, John donated about twenty-five thousand dollars to the convention (big money in those days) that then took the clause out of the church deed, and Lockland Baptist became independent.

Previously, during John's ministry in Tyler, Texas, he had become acquainted with the owner of Aquila Priscilla Tent Manufacturing Company in Waco, Texas, the man who provided tents for B. B. Crimm and his tent meetings. John had asked the man, in his spare time when he was not busy with other contracts, to provide his ministry with a tent as well. When the tent was finished, Dr. John would then hold tent revivals for a couple of weeks, and by the end of the revival, a new church had been born. This work marked many years of John's ministry. In 1962, Dr. John launched a tent-revival meeting in Cincinnati, Ohio, where a four-center post tent was raised at the end of Paddock Road. The tent was so large—enough to seat nearly fifteen hundred people—that setup lasted up to three months. In the same year, John launched a tent ministry in Pennsylvania in three or four different areas. The tent then traveled by flatbed trailer—it was so large, that was the only way to transport it—to Arkansas; to Somerset, Kentucky; to Monticello, Kentucky; and finally to Albany, Kentucky.

26

The Matthews Property

Located in a residential area, Lockland Baptist Church had already bought nine adjoining 50-by-150 foot parking lots, but the rest of the neighbors had raised their prices, so Lockland could not afford to buy any more. G. B. Vick came to help assess their situation.

Dr. John knew the church might have to move to a new location, but in his wisdom, he introduced this concept to his congregation slowly. At first he said, "We *probably* will have to relocate," but as time passed, he began saying, "We will *have* to relocate." Dr. John knew that to lead people, you must know how to express yourself; people can't become angry when you say "probably" before "must."

When the time had come for Dr. John to tell the church members they should start looking for property, he reminded them, "The Catholic people bought the highest hill in town; we Baptists ought to be as smart as the Catholics. We're going to get our property shortly." He discussed different pieces of property and allowed others to express themselves. He talked about it in such a fashion that half the congregation thought they had already purchased property! So when the right property became available, only two men voted against it. John kept his people fully informed, and when the time was right, they were ready and unified with him in spirit.

Leadership should not be fearful. John was not *forcing* the church to do something; rather, he was *leading* them to do something. He knew what needed to be done because it was his job to know as the shepherd of the flock—sow grass and mend fences. Of the two men who voted against the purchase of new property, one passed away soon after, and the other became friends with Dr. John. He got over it.

Rapid growth led the church to purchase about 170 acres of land off the Glendale-Milford Exit on Interstate 75 in 1957. Ms. Matthews, the elderly woman who had lived in the estate house called the Mansion, had passed away in June of 1957. She was part of the Burchanall family, the granddaughter of the founder of Proctor & Gamble, and had married into the Matthews family.

One day in the autumn, Dr. John and Mrs. Rawlings were driving home from a funeral down Springfield Pike when they spotted a woman wearing a nurse's uniform stepping off a bus and starting down the lane.

"Honey," Dr. John said. "Let's drive down and see if that lady owns that property." He was referring to the beautiful piece of land across from a drive-in theater that he was interested in purchasing for the new church building. He pulled off the road alongside the woman. "Lady, do you and your people own this farm?"

"Hello, Dr. Rawlings! I recognize your voice; I listen to you on the radio. But no, we don't own it We just rent this house back here. See that other house down at the lower end of this field? Mr. Burchanall lives there, and you can find out about the property."

After thanking her, he drove to the lower end of the field. As he pulled up to the huge house, Irish wolfhounds and other dogs flooded into the yard; he had never seen so many. They swarmed the car, howling, leaving Dr. John a bit scared.

Suddenly a tall, handsome fellow emerged from the house, yelling at the dogs to keep quiet.

"You're Mr. Burchanall," Dr. John asserted.

"Yes, I am."

"I'm Dr. John Rawlings with Lockland Baptist Church."

"Well, Reverend, come on in!" the man said. "I've heard your program. What brings you this way?"

"I want to talk to you about this property out here. We're being forced to move, and we can't buy land around our church. I've been looking at this property and praying about it, but I didn't know who owned it. Would you be interested in selling it?"

The man thought for a moment. "Well, we're retired, but I've already got my will made out, and we're not going to change it. But I'll tell you what,

Reverend. I've got a cousin who's got some land. His mother just died, and he might be interested."

Dr. John asked, "Where is he?"

"Up behind Saint Rita's School for the Deaf."

Dr. John answered that he thought that property belonged to the Catholics, but Mr. Burchanall assured him that wasn't so. "His name is Bill Matthews. His mother was the granddaughter of the founder of Proctor & Gamble." With offices in Columbus, Springfield, Hamilton, and Cincinnati, the Matthewses dealt in land management, owned ranches in Montana and other places, and were very affluent.

"Would you mind calling your cousin and telling him that I'm interested, and then I will call and try to get an appointment?" asked Dr. John.

Mr. Burchanall agreed, and the next day, John called Bill Matthews's office in Hamilton, Ohio, and made an appointment for a few days later.

It wasn't a very pretentious office, Dr. John thought as he entered the building. "Is Mr. Matthews in?" he asked at the front desk.

"No, he's in his downtown office today."

"But I have an appointment. I'm Reverend Rawlings." He was obliged to take a seat and wait for quite a while.

Finally, the secretary said, "Well, Mr. Matthews has been delayed. Would you like to set another time?"

But Dr. John knew Mr. Matthews would have to come eventually. "No," he said after a moment. "He'll most likely come. I'll just wait it out." Two hours passed until, at last, a well-built, handsome man entered the office. He stood at about six-three with iron-gray hair. An impressive figure.

"Good afternoon," said Mr. Matthews. He passed the secretary's desk, went into his office, and shut the door.

"Reverend Rawlings," the secretary called after a pause. "Mr. Matthews will see you now." She escorted him into the office where Mr. Matthews sat behind his desk. He didn't offer to shake Dr. John's hand.

After the secretary left, Dr. John said, "Mr. Matthews, I met your cousin, Mr. Burchanall, and I expressed an interest in his property over on Springfield Pike. He said he wasn't interested but that you were his cousin, and you might be."

Mr. Matthews was opening his mail and reading over some letters, not in the least attentive to Dr. John.

"Mr. Matthews, look at me."

He looked up.

"I'm not accustomed to people reading their mail while I'm talking to them."

"Reverend Rawlings," Mr. Matthews answered, "I'm sorry. That's very ill-mannered of me."

"You're busy, and I'm busy, but I need your attention."

"We might be interested. My mother died, and I don't know what we're going to do with the land. How much property did you want?"

Dr. John shrugged. "As much as we can get."

"What do you want to pay for it?"

"I don't want to pay for anything if I can get somebody to give it to me. But whatever the price is, if it's reasonable, we'll buy it!" Mr. Matthews smiled as Dr. John continued. "I tell you what. You think about this, and I'll talk with my men, and we'll look at the property."

"You know that interstate is coming through there, and we don't know how much we're gone to have left. We just don't know much about anything yet. My mother just died awhile back."

"Alright. Here's my telephone number; you call me." Dr. John handed it to him along with a Gospel tract. "Mr. Matthews, this is so serious. There will be lost people who will be saved. Now I'm told that you're a man of character and leadership."

"I appreciate somebody expressing it like that."

"You wouldn't mind if we had prayer, would you?" asked Dr. John. They prayed together, and that day was the beginning of their friendship.

A few days later, Mr. Matthews called Dr. John. "I talked to my sisters. Are your people interested?" Mr. Matthews had three sisters, two of whom were nuns and one was Episcopalian.

"Yes, we're interested. I've been looking at it. We would be most delighted to have the property from Oak Road over to the Catholic property, at least fifteen acres. I've already checked with the engineering company about the new highway."

"I'm going to be downtown tomorrow, and we'll get together."

Dr. John suggested, "I'll come to your office."

"No, I'm going to come to your office."

The next day, in Dr. John office, he and Mr. Matthews talked. "If the price is right," Dr. John said, "we'll do something about it. We have to move. I'd like to have that whole section, probably fifty acres more or less, the best I can tell."

"You talk to your men, I'll talk to my sisters, and we'll get a price."

Less than a week later, Mr. Matthews called. "Are you ready to talk business?"

"Yessir, I've been waiting."

Mr. Matthews came to Dr. John's office the next day. "We will take $150,000 for that acreage, not including utilities."

This necessitated another meeting between John and his men. "Let's buy it!" they said.

"No, no, no, fellows. Let me handle this. I'm a horse trader, after all. Now Mr. Matthews asked $150,000 for twenty-five acres. I tell you what let's do: We'll give him that for the whole thing *if* they'll add the utilities. If he won't do that, we'll offer to give him $125,000, and *we'll* put in the utilities." They closed the meeting in prayer, and Dr. John met with Mr. Matthews again with this new proposition. Again Mr. Matthews had to take the matter to his sisters, but the next time they met, they were ready to settle the matter.

"Do you think we ought to get our lawyers now?" asked Mr. Matthews.

"Well now, I'm a Christian, and you're a Christian. I'm honest, and you're honest. And honest people don't really have to lean on lawyers. But yes, we need the papers drawn up." Dr. John told to his secretary, "Make out a check for five thousand dollars as earnest money."

"You don't need to do that," Mr. Matthews said, but Dr. John didn't want him to back out. In the lower-left corner of the check, he wrote the words *for property.* That was October 1958.

It wasn't until February 1959 before the church took ownership of the property. One year and five months later, 110 more acres became available. Mr. Matthews called Dr. John and told him that his sisters wanted to sell it. "There's a corporation in New York City trying to buy it, but that's my home. I'd like the church to have it. Would you like to buy it?"

"Yes, we'll take it," Dr. John replied. "How much?"

"I talked to my sisters, and I think I can sell it to you for $240,000 with additional property."

The 170 acres located in Evendale, Ohio, including portions of Glendale and Woodlawn, cost Lockland Baptist about $440,000 total. The church did not begin constructing a new building right away but in the summertime used the property to host outdoor meetings and tent meetings.

Groundbreaking for the new field house was in July 1963, and Lockland Baptist Church became Landmark Baptist Temple. The first service in the field house was held on December 25, 1963, and "Lockland Baptist Church had been phased out of existence and into the history books."[23] In an article that appeared in *The Millcreek Valley News* in December 1963, it was written that, "In essence the Landmark Baptist Temple is returning close to its original home. And since the frontier days of the Northwest Territory, the membership has always held the Bible as their sole authority for existence and their mission to proclaim the Gospel of Jesus Christ to the world."

The field house allowed for several full-size basketball courts because the multipurpose building was intended to house a sports complex and possibly later serve as a school. Dr. John's vision was to build an even larger building on the hill above the field house. Detailed architectural drawings were rendered, but the building was never built. However, attendance continued to swell so much so that twenty-one entire acres were paved for parking.

In 1989, Dr. John estimated the value of the land and buildings exceeded twenty million dollars. The 160 rolling acres eventually consisted of a park and inviting woods, a large fishing lake, baseball diamonds and athletic complex, the renovated Mansion that was converted into the church offices, an apple orchard and an apple-processing barn (which existed on the property at the time of purchase), and a sunken garden that provided a beautiful setting for outdoor weddings. Dr. John's grandson Steve and his wife, Melody, were married there on September 20, 1980.

The youth center was completed in July 1972 and at the time was advertised as a "one-million dollar building." It was forty feet longer than a football field. As with the building of the field house, much of the labor was done by volunteers, many of whom worked day and night to complete the building in good time—as the old country saying goes, many of the men worked "half a day," meaning twelve hours. A lot of the contractors gave up work for their own businesses to help the church because of their dedication to Dr. John and their belief in him and the Lord's work.

When Landmark Baptist Temple built their family life center, the mayor of Evendale and the city council accused the church of violating local building codes. Two years later, the issue went to court. The mayor of Evendale, the city council, and five inspectors were going to witness against the building under the assertion it was unsafe.

On the day of the hearing, every corner of the courtroom was packed. Dr.

---

23   James L. Adams, "Landmark Baptist Temple: Plan it big, keep it simple," *The Cincinnati Post*, (August 21, 1976): 1, 31.

John brought with him three buses of high school students who took over the courthouse singing, handing out tracts, and talking to people. Mrs. Rawlings also accompanied her husband and found a seat beside two of the councilmen's wives.

The bailiff in the courtroom knew George Rawlings, who was now an attorney and had represented clients in the Hamilton County Courthouse. "Mr. Rawlings," said the bailiff, "anything I can do for you?"

"No, I don't think so," George answered nervously.

The mayor and the councilmen walked into the courtroom where the inspector from Evendale and his lawyer were preparing for the hearing.

"George," whispered Dr. John to his son, "call the bailiff back. Tell him you want to speak with the judge."

The bailiff agreed. When he returned, he said, "The judge wants to talk to you." George followed the bailiff into the judge's chambers, where the village inspector and the lawyer were also present.

George listened and the judge yawned as the inspector railed on and on about how the Landmark building was unsafe. At last, the inspector turned to the lawyer and asked, "Have I left out anything?"

"No, you've covered it all," the lawyer said. "We can proceed."

The judge paused. "I tell you what. Mr. Rawlings tells me they've been using this building for two and half years. Nothing's happened. And Easter is coming up—Good Friday. Mr. Rawlings?"

George glanced up.

"Could you do these two things that the inspector's asked for?"

"Sure we can," George said. There were only two out of nine items that had not yet been corrected to code.

"Mayor," the judge said, "I'll hear this case the fourteenth of July. Landmark can go ahead and use the building because Good Friday and Easter are coming up. You're the fifth inspector to look over this building anyway."

The inspector and lawyer exchanged bewildered glances.

In the courtroom, Dr. John waited as the Landmark youth continued to sing choruses. Forty-five minutes had passed when George finally emerged from the judge's chambers and gave his father a thumbs-up. Baptists shouted victoriously all throughout the courthouse!

27

Mockingbird in the Twilight

There will never be a night so dark that [God] can't be the light. There will never be a desert so dry that He can't give water. There will never be a sun so hot that He can't give a shadow.

—DR. JOHN W. RAWLINGS

Early during his ministry in Cincinnati, Dr. John was overcome with a serious illness and was taken to Holmes Hospital. In a sermon delivered July 9, 1978, Dr. John spoke of the time he spent there. "I sat and looked over at Kettering laboratory one afternoon. A little mockingbird was singing in the twilight of that September evening. I had been out walking in the parking lot, as I had made friends with the nurses and just about did as I pleased there. I told them I was going to dress and walk around awhile. I had to try and pull my thoughts together. I had been preaching every night in the tent meetings, traveling thousands of miles, from the first of June until September. Herb and I had started down in Kentucky with three meetings—one in Monticello, one in Albany, and the other back up in Somerset. Then we went to Collegeville, just outside Philadelphia, came back to Cincinnati, and went back to Batesville, Arkansas." Batesville was close to Dr. John's birthplace. They set up the big tent on the bank of the White River but the onslaught of mosquitoes cut the meeting short.

While working hard on the family farm as a young man, Dr. John had suffered an accident that left him with what he believed to be a ruptured appendix. He believed that God had sustained him supernaturally through this condition that now left him quite ill at Holmes Hospital. "I was broken in health," he says. "The years of illness had finally taken their toll. I sat there and listened to those birds sing, and I thanked the Lord that I had been saved and had a rich ministry. I hadn't done much, but I said, 'Lord, if this is the end, it's in Your hands.'

"I had great peace, and God has the last word. He will be there in the desert. Some of you listening to my voice, your home was broken up, the lover of your heart walked out, you were left alone, and you said, 'It's not worth it.' Oh, listen! God is sufficient. There will never be a night so dark that He can't be the light. There will never be a desert so dry that He can't give water. There will never be a sun so hot that He can't give a shadow."

28

Landmark Baptist Church

It is the oldest active church in America today.
—DR. JOHN W. RAWLINGS ON LANDMARK BAPTIST

Like the former property in Lockland, the new Landmark property also had a rich history. It was the former location of a dairy farm called Opekasit, an Indian word meaning, "looking toward the dawn." The parsonage was called the Eliza House, where Dr. John and Mrs. Rawlings lived. A historical marker located in Glendale at the Landmark property describes the Eliza House and its history:

> Three hundred yards east of this location on Oak Road, overlooking the Miami & Erie Canal, was the house of abolitionist John Van Zandt (1791–1847). For years this house was known as one of the most active "stations" on the Underground Railroad. In 1842, two bounty hunters from Sharonville caught Van Zandt helping eight runaway slaves who had escaped from owner Wharton Jones of Kentucky. Defended in court by Salmon P. Chase, who became Chief Justice of the Supreme Court of the United States from 1864–1873, Van Zandt was convicted and fined. Chase appealed the case to the U.S. Supreme Court, where

he tested the constitutionality of the 1793 Fugitive Slave Law. When writing her novel *Uncle Tom's Cabin*, Harriet Beecher Stowe used Van Zandt as the abolitionist character John Van Trompe. Van Zandt's house became associated with the book and was known as "The Eliza House," named for one of the novel's main characters.[24]

A black slave woman and her daughter Eliza escaped slavery after they traveled from Kentucky to Ohio across the Mason-Dixon Line and the frozen Ohio River. The mother and daughter found refuge in the Eliza House, which stood across the road from Opekasit Farms. Harriet Beecher Stowe incorporated their story in her novel *Uncle Tom's Cabin,* a book that evoked sympathy and support for the abolitionist movement, thus triggering the Civil War. This war not only divided the nation between North and South but also divided the Baptists by North and South, the

Historical Marker for the Eliza House

latter of which became Southern Baptists. The Northern Baptists were later called American Baptists.

Van Zandt was buried in Wesleyan Cemetery on Colerain Avenue in Cincinnati, Ohio, and upon his tombstone these words are inscribed:

---

24   "Marker #66-31 The Eliza House." *Remarkable Ohio Marking Ohio's History:*
     *http://www.remarkableohio.org/HistoricalMarker.aspx?historicalMarkerId=1081&fileI
     d=6775* (March 8, 2011).

In him Christianity had a living witness. He saw God as his
Father and received every man as a brother. The cause of the
poor, the widow, the orphan and the oppressed was his cause.
He fed, clothed, sheltered and guarded them. He was eyes to
the blind and feet to the lame. He was a tender father, a devoted
husband and a friend to all. He is what is here described because
he was a Christian philanthropist who practiced what he believed
and he thus lived practicing his faith.[25]

Like Van Zandt, Dr. John was a living witness for Christ. One of his
neighbors in the city of Glendale was a semiretired judge from the Sixth Circuit
Court of Appeals who had heard Dr. John preach. Dr. John, a diligent soul
winner and bold proclaimer of the Gospel, knocked at the judge's door one
night. "If you're not busy," he said, "I'd like to talk to you."

The judge invited him inside as Dr. John continued, "I'm your neighbor,
and I don't want any of my neighbors going to hell. I felt led to come and talk to
you. You're a judge; you're going to stand before the Supreme Court of heaven
one day, and you're going to have to give an account of what you've done with
Jesus."

"Reverend, you put it straight, don't you?"

"Straight as a gun barrel," Dr. John answered. "Have you or have you not
accepted Jesus Christ?"

The judge's face reflected his sobering mood as he humbled himself and
said he was Episcopalian. "I'm not sure you'll understand this," he said and
continued to explain his salvation experience as a young boy. Though Dr. John
didn't notice at first, the judge's wife was standing at the door.

"Mrs. Peck, come on in," said Dr. John. "This is for you too. You're my
neighbor."

"Brother Rawlings, I've been saved."

Dr. John turned to her husband. "Judge, isn't it true that my preaching is
so straight that you're uncomfortable with it?"

"Yeah," he agreed.

"But we can be friends. You can go to heaven dry-cleaned. Meaning

---

25   Teddy Gray Brock, "John VanSandt 1791-1847." June 10, 2010. *Hamilton County*
      Biographies: http://ohiobios.ancestralsites.com/hamilton_co/b00097.html (February 22,
      2013).

sprinkled, you know. You and your wife can go to heaven dry-cleaned, but it'd be a whole lot better if you'd let me baptize you both."

Baptisms were performed after almost every service at Landmark. Many people even today have testimonies of being baptized by Dr. John at Lockland Baptist, Landmark, or under his ministry. Baptisms were an integral part of the church service, and for several years, the church reported eighteen hundred to twenty-two hundred baptisms per year. During baptismal service, Dr. John would ask the person if he or she had accepted Jesus Christ as his or her Savior and would then immerse the person into the water, saying, "Buried in the likeness of His death," and then lift them up, saying, "Raised in the likeness of His resurrection." In early October 1965, Dr. John had the pleasure of baptizing his two oldest grandchildren, Steve and Jon. They were both namesakes of Dr. John, as Steve's birth name was John Steven.

Steve had gone forward for a salvation decision on Wednesday evening when special speaker Bill Glass, an All-Pro defensive end for the Cleveland Browns gave the invitation. Jon made his salvation decision shortly after. Landmark always invited interesting people to speak to the congregation, such as Bill Glass. At the end of his professional football career, he took on the role of a full-time evangelist and spoke several times at Billy Graham crusades where he shared his testimony. In 1969, he began the Bill Glass Evangelistic Association, later called Champions for Life.

On the day of their baptism, Steve and Jon shared the baptismal pool. Jon's baptism went smoothly, but Steve's involved a bit of a struggle. As Dr. John quickly dunked Steve into the water, rather than breathing air, Steve gulped water, and when Dr. John raised him, he came up sputtering and coughing. Dr. John remarked, "He must be a Methodist" because his audience knew that Baptists were baptized by total immersion and Methodists were only sprinkled. The crowd laughed heartily.

Over forty years later, Dr. John baptized Steve's daughter Kaitlyn when he was in his late eighties at Highland Hills Baptist Church in Fort Thomas, Kentucky, and her sister Meredith when he was ninety years old at Big Bone Baptist Church in Union, Kentucky.

But baptisms did not always go according to plan. A deaf man involved with the deaf ministry at Landmark once walked into the baptistery after a church service as preparations were being made for baptisms. Brother Harold—who had moved from his pastorate at a church in Saint Louis, Missouri, to join Dr. John as Associate Pastor at Landmark—was to perform the baptismal service.

As the deaf man walked past the baptistery, he was herded into the changing room and then led to the baptismal pool where Harold baptized him.

Later, one of the leaders of the deaf class asked the man about his experience. "I thought you were already saved and baptized."

The man signed, "I am. I just went upstairs to go the bathroom!"

The deaf ministry was one of the many outreaches at Landmark. Others included the bus ministry, radio ministry, a bookstore, Bible study curriculum, recording studio, and more.

The bookstore was managed by Mrs. Elizabeth Downey and was opened shortly after the church was built. During these early years, it was the only Christian bookstore in the entire Cincinnati area, and people traveled from great distances for the Christian resources offered by the Landmark Bookstore that were not offered elsewhere. At the time, no national chains, such as Berean or Family Christian Store, were in the area. It was open after regular services at Landmark but also from Monday through Saturday from 10:00 a.m. through 6:00 p.m.

Mrs. Downey was a beloved and well-known figure at Landmark. An organized and demanding boss, she expected others to do their best and was frustrated when she would ask for someone's help and they would answer, "That's not my job." When Mrs. Downey saw that something needed to be done, she did it whether it fell under her job description or not. Harold recalls one particular instance when he was looking for her and could not find her in the bookstore as usual. He did an extensive search of the building and finally found her in the lady's restroom, where she had fallen asleep on the throne.

Among the many resources available in the bookstore was Home Bible Studies, a curriculum distributed by Landmark to provide pastors with biblical studies help. This included cassette tapes with recorded sermons from famous pastors and evangelists, such as R. G. Lee's "Payday Someday." Lee was the pastor of Belleview Baptist Church in Memphis, Tennessee.

Another outreach that originated at Landmark was the Artist Recording Studio, which both recorded and pressed vinyl albums. These included albums for the Cathedral of Tomorrow under the ministry of Rex Humbard from Akron, Ohio, one of the top television broadcasts in the entire nation at the time. The studio also produced albums for Jack Van Impe. Later, Dr. John's son Carrol took the leadership of the studio, which continued to operate until vinyl records were replaced with more modern and popular technology, such as eight-track tapes in the 1960s and cassette tapes starting in the early 1970s. Landmark later produced cassette tapes of Dr. John's sermons.

In 1973, Dr. John spearheaded the founding of Landmark Christian School, which offered grades kindergarten through twelve. Enrollment at its peak reached 650 in 1976 from kindergarten to high school seniors. Dr. John founded Landmark Christian School to provide a thorough and Christian education for the Greater Cincinnati area. An emphasis was placed on sports programs in an effort to minister to and draw young athletes to the school. In the school's early years, Dr. John frequented the sporting events, including basketball games, and enjoyed interacting and bantering with the players. Fans could hear him cheering for his home team, and often his cry would ring throughout the gymnasium, "Righteousness shall prevail!"

At Landmark, there were many different programs and ministries to serve the needs of a diverse group of people. Dr. John also continued to plant dozens of churches throughout the region, and under his leadership in the 1970s, Landmark became one of the ten largest churches in the nation. A *Christian Life Report* in 1968 listed Landmark Baptist Temple as the sixth largest Sunday school in the United States. The top five were Akron Baptist Temple in Akron, Ohio, pastored by Dr. Dallas Billington; First Baptist Church in Dallas, Texas, pastored by Dr. William Criswell; Temple Baptist Church in Detroit, Michigan, pastored by Dr. G. B. Vick; Canton Baptist Temple in Canton, Ohio, pastored by Dr. Harold Henninger; First Baptist Church in Hammond, Indiana, pastored by Dr. Jack Hyles; and Landmark Baptist Temple in Cincinnati, Ohio, pastored by Dr. John Rawlings. Dr. Jerry Falwell's church in Lynchburg, Virginia, Thomas Road Baptist Church, followed at number eight.

29

Life at Landmark

Although many may describe Dr. John as a "hellfire and brimstone" preacher, he once said of himself in a sermon on November 6, 1977, "I don't think anybody can ever accuse John Rawlings of not being a positive preacher! I am so positive I can tell you that 'all things work together for good to them that love God, to them who are called according to His purpose!' You can't be any more positive than that."

Dr. John's sermons at Landmark were almost always evangelistic in nature. His sermons were based upon Scripture from the King James Version of the Bible. He would often cite well-known verses such as John 3:16, "For God so loved the world, that he gave his only begotten son, that whosoever believeth in him should not perish, but have everlasting life," and Romans 3:23, "For the wages of sin is death, but the gift of God is eternal life through Jesus Christ our Lord." He had the ability to feel what the Holy Spirit was telling him. He always gave the men working the sound booth a sermon title because they asked, but his title was rarely related to the sermon. At times, he changed his sermon while walking down the aisle because the Spirit changed his message.

One example can be found in a sermon from May 7, 1978. "Go out some night and look at the stars with their ten thousand, yea, ten million voices," Dr. John told the congregation. "Out yonder somewhere beyond stars and planets and moons and galaxies, God is. He has always been and will always be. He is my Father. Just think how He [descended] to earth and became a little baby in a manger in Bethlehem. He wrapped Himself in flesh, yet without sin. [Later] He was spit upon, his beard plucked out, cursed and reviled. Then He said before He died, 'I lay down my life, that I might take it up again.' He carried that old rugged cross up the hill of Calvary and there submissively laid down upon that cross. Those Roman soldiers drove the nails in His hands and in His feet. They put that crown of thorns upon His head. He hung suspended between heaven and earth and then pushed His spirit out and died. His body was laid in the grave where no man had yet laid. Then in seventy-two hours, He came out of that grave. He defied gravity and ascended on high. He saves us and calls us to serve Him … No wonder He said, 'Thou shalt love Thy God with all Thy heart and with all Thy soul and with all Thy mind.' Why? Because He is everything, He is everywhere, yet He is so small He can dwell within my heart. I … pray … 'Even so, come, Lord Jesus.'"

After the sermon, the hymns sung during the invitation, such as "Just as I Am," reflected Dr. John's previous message with verses like: "Just as I am without one plea, but that Thy blood was shed for me." Dr. John, unlike many other preachers, knew how to give an invitation. He would ask the congregation to bow their heads and close their eyes in quiet prayer. Then he would ask those who were saved and born again to raise their right hand high as a testimony of their faith in Christ.

While their eyes were still closed, he would then ask for those who did not know the Lord to raise their hands for prayer. He would say "thank you" as he acknowledged each individual. There was always someone in the rear of the church, as Dr. John would often say, "Yes, you in the back …" Many people had not heard such power from the pulpit, and at the invitation, many would often make decisions for Christ. Dr. John's messages deepened the spiritual lives of believers.

Then Dr. John would call those who had raised their hands to come forward. It was a compelling and emotional time as the Holy Spirit would "tug on [their] heartstrings." Dr. John would say something like, "God means business when He calls. Will you hear His voice? Will you yield? Will you come? Will you bend a knee at this altar and say, 'Oh, God, have mercy on me?'" He would tell them to repent, saying, "Have the peace of God given to you. Then you will have something worth living for and something worth dying for."

During this time, an invitational hymn was sung, such as, "Softly and Tenderly." As he invited people to come to the altar, Dr. John would echo the words of the chorus of this hymn, "Come home, come home." He would say,

"Step out, young man, young lady. Step out from wherever you are, and come home."

Some deacons and church leaders would walk amongst the crowd to see if there was anyone who had questions or wanted to be accompanied to the altar. People would go forward for salvation decisions, for rededications, for full-time service to the ministry, or to "move their letter (membership)" from another church. Lockland Baptist and Landmark Baptist were widely known for the numerous decisions made in commitment to Christian service.

Dr. John was known as having keen eyesight, and even though the auditorium was expansive, he was quite aware of every individual in attendance each Sunday. Some described him as having an "eagle eye." Ms. Heitkamp, a very large woman, always sat in the third row from the front. Every time Dr. John would finish preaching and start the invitation, his eagle eye would spot her rising from her pew and walking all the way across the front of the church, in front of everyone, to visit the ladies' restroom on the other side.

Finally, Dr. John confronted her about it. "Ms. Heitkamp," he said, "why do you go to the restroom every service?"

She answered, "Well, preacher, us old women just can't hold our water like we used to."

Dr. John's sermons were such that individuals would feel as if he were speaking directly to them. By telling colorful stories and often "breaking the Queen's English" while preaching, Dr. John made biblical truth clear and relevant to all his listeners. He knew how to move each person according to their conscience and their walk with the Lord. If a person had a hidden sin in their lives, they would often be deeply convicted during Dr. John's sermons.

Dr. John became one of the first preachers in the Greater Cincinnati area to televise his Sunday morning worship service, and his publication, *The Landmark Journal*, made its way into thousands of homes each month. At one time, it was mailed monthly to thirty-five thousand people in all fifty states of the Union as well as to homes in many other countries.

The bus ministry was a major twentieth-century church innovation, and Dr. John grew one of the nation's largest transportation ministries at Landmark with around one hundred buses encircling the Cincinnati area, bringing twenty-eight hundred to thirty-two hundred people to church each Sunday. At its peak, the bus ministry resulted in half of over the total attendance for Sunday school, and average weekly attendance of Sunday morning service reached a high of over five thousand! The Landmark buses transported kids from the entire greater Cincinnati area, which included southwestern Indiana and northern Kentucky, to Sunday school. The children who rode these buses were often termed "bus kids."

Willie Holt and others purchased many of the buses from schools in the tristate and around the country, such as from southern Indiana. The church would purchase about ten to twelve buses at a time as the schools retired their fleets and sold their old buses. This allowed the church to pay for the cost of maintaining the bus fleet, and an onsite bus garage would service and paint the buses. There were many dedicated bus drivers, such as Willie Holt, Sonny Neal, Tommy Neal, Gene Ellis, Curtis Sample, Clarence Worley, Hargis Reynolds, and Llano Bell, who drove a bus for over thirty years. There were also many wives and other ladies who visited the neighborhoods, announcing the bus routes to the citizens. Dr. John once sent one hundred Landmark buses to downtown Cincinnati, blocking Interstate 75, to protest a decision made concerning a requirement for bus safety.

In late 2010, Herb attended a Southern Gospel concert by Signature Sound at Florence Baptist Church in northern Kentucky, where he happened to be sitting beside a man who had once been a "bus kid." When he was seven years old, a woman dropped by his house to invite his family to Sunday school at

Landmark. The boy promised he would go, and on Sunday, he stood outside on the corner, waiting for the bus. A kind woman helped him aboard, and when the bus arrived at the church, he climbed off after the woman directed him to the children's Sunday school class. At the end of the service, he hurried back outside to board his bus but was shocked and intimidated to see a long row of sixty buses lined up. He could not distinguish his bus from the many others, which terrified him. Frantic, he ran up and down the row of buses until he finally spotted the kind lady whom he had met earlier that morning. Relieved, he climbed on the bus and rode home.

"Did you enjoy Sunday school?" his father asked him when he arrived home.

"Yes," the boy answered. "But I'm never going back again." When his father asked why, he said, "There are too many buses! I couldn't find my bus!"

But his father wanted him to go back and thus devised a plan. When Saturday rolled around, his father instructed him, "I'm going to give you some money, and I want you to go to the store and buy some bubble gum. When the bus picks you up tomorrow, I want you to chew the bubble gum. When you get to church, take the gum out of your mouth and stick it to the front fender of the bus, close to the headlight where you can see it. When you come out of the church, look for your gum, and *that's* your bus."

His plan worked to perfection, and the boy enjoyed chewing his gum again on the way home. And not only was he able to find his bus after the service, but during the service, he found Christ. He invited Him into his heart and remained faithful to God for the rest of his life.

Another example of a "bus kid" was Kim Johnson, a girl who was once invited to a Landmark Baptist satellite church in Monfort Heights in 1980. She writes that she grew up in a non-Christian home, and "the night I was invited by a friend to Landmark Monfort Heights was the night that the Liberty Players were performing a drama about the realities of heaven and hell." Dr. John's oldest granddaughter, Catherine, was performing that evening. Kim remembers "sitting in the pew and realizing that if I were to die that night, I would spend eternity apart from God. That night I accepted Jesus into my life, and my life has never been the same since then." While attending Ohio State, she became involved with Campus Crusade for Christ and joined its staff once she had graduated. Her first assignment was in Zambia, Africa.

Kim enjoyed sharing her faith with college students and reaching them with the good news of Jesus Christ. Her life was changed as a result of Dr.

John and Dr. Harold's faithfulness to the Lord over the years. "I have seen my entire family come to know Him. I've been on missionary journeys to Egypt, Kenya, Zambia, Turkey, Azerbaijan, China, Thailand, and France. I love being an ambassador for Him."

These stories are examples of the many lives impacted by the bus ministry under Dr. John's leadership. One day in his later years while living in Union, Kentucky, Dr. John was going for a walk in his neighborhood in Triple Crown. A man who was a former "bus kid" stopped him and asked, "Are you John Rawlings?" He then told a story from his childhood. One day, he saw a flyer from Landmark for "Kite Sunday," a day when children attending Landmark received a free kite. "I brought home more than a kite," the man told Dr. John. "I brought home Jesus that day."

30

The Finest Lady Soul Winner

During the forty-three years Dr. John served as pastor of Landmark Baptist Temple and the nearly seventy-five years they were married, Orelia Rawlings was the epitome of a pastor's wife. Her cooking was legendary among those privileged to enjoy one of her delicious meals.

In addition to cooking, she loved gardening. Every spring and summer, her gardens blazed with color. She was always impeccably dressed, as she tailored many of her own clothes. She was keenly interested in politics and world events and always interpreted those happenings in the light of Scripture. She loved music and could play the piano (she learned on a pump organ) and wrote a number of songs, some of which were performed by the Landmark Church Choir. Each Christmas season for a number of years, she wrote a little drama that her grandchildren were expected to

act out before the gifts were opened. This was one of the eagerly anticipated events of the season. Another of her writing accomplishments includes her poem about her childhood at Aetna School. Dr. John's grandson Steve recalls sitting with his grandmother at the kitchen table in the Mansion as she typed the poem on her old black Royal manual typewriter.

Mrs. Rawlings was not as rough as her husband, but she was just as tough. During their ministry in Cincinnati, at one time the Landmark property was home to Dr. John's twenty-five head of horses. One day, when he was riding an especially frisky Tennessee Walker stallion, Mrs. Rawlings looked out and saw that her husband was in a dangerous situation. "You get down off that horse!" she yelled. "One thing I am *not* going to do the rest of my life is take care of a crippled preacher!"

Whether Dr. John needed a word of encouragement or a gentle reprimand, Mrs. Rawlings seemed to always know just what he needed to hear. While living in Tyler, Dr. John went through a brief period of discouragement. On a dark, rainy day, when he walked into the house, Mrs. Rawlings could tell from his expression he was downhearted. Rather than commiserating with her husband, she encouraged him to keep going and to never give up by posing a searching question, "Have I married a quitter?" This prompted John to carry on despite difficulties and dejection. Mrs. Rawlings's wisdom and encouragement often carried him through trying times.

Pastor Jerry Falwell said of Orelia Rawlings, "She was a beautiful and dignified lady."[26] Falwell met her in August of 1952 when he had just turned nineteen years old and Mrs. Rawlings was forty years old. Reverend Charlie Harbin thought she was the finest female soul winner he had ever met. She had a true inward as well as outward beauty; Dr. John believed there was no Hollywood star of her age more beautiful. She was not afraid of confrontation or of going to battle for her Lord. As a soul winner, friend, and example to the women of Landmark, Orelia Rawlings was the embodiment of the Proverbs 31 woman:

> Who can find a virtuous wife? For her worth *is* far above rubies.
> The heart of her husband safely trusts her; so he will have no lack
> of gain. She does him good and not evil all the days of her life.
> She seeks wool and flax, and willingly works with her hands. She
> is like the merchant ships, she brings her food from afar. She also

---

26   Reverend Jerry Fallwell, "About Mrs. Rawlings." February 17, 2007. *World Net Daily:* http://www.wnd.com/index.php?pageId=40222 (March 14, 2009).

rises while it is yet night, and provides food for her household, and a portion for her maidservants. She considers a field and buys it; from her profits she plants a vineyard. She girds herself with strength, and strengthens her arms. She perceives that her merchandise *is* good, and her lamp does not go out by night. She stretches out her hands to the distaff, and her hand holds the spindle. She extends her hand to the poor, yes, she reaches out her hands to the needy. She is not afraid of snow for her household, for all her household *is* clothed with scarlet. She makes tapestry for herself; her clothing *is* fine linen and purple. Her husband is known in the gates, when he sits among the elders of the land. She makes linen garments and sells *them,* and supplies sashes for the merchants. Strength and honor *are* her clothing; she shall rejoice in time to come. She opens her mouth with wisdom, and on her tongue *is* the law of kindness. She watches over the ways of her household, and does not eat the bread of idleness. Her children rise up and call her blessed; her husband *also,* and he praises her: "Many daughters have done well, but you excel them all." Charm *is* deceitful and beauty *is* passing, but a woman *who* fears the LORD, she shall be praised. (Vv. 10–30, original emphases)

Mrs. Rawlings with Dr. John and Their Sons on her 90th birthday in August 2003

31

The Place to Be

"It's Better to Build Boys & Girls Than to Repair Men and Women."

—MESSAGE INSCRIBED ON FREE PENCILS FOR
ADVANCING THE LANDMARK BUS MINISTRY

The *Cincinnati Post,* Cincinnati's largest daily newspaper in the mid-1970s, highlighted Landmark Baptist Church in a front page spread on Saturday, August 1, 1976. In this article, *Post* reporter James L. Adams describes Landmark:

> Driving up the curving, blacktopped driveway, flanked by a gleaming white slat fence, leading to the Landmark Baptist Temple, one gets the feeling of entering a Bluegrass horse farm rather than approaching a church. The lane opens into a sprawling 15-acre paved parking lot that seems to disappear over the horizon. Two huge buildings anchor the paved expanse. One-hundred-ten buses used for Sunday School and the Landmark Christian School are parked in rows on a rise. (The Landmark fleet is one-fourth as large as Queen City Metro's.) One looks in vain for a "temple" or a church building with a steeple. Sunday school—and Landmark

Baptist Temple is more of a mammoth Sunday School than anything else—and evangelistic services are held in the cavernous 2278-seat "field house," which looks like an airplane hangar from the sky and a civic auditorium from the inside.[27]

Average attendance at this time was forty-one hundred, and there were often not enough seats to accommodate the Sunday school attendants. The overflow attended classes at the old Lockland Baptist Church on Mills Street. The church was gaining national attention. One attendee at Landmark was Buz Lukens, a United States Representative for the state of Ohio. In a private meeting with President Richard Nixon, Rep. Lukens scribbled "Harold Rawlings" and "Landmark Baptist Temple" on a piece of paper, saying, "You ought to hear my pastor." Nixon stuck the note into his pocket.

Some weeks later, Harold received a call from one of Nixon's assistants from the White House. Of course, there was no hesitation on Harold's part to preach at the White House. He didn't have to pray about it—he accepted the offer.

Adult Sunday School Class at Landmark

---

27   James L. Adams, "Landmark Baptist Temple: Plan it big, keep it simple," *The Cincinnati Post*, (August 21, 1976): 1, 31.

During the late 1960s and into the 1970s, Landmark Baptist was "the place to be" for Independence Day celebrations, as Dr. John was quite the organizer of lavish events. A sign near the church with invitations like the following welcomed visitors:

July 4th Patriotic Festival

Everyone Welcome

Softball Tournament • Arcade • Delicious Foods

Gospel Sing • Bluegrass Music • Lake Boat Rides • Wagon Rides

The church grounds were teeming with church members, families, and visitors. There was more food than the entire crowd could eat, including Texas barbeque, corn on the cob, hamburgers, hotdogs, pinto beans, cornbread, and large, juicy, watermelons bought from the Amish in southern Indiana.

In the August 1976 *Cincinnati Post* article, James L. Adams wrote:

> On July 4, church members met in their own park for a God-and-country program that included patriotic preaching soft-drink wagons, a smorgasbord of sports for the children—baseball, fishing, volleyball—and helicopters offering rides for those wanting to rise above the mundane.[28]

Children loved the helicopter rides, a unique attraction for that area. There were also car shows, which included Model A, Model B, and Model T cars. Church teams from all over the region, including Indianapolis, Indiana; Nashville, Tennessee; and Detroit, Michigan, played in a large softball tournament. The greased pig contest was quite popular, as the crowd enjoyed watching the young competitors quickly become soiled by grease and mud. A change of clothes was a necessity once the event was over.

The donkey softball game was also a big attraction. Players would hit the ball, jump hastily onto their donkey's back, and attempt to ride it around the bases. On one memorable occasion, a "jack" tore straight past the pitcher's mound and second base to center field, where a "ginny" that had caught his eye was standing. The jack tossed his rider, Carrol Rawlings, along the way. At once, Dr. John took charge and changed both the donkey's mind and direction—with the help of a cattle prod.

---

28   James L. Adams, "Landmark Baptist Temple: Plan it big, keep it simple," *The Cincinnati Post*, (August 21, 1976): 1, 31.

Pony rides were also offered. Ponies would pull carts to areas around the grounds, such as the ball fields. Carrol recalled a time when he was in the driver's seat of one such pony cart, and Dr. John encourage the wife of a visiting preacher to take a ride. Carrol looked on as the very sophisticated woman took her seat in the cart. When she was settled in, Carrol gave the reigns a flick, and as the pony went forward, it passed gas with each footfall for several feet. Amused, Carrol glanced back at the pastor's wife and laughed inwardly at her indifferent expression.

Other events of the Fourth of July celebration included hot air balloon rides, crafts, concerts with old time Gospel and bluegrass music, canoeing and kayaking in the church lake, clowns, and puppet shows from members of the church, such as the Bowling family. Because Dr. John had always loved animals, a petting zoo was also always part of the celebration.

The church also celebrated an event called "Old Fashioned Day" once a year, the one time when Dr. John would not wear a suit to Sunday service. Instead, he often sported a cowboy hat and boots. The members of the church would dress in their finest old-fashioned clothes or western wear. And a visiting "hillbilly" family would ride to church in a Model T Ford.

Those were happy times at Landmark, when believers from near and far came together to worship and fellowship. Many felt those times were glimpses of the joy they would experience in heaven, and the memories they made were enduring.

32

Speakers at Landmark

Many evangelists and pastors visited Landmark, including Jerry Falwell, Jack Van Impe, Dr. Tim Lahaye, Dr. Martyn Lloyd-Jones, B. R. Lakin, Bob Harrington, and Dallas F. Billington.

Jerry Falwell was perhaps one of the most well-known evangelists to visit Landmark and used to call Dr. John regularly. Jerry met Dr. John originally through Herb when they were roommates in college in 1953 at the Baptist Bible College in Springfield, Missouri. During that time, Dr. John was vice president of the Baptist Bible Fellowship and was around the college quite often. Jerry heard many sermons from Dr. John, and the respect between them was mutual.

In later years, after establishing Liberty University in Lynchburg, Virginia, Jerry Falwell grew especially close to Dr. John and would often visit Landmark to speak, including Fourth of July celebrations. Church members at Landmark enjoyed hearing about the progress of Falwell's Moral Majority, which he founded in 1979. The last visit Falwell made to Landmark was to bring the eulogy at Mrs. Rawlings's funeral service in 2007. He was a friend of the family until his own death shortly thereafter.

Dr. John came to respect Falwell's ministry with the *Old-Time Gospel Hour* telecast and for developing a deep consciousness in preachers for their cities in the 1970s, coining the phrase "Capture your city for Christ." Dr. John valued this approach to evangelism because he felt if a preacher did not respect his city, try to honor Jesus Christ in his city, and beg men and women to be saved, "We are not the kind of citizens we ought to be!" he says. "We ought to love our city! We ought to care for our city because our city is made of people!"

Jack Van Impe, another visitor to Landmark, had a ministry whose mission included confronting the culture, such as getting young people to turn away from hard rock music. A friend of the Rawlings family, Pastor Cecil Eggert, shares his testimony of being influenced by Jack Van Impe's message. He recalls that after listening to a sermon he threw away all of his hard rock albums and quit as the bass guitarist of his rock 'n' roll band.

The Landmark audience was astounded by Jack Van Impe's memorization of Bible passages. As a televangelist teaching Bible prophecy, he is became known as the "Walking Bible" because of his "ability to quote 14,000 Bible verses."[29]

Dr. Tim Lahaye once spoke at Landmark. He had a record album released as part of the "Great Sermons of the 20th Century" series. The record was titled "The Battle for the Family" and was released by the Artist's Recording Company in Cincinnati, Ohio, a record company owned by Dr. John's son, Carrol. Dr. Lahaye became best known for *Left Behind*, the book series of apocalyptic fiction he cowrote with Jerry B. Jenkins. "The *Left Behind* fiction series ... have broken all publishing records with a total of 80 million in print."[30]

Dr. Martyn Lloyd-Jones was a British evangelical preacher who was minister of Westminster Chapel in London, England, for almost thirty years where Dr. Harold Rawlings once preached. Also a medical doctor, Dr. Lloyd-Jones stood in strong opposition against the liberal theology that was permeating the church. Like Dr. John, he was an influential preacher of the twentieth century. His sermons were widely published, studied, and quoted by many.

B. R. Lakin spoke effectively to all audiences, youth as well as adults. When he came to Landmark, he was well received, and people looked forward to his appearances. For a time during the 1960s, he was actually a member of Landmark. Like Dr. John, "Dr. [B. R.] Lakin was polished, dynamic, eloquent, and witty. His voice was captivating, and his delivery was flawless." And as Dr. John did, "He was a great preacher, and he knew that he was." During a conference in Louisville, Kentucky, in his later years, he shared the platform with Dr. John R. Rice. "Dr. Lakin was always at his best when he preached to

29   "Scripture Memorization: The Walking Bible." *Jack Van Impe Ministries International: http://www.jvim.com/scripturememorization.htm* (August 18, 2011).

30   "Tim LaHaye's Biography." *Tim La Haye Ministries: https://timlahaye.com/shopcontent. asp?type=Biography* (August 18, 2011).

preachers. That night in Louisville was no exception. When Dr. Lakin finished preaching and sat down, Dr. Rice said, 'You stole the show.' Dr. Lakin replied, 'I intended too.'"[31]

In a well-known sermon entitled "Why I Know There Is a God," B. R. Lakin confronted atheism. "To be an evolutionist," he said, "you'd have to switch your brain out of reason and throw it into neutral. Listen to what they say:

> Way back yonder sometime, somewhere, somehow, nobody knows when, how, where, or why, nothing got in nothing and nothing formed a something. A germ got in the water somehow. Then the water developed it into a tadpole, and one day, the tadpole swam to another bank and got stuck in the mud and dried there. Wriggling around in the mud, he formed warts on his belly that later became legs. After he developed legs, he was climbing through the trees one day when his foot slipped. As he fell, he wrapped his tail around a limb. The jar of it broke off his tail. He hit the ground, stood up on his hind feet, walked across the street, bought him a suit of clothes, went to teaching in the university, and said, "Thank God, I'm a man at last!"

Before his call to preach, Reverend Bob Harrington was a successful insurance salesman who wore a red tie and carried a red-covered Bible. When asked why he carried a red Bible, he would say, "Because the Bible ought to be *read*." After establishing himself as an evangelist, he appeared on TV shows, including *The Mike Douglas Show*, *The Phil Donahue Show*, and *Oprah*. He had famous debates with American atheist and Communist sympathizer Madelyn Murray O'Hare, including several on *The Phil Donahue Show*.

Bob Harrington first spoke at Landmark in 1966. Billboard space was purchased strategically around the Greater Cincinnati area in anticipation of his visit. Record albums that included his testimony were given out to promote his visit. At the peak of his ministry, he was the biggest draw to ever speak at Landmark. The attendance was around three thousand each night. Chairs were carried in to accommodate the crowd in the two balconies on either side of the

---

31   Dr. Louis Arnold, "Dr. B. R. Lakin." *Let Us Not Forget Our Roots: Great Preachers I Have Known: http://www.louisarnoldministries.org/preachers.html#anchor569905* (February 22, 2013).

church. Additional chairs were put in every aisle, which would probably easily violate modern-day fire codes.

Bob Harrington came to Landmark three times. The second time he visited, the meetings were held outside, where he spoke from a special platform, and the crowds were even larger. According to the July 1972 *Landmark Journal*, sixty thousand people heard Bob Harrington preach and said he lived up to his reputation as "the world's most unusual evangelist." It was believed to be the largest revival crusade in the city of Cincinnati since Billy Sunday's visit in 1922.

During one slightly controversial visit, Harrington traveled to the heart of Newport and preached uninvited at the Pink Pussycat Lounge, witnessing to the dancers. He also visited the high schools, local TV stations, and the Beverly Hills Supper Club in Southgate, Kentucky, where on May 28, 1977, more people had been killed in a nightclub fire than in any other in the United States, with a fatality count of 165 people and 200 injured.

Dallas F. Billington, another visitor to Landmark, was the pastor of Akron Baptist Temple in Akron, Ohio, which many considered to be the largest church in America in the 1960s and early 1970s. In the foreward to *God Is Real,* B. R. Lakin states that Akron Baptist Temple had the largest Sunday school in the world with missions and churches around the globe. When he founded the church, it had eighty charter members, but the church grew until it had sixteen thousand members. In 1960, when the church celebrated its twenty-fifth anniversary, fifty thousand people came to Akron to hear Pastor Billington preach. Billington was a great church-planter; his ministry was instrumental in the founding of two hundred churches. (Autobiography *God is Real*).

These were the kinds of people Dr. John brought in to speak—unusual, controversial, and colorful evangelists. Other visitors included G. B Vick; John R. Rice; Captain Edgar Bundy, former US Air Force intelligence officer; Bob Jones Jr., President of Bob Jones University; Monroe Parker; R. G. Lee; Curtis Hudson; Jack Wyrtzen, founder of Word of Life at Schroon Lake in upstate New York; Tom Malone; Buffalo Bill of Nashville, Tennessee; Holland London; Carl Hatch; Dr. Jim Vineyard; Jack Hyles; Howard Sears; J. O. Grooms; "Doc" Rusk; Alvin Dark, manager of Oakland Athletics; evangelist Jim Delashmit, former President of Hell's Angels motorcycle gang; Colonel Oliver North; Stephen Alford; Frank Collins; and Jackie Burress; among others.

Paul Anderson, internationally renowned strongman, thrilled the audience at Landmark. The young man from Georgia became the:

> World (1995) and Olympic (1956) weightlifting champion—and holder of all the world records at the time … Paul Anderson … was probably the strongest man who ever walked the face of the earth. One of the best known athletes of his time, no other strongman, before or since, has captured the imagination of the world the way Anderson did … As a member of the first U.S. sports team to visit the Soviet Union during the Cold War, the 5'9, 363-pound Anderson thrilled the 15,000 strength-and-power-loving Muscovites—plus many more on television—who sat outdoors for hours in a drizzling rain to watch him trounce their champion. The Moscow newspaper the next morning called him "The Wonder of Nature."[32]

Anderson later began his own ministry, called Paul Anderson Ministries, which included a youth home founded in 1961.

Another interesting character to visit Landmark was the tallest man in the world whose Philippine wife, Herb recalls, was quite short. As he put it, she "only came to about her husband's belt buckle."

Well-known political commentator and former US Marine Corps Colonel Oliver Laurence North spoke at Landmark in the 1990s. Millions watched as he testified before Congress in regard to his involvement in the Iran-Contra Affair.

Charles "Tremendous" Jones, a successful insurance executive before he became an inspirational speaker, was well received at Landmark and spoke twice. One of his famous motivational quotes is, "If you can't be happy where you are, it's a cinch you can't be happy where you ain't."[33]

Peter Ruckman was very popular with the youth and was known for his chalk drawings. He would begin a sermon with drawings on a chalkboard, and as he spoke, the picture would come together. By the end of his talk, the picture he had drawn tied in perfectly with his sermon. Peter Ruckman was known for his strict adherence to the 1611 King James Bible.

32   Clarence and Carol Bass, "Paul Anderson, King of the Squat." 1999. *Ripped: http://www.cbass.com/ANDERSON.HTM* (February 22, 2013).

33   Gary P. Guthrie, *1,600 Quotes & Pieces of Wisdom That Just Might Help You Out When You're Stuck in a Moment (and can't get out of it!).* (iUniverse, Inc., 2003), 10.

Landmark guest speaker Tony Cloninger pitched for the Cincinnati Reds and Milwaukee Braves, the team who later became the Atlanta Braves. Cloninger's two sons attended the summer church camp Chautauqua with other kids from Landmark. On July 3, 1966, Cloninger hit two grand slams and drove in nine runs, setting a major league record for pitchers. He later became a pitching coach for the New York Yankees and Boston Red Sox. He earned four World Series rings.

Both David Canary and Max Messner played football at the University of Cincinnati (UC) and attended Landmark Baptist Temple during their college days. David Canary attended the University of Cincinnati on a football scholarship and was the first UC football player to attend the UC College-Conservatory of Music (CCM). He later starred in the hit TV series *Bonanza*, in which he was cast as "Candy" Canaday, foreman of the Ponderosa ranch. Since 1983, he plays a leading role as twin brothers Adam and Stuart in the daytime soap opera *All My Children* and has won five Emmy awards.

Max Messner later played professional football for the Detroit Lions but suffered an injury during his first season and was forced to retire. For six years, he was a famous NFL football player for three teams: the Pittsburgh Stealers, the New York Giants, and the Detroit Lions. Carrol Rawlings remembers that Canary and Messner sang a duet to the African-American spiritual "There Is a Balm in Gilead" at a Lockland service.

Refrain
There is a balm in Gilead
To make the wounded whole;
There is a balm in Gilead
To heal the sin-sick soul.

Sometimes I feel discouraged,
And think my work's in vain,
But then the Holy Spirit
Revives my soul again.

Refrain
If you can't preach like Peter,
If you can't pray like Paul,
Just tell the love of Jesus,
And say He died for all.

33

"The Nation's Station"

While pastoring Landmark, Dr. John grew his radio ministry in the early 1950s to reach fifty-three stations. By 1958, it was broadcast on two hundred stations and reached nearly three hundred stations in the 1960s. Weekly television programs were also broadcast from the church. For a time, the *Landmark Baptist Hour* was broadcast internationally on a cable network. The broadcast blanketed the East coast of the United States and was mostly aired on Sunday evenings. A primary objective of the Landmark broadcasts was to establish new churches and to help strengthen existing ones.

In May 1932, radio station WLW of Cincinnati, Ohio, made history and shocked other radio stations around the country by transmitting over the air five hundred thousand watts of power. It became "The Nation's Station" and remains the only commercial station in North America to ever transmit such power.

> The signal was so powerful that WLW programming emanated from metal fences and downspouts for miles around the transmitter. Farmers couldn't shut off their barn lights. A motel in the neighboring town of Mason, Ohio, found that its neon sign glowed brightly even when it was turned off.[34]

---

34   Michael Banks, *Before Oprah: Ruth Lyons, the Woman Who Created Talk TV*, ed. John Baskin, 1st edition. (Wilmington, Ohio: Orange Frazer Pr., May 2009), 62.

174

The transmission power was cut back to fifty thousand watts on March 1, 1939, as the FCC did not renew WLW's high-power permit.

Another station that broadcasted the Landmark program was WCKY 1560 on the AM dial. WCKY was directional in its broadcast, so there were many listeners far to the south and north as well, whereas WLW was nondirectional.

WCKY could be heard as far south as Bonaire, South America, and as far east as Bermuda. Herb recalls that visitors from different parts of the hemisphere, such as Bermuda and the Bahamas, listened to the *Landmark Baptist Hour*. Some of these listeners even traveled long distances to hear Dr. John preach in person. Even on the small island of Spanish Wells, Dr. John's radio program could be heard throughout the streets, as shared by Kirtland and Sally Robert, residents of the island. They listened to WCKY in the early 1970s and remain friends of the Rawlings family to this very day. Kirtland and Sally recall a time when one could walk through their neighborhood on Sunday evenings and hear the *Landmark Baptist Hour* through the open windows of the houses lining the street, reminiscent of how listeners in East Texas tuned into Central Baptist's broadcast. At that time, there were about nine hundred people living on the island of Spanish Wells. WCKY could be heard clearly all over the Bahamas, and many families there were very supportive of the radio ministry.

The church also received letters from navy personnel who listened to Dr. John's Sunday night broadcast while sailing on the Caribbean, and there were many supporters of the radio ministry in Canada as well. Dr. John's son Carrol, while working at Landmark, remembers reading a letter from a lady from a remote area in Canada who received the broadcast even though she lived fifty miles from the nearest railroad.

Pennsylvania was one of the largest contributing states. Many Amish and Mennonite visitors traveled from Pennsylvania to see Dr. John in person. Many of the Pennsylvania contributors lived in towns like York, Boyertown, Pottstown, and Kutztown.

Many people wrote into Dr. John's radio ministry, and some of the letters were quite amusing. One lady wrote that she was tired of being "pore" and asked Dr. John to send her three dresses, size twelve; two pairs of shoes, size seven; and five pairs of "step-ins." One person wrote in saying that Dr. John and Herbert W. Armstrong, founder of the Worldwide Church of God in the late 1930s, were her two favorite preachers.

Carrol recalls the story told by a Kentucky state trooper from northern Kentucky. The officer related that he listened regularly to Dr. John's Sunday night radio broadcast, but to receive the best signal, he had to be on a certain hill at a high elevation. He noticed that during those times he never once received a call from the dispatcher.

The Gospel reached many people through Dr. John's radio ministry, as Dr. John did not withhold his fiery preaching from his radio listeners any more than he did from his parishioners. In his radio broadcast of June 18, 1978, he said, "You people listening to me on the radio, I want to jack you up a little bit. You can sit at home and turn your toes up toward the ceiling and say, 'Well, I listen to Dr. John. I can be a good Christian and stay at home.' That is not so. That is the Devil talking. That is not right! If you are able, you ought to go to church! Get skinned in the morning, and let me skin you at night! Or let me skin you in the morning, and let your preacher skin you night! That is the way you need it! Christians need to be preached to! We need to see the fruit! Moses' crowd couldn't see the fruit! Joshua's crowd couldn't see the fruit! Caleb's crowd couldn't see the fruit! All they could see were these giants. 'Well, we can't do it. Do you think it will work? Dr. John, do you think people will go to a tent meeting?' ... No! They won't go unless somebody will challenge them! No! People will not get right unless somebody tries to reach them! People will go to hell unless God's people go out where the people are! Did He give us an assignment? 'Go out quickly into the streets and lanes of the city ... and compel them to come in!' Did He not say, 'Go out into the highways and hedges, and compel them to come in, that My house may be filled'? God tells us how to do it. In the book of Acts, He sent them out two by two. He said, 'Go, and I will be with you. Go, and I will be with you even unto the end of the age!'"

Linda Whanger of northern Kentucky and her family, like many others, were deeply impacted by Dr. John's firebrand style of preaching, including through his radio ministry. She writes:

> It all began in Cincinnati, Ohio, when my Dad listened to a radio broadcast and heard Dr. John W. Rawlings telling the good news on the airwaves. Our family had been attending a church on most Sundays, but I can only recall going to a downstairs room and coloring or doing other activities for children at the previous church. My dad was excited enough about the pastor on the radio broadcast to take all of us by city bus from the Clifton area in

Cincinnati to Lockland, Ohio. We began attending Lockland Baptist Church three times a week by city bus: Sunday mornings, Sunday evenings, and Wednesday evenings. After attending regularly for a few months, I remember seeing my Dad go down the aisle at the end of a service. I did not understand what he was doing at the time, but his decision began a whole new chapter in our family. It began the practice of regular, steady attendance in church, one of the mainstays of our family life.

While preaching in North Carolina, Dr. John happened to be visiting an area in which he was very well known and had been for the past thirty years. During a marvelous altar service in a packed house, Dr. John greeted the people who had heard him on the radio and had come to see him preach. After the service ended, a long line of people stood before him, at the forefront of which stood a tall, handsome man of about six foot three—a very strong individual. He reached out with his big hand to Dr. John. "I want to thank you for your radio program and for turning my life around and helping me to get right with God." As the two shook hands, the man slipped a crumpled piece of paper into Dr. John's palm and said, "Put that in your pocket." After the man left, Dr. John turned to the next person and continued shaking the hands of his supporters.

About an hour later, Dr. John went home as a houseguest of the man who sponsored his program. Dr. John went to his bedroom, and when he changed clothes, he found the crumpled piece of paper in his pocket. *What's that?* he wondered as he took it out of his pocket. It was a large envelope with "Dr. John Rawlings" written on it. He opened the envelope. Inside was a stack of one hundred dollar bills!

During the service hours earlier, Dr. John had mentioned in his message that he had been on the radio for fifty years. He told the audience he had never taken any of the contributions for himself but had given everything that came in the way of gifts toward the expenses of the broadcast. Though he had made the comment in passing, now he stood with a handful of one hundred dollar bills.

Dr. John had always considered himself an instrument of God and had looked at his radio ministry as merely a mouthpiece of the Lord. He was not his own; he belonged to God. Yet while looking at this money, something was bothering him. He and Mrs. Rawlings's wedding anniversary was fast approaching, and he felt a wave of temptation sweep over him. As he climbed into bed, a small internal voice whispered, "I would keep that."

Then a second still, small voice answered, "Don't you remember what you said to those people?"

It didn't take long for Dr. John to settle the matter. He sat up in bed, flipped the light on, took his coat out of the closet, and dropped the envelope into the pocket, telling himself, "This belongs to radio." He climbed back into bed and went to sleep.

Dr. John had promised God that he would give everything he had back to radio. He could have kept the money and maintained a clear conscience because it *was* given to him as a gift. Yet he could not break his promise to almighty God and purposed in his heart to do what he knew was right according to his promise.

34

Music at Landmark

As a visionary, Dr. John saw the potential of Southern Gospel music to engage the community and draw people into church. Landmark was thought to be the first to bring in handheld microphones for each singer. The new style of music was at first controversial because of its loud volume and liveliness but caught on quickly as new Southern Gospel groups began touring the country.

In the mid-1960s, Landmark invited a Gospel group known as The Spurlows to perform. Contemporary and considered controversial by many, the group consisted of a band and chorale group that included instrumentation, such as trumpets, trombones, and drums. In times past, this type of music had been frowned upon by the church, including many fundamentalist Baptist churches, but Dr. John's church was, in many ways, a forerunner of things to be, as was Dr. John's visionary thinking.

The Landmark Quartet became a popular part of Dr. John's radio show. Founded after the church moved from Lockland to Evendale, a suburb in the northern part of Cincinnati, the quartet was originally formed for the purpose of evangelistic meetings around the country and to build and strengthen an audience for Dr. John's radio ministry. A large bus was purchased to transport the quartet to the evangelistic meetings.

The original members of the quartet were Carl Noe, Carrol Rawlings, Don Norman, and Mack Evans, with Jack Clark at the piano. Buddy Liles later replaced Carl Noe at bass. A preacher named Chuck Ramsey followed Clark at piano, and then Loren Matthews succeeded Ramsey. The group made popular such songs as "Shout Brother Shout," "On the Sunny Banks," and "He Looked Beyond My Faults." The quartet recorded for Heartwarming Records, which at the time was the top Gospel-recording label, and received much airtime on Christian radio stations. They recorded about ten albums and regularly appeared on *Landmark Baptist Hour*.

Don Norman and Mack Evans later accepted ministry positions with Jerry Falwell and the Thomas Road Baptist Church in Lynchburg, Virginia. Buddy Liles spent twenty-five years with the Florida Boys Quartet, performing on the *Gospel Singing Jubilee* for many years and has appeared on Nashville television programming as well as on national television. He sang at a congressional breakfast in Washington, DC and was inducted into the Gospel Music Hall of Fame.[35]

Loren Matthews, after spending some time away from the faith, began a ministry with his wife that sought to renew marriages. Carrol Rawlings later joined the Rhythm Masters, with his wife, Linda, at the piano/keyboard. One year, the group won the top national award in the part-time/professional Gospel group category at the quartet convention in Tennessee. Carrol's son Scott also sang with the group. More recently, Carrol and Linda founded the Harvesters, a group based in Florence, Kentucky, with their daughter Lindsay, Dr. John's youngest grandchild, on bass guitar.

Perhaps the most well-known and cherished performance under Dr. John's ministry was that of "Till the Storm Passes By," a song featuring choir director Herb Rawlings accompanied by the large Landmark choir, which included choir members from several neighboring churches. The album sold large numbers, but because records of such things were not kept during those days, it is unknown just how many were sold.

While attending a Massachusetts fellowship meeting sometime around 2005, Herb discovered upon checking into a bed-and-breakfast in Falmouth, Massachusetts, that the owner recognized the Rawlings name. "Are you from the Rawlings family in Cincinnati?" he asked.

Herb answered, "Yes, I am."

"You're Herb who sang 'Till the Storm Passes By'!" the man exclaimed. "That's my favorite song."

Herb was pleasantly surprised, as the album had been released about forty years earlier!

One of the most popular Southern Gospel groups to visit Landmark was the Imperials, who enjoyed the peak of their career between 1964 and 1970. The members at the time were Sherrill Nielsen, Gary MacSpadden, Henry Slaughter, Jake Hess, and Armond Morales. Jake Hess, the leader of the group, would later tell Herb and his wife, Pat, as well as Carrol Rawlings, that Dr. John saved their career. In the mid-1960s, Dr. John called Jake to schedule the group for a concert at Landmark. When he asked Jake what dates the group had available, Jake looked at its completely open calendar and agreed to a date with Dr. John. After the group performed at Landmark, Dr. John said to Jake, "The truth of the matter is you don't have any bookings, do you?"

Jake responded that he had not been totally honest when he looked at his schedule before and confirmed the group's entire year was open.

Dr. John then went about calling his pastor friends around the country, telling them to schedule the Imperials. Jake Hess later related that Dr. John helped book the group for the remainder of the year.

Later on, the Imperials went to a more contemporary sound and were hired to sing backup for Elvis Presley. Elvis idolized Jake Hess and was thrilled to sing on the same recordings with his hero. "The classic Elvis recording, 'His Hand in Mine,' prominently features Jake Hess and the Imperials."[36]

Other popular groups that sang at Landmark around this time included the Cathedrals, Whetherfords, Statesmen Quartet, Oak Ridge Boys, Stamps, Rambos, Speer Family, Blackwood Brothers, Tony Brothers, Dixie Four, and Henry and Hazel Slaughter. Claude Hopper of the Hopper family singers sang at Landmark, whose son Dean played drums—the first time the Landmark congregants saw drums on the platform! Drums and loud music as a whole was considered controversial at the time, so Claude asked Dr. John for approval to bring the drums into the church. Dr. John responded, "Sure, bring them in and have him beat the Devil out of them! If anybody doesn't like it, they can leave!" Dean became the lead singer of the Hoppers.

Large outside open-air concerts and services were held on the Landmark grounds. A special choir platform with a shell overhead was built to protect the performers from the weather. This was done while the new church building, called the field house, was being completed.

---

36   "GOGR Music History: The Imperials." *Southern Gospel Music Association: http://www. sgma.org/gogr_history/imperials.htm* (February 22, 2013).

These were exciting and exhilarating times for church members and visitors of all ages and for connoisseurs of Southern Gospel music. On one occasion, a large contingent of Gospel groups, including the Statesmen and the Blackwoods, performed before a crowd estimated to be nine thousand. There were so many cars that they were backed up onto Glendale-Milford Road, the primary entrance to Landmark, and even back to the exit ramp of Interstate 75.

Probably the most popular quartet to visit Landmark in the late seventies and eighties was the Cathedrals, whose name originated from its time at the Cathedral of Tomorrow in Akron, Ohio. The group began as the Cathedral Trio but became a quartet when George Younce was added at bass. They often traveled with their pastor, evangelist Rex Humbard.

The group had a unique sense of humor, which made them even more entertaining and popular, and onstage the group members would banter amongst themselves that later many other Southern Gospel groups would mimic. The congregation loved the quartet's delivery and charisma.

The Cathedrals sang memorable hymns such as "Rock of Ages," "In the Sweet Bye and Bye," "What a Friend We Have in Jesus," "Sweet Hour of Prayer," and "The Old Rugged Cross." But the group also was uniquely entertaining in the variety of its repertoire. They performed songs outside the Gospel mainstream as well, such as "He's Got the Whole World in His Hands," "Yesterday," "When the Saints Go Marching In," and the unique "The Laughing Song," which congregations around the country enjoyed. As George Younce delivered it, the crowd would laugh more and more along with him. By the end of the song, he had everyone laughing (at him!). Recordings of "The Laughing Song" can still be viewed on YouTube. This laughter, of course, is not to be confused with the modern phenomenon known as "holy laughter."

The Cathedrals were also known for their strongly patriotic numbers, such as "The Battle Hymn of the Republic" and "America the Beautiful." The group retired in 1999 due to George Younce's declining health after he had suffered a heart attack in 1987. Glen Payne contracted cancer and passed away while on the Cathedrals' farewell tour. "Being in existence from 1964 to 1999, many consider the Cathedrals the best Southern Gospel group ever to tour the nation and the world."[37]

The members of the Cathedrals were good friends of Landmark and of

---

37   "The Cathedral Quartet." *Southern Gospel Blog.com: http://www.southernGospelblog. com/reference/cathedral-quartet* (February 22, 2013).

Dr. John. They seemed to especially enjoy visiting Landmark, and on more than one occasion, they presented Dr. John with a brand-new pair of cowboy boots.

35

A Day of Darkness

In the mid-1970s, Dr. John described one of the darkest days he had ever experienced, a day he visited a specialist in Cincinnati. The doctor examined his throat and vocal cords, and what the told Dr. John shocked him. He then became so depressed that after leaving the doctor's office he drove and drove for so long that he lost track of time.

Dr. John's son Harold had recently gone through indescribable trauma with the loss of his own voice. Harold went through an entire year without being able to speak. Dr. John wondered how difficult that must have been for such a brilliant young preacher as his son and imagined that Harold must have spent some lonely nights wondering if he would ever preach again. Yet Dr. John could not recall ever hearing Harold complain.

Is it possible that I may come to an hour when I'll never be able to preach again? Dr. John wondered. "Lord," he prayed, "is this what I have come to? I have tried to serve You. Now, Lord, I am going to make a vow that I will use it [my voice] until it is worn out. Then I will finish my days, whatever they are."

Never one to give up, Dr. John continued on in the Lord's strength. "I want to preach as a dying man to dying men and women and young people!" he said in a sermon to the congregation of Landmark in 1978. "I would like to take every one of you and counsel you that your life is important! It is the most valuable possession other than your soul. Use it for the glory of God. Don't let the Devil cheat you. Don't let him rob you … Don't let him strip you of everything you have. Please don't let the Devil do you that way. Make a vow to God, before God and His holy angels, 'My life is mine! God has given it to me. I will use it for His glory.'"

And the Lord continued to sustain Dr. John's voice for many years after.

36

The Mongrel Dog

I was wounded, and He healed me. I was lost, and He saved me. I was lonely, and He comforted me. I was broken, and He sheltered me.

—DR. JOHN W. RAWLINGS

Many members and visitors of Landmark traveled long distances to attend. Therefore, as a visionary, Dr. John sought to reach the entire region around Landmark. During the 1970s, he planted satellite churches in the area, and eventually, there came to be seven of these churches in total, five in Southern Ohio: Montford Heights, Delhi Township, Clermont County, Hamilton, and Lockland (a location that welcomed eight hundred people on Sunday mornings in 1976), and two in Kentucky: one in Covington and one in Newport. Some of these churches exist to this day.

On February 12, 1978, Dr. John delivered a powerful sermon, "The Mongrel Dog," at Landmark in which he shared an interesting story concerning the founding of the satellite church in Newport. This sermon had a great impact on many listeners to the *Landmark Baptist Hour*. One such listener was Aziel Pinder of Spanish Wells, Bahamas, a well-known fishing guide with a radiant Christian testimony. Pinder later testified to Dr. Harold Rawlings that this sermon was one of the most powerful stories he had ever heard. He was impressed by Dr. John's vivid illustration in the sermon of Christ's coming into the world to save sinners, who Pinder described as "those mongrel sinners."

Dr. John dedicated the sermon "The Good Samaritan" to Mayor Johnny Pelusso of Newport, Kentucky. Johnny J. Pelusso Jr. was the son of Italian immigrants and one of nineteen children. He later started his own television repair shop and thus received the nickname Johnny "TV" Pelusso. He served the citizens of Newport as mayor for two terms beginning in 1964 and 1976. He also served four terms as a Newport city commissioner (*Images of America Italians of Newport and Northern Kentucky*). Like Dr. John, Johnny Pelusso was a colorful and controversial figure. It is believed that he came to know the Lord Jesus Christ in a personal way under Dr. John's influence.

One day in the winter of 1978, Dr. John was visiting Mayor Pelusso for a piece of property for the Newport church. With Dr. John were two men on staff at Landmark, Bob Johnson and Willie Holt. Bob Johnson was an associate in the Sunday school division and headed up the bus ministry at the time when there were over one hundred buses.

Willie Holt had been a used car dealer in Lockland and had the stereotypical reputation of those who work in the industry. His daughter Landa Gayle, through persistence and prayer, finally convinced him to drive a bus for Landmark, where she was a bus captain. Although unsaved at the time, Willie finally consented. After serving there a short time, he was saved and baptized under Dr. John's leadership.

Willie served on staff at Landmark as Memorial Gardens director, where he managed the cemetery operations and was in charge of burials. He also bought and sold the buses in support of the bus ministry. About a year after Willie had accepted the Lord, Dr. John called him to the platform during a church service to have him give a report on the status of the cemetery. Not one trained in "preacher-speak," Willie blurted out, "Well, Dr. John, praise God! We've already got a hundred in the ground." Many in the audience snickered to themselves, possibly in consideration of others' lost loved ones.

Willie Holt often accompanied Dr. John on such visits as the one to Newport, as Willie was a valuable contributor to the ministry with his experience as a salesman and dealer.

The following is related directly from the transcript of Dr. John's sermon, "The Good Samaritan," dedicated to Mayor Pelusso where he tells the story of "the mongrel dog":

The snow was deep. It was so cold. We were on a high hill. After looking at this property, we started winding our way down that cold, icy street. Driving was hazardous. Suddenly, all of us looked out the left side of the car. There was a mongrel dog staggering down [the] sidewalk. Immediately, you could see the dog had something wrong with it. It was not a large dog, a black-and-white fellow. You could see the blood streaming. He had crossed the street.

Mayor Peluso said, "Wait, wait! Wait just a minute! Wait a minute!" Before we could get the car stopped, he had opened the door and jumped out of the car. I thought it was so strange. He is a mayor of one of our fine cities, and he was as pale as if a child had been run over.

The dog snarled at him. Then he wobbled across the street and wouldn't let the mayor catch him. I opened the door and said, "Mayor, he will bite you! You had better leave him alone!"

"No, no! He has got to have help!" He started walking on.

Bob Johnson was driving the station wagon. He drove on down the street. The dog would go faster, he would fall over and get up. The mayor was trying to catch the dog. The street was icy. We must have driven half a block. The rich, red blood was streaming from that dog's neck. We found out he had been shot. So we parked. The dog finally laid over. He couldn't go any farther.

The mayor looked at us and said, "Bring me a blanket! Have you got anything in the car?"

All we had were some old, dirty rags the mechanics had left in the station wagon. I noticed the mayor taking those rags, and gently as a mother with a little child, he put them around that dog's neck and took the dog in his arms.

There was a fire station just across the street. The mayor rushed across the street. He kicked the door with his foot while holding the dog in his arms. A big, strong fellow opened the door. Of course, the fireman recognized the mayor.

The mayor went right on in. He didn't pay any attention to us. We waited because he was riding in our car. Several minutes went by. I looked out and saw the mayor coming. He had a clean, white bed sheet wrapped around that dog. He came back.

Brother Willie Holt opened the door. The mayor got in. I noticed a look in his face that I couldn't understand. Why would a mayor of such a large city have such a concern? I saw his hands trembling.

I will be honest and frank with you. I would have gone by and left the dog. The fellows who were with me would have. I was in the front seat. The mayor was in the backseat with Mr. Holt. He was giving instructions. I was trying to talk to him about something else. I could tell he was not listening. He was urging Mr. Johnson to hurry. "Go on down to the foot of the hill. On the main street, turn right. We must get this dog to the veterinarian."

So just as quickly as we could, we rushed to that building where the veterinarian was located. You know, while going down that hill, I looked back. I saw Mayor Peluso kissing that dog. He would put his cheek against that dog—that dog that snarled and snapped at him before. His eyes were glazed. He was still bleeding. That white sheet was covered in blood. I saw that dog lean his head over against the mayor's cheek—just a mongrel off the street.

He rushed on in and took that dog to the veterinarian. After awhile, Mayor Pelusso came out. He got in the car. There was a look of relief on his face. He said, "I think we have made it. They are giving him IVs. They are going to give him blood. They are going to take care of him."

He said the veterinarian had asked whose dog it was. The mayor said, "It doesn't make any difference. The dog is wounded. Somebody shot him."

He had been shot through the neck. I looked at the mayor. I saw a look of relief on his face. Then I remembered something. A mutual friend had told me just two days before that Mayor Johnny Pelusso as a young lad was in World War II. He had been in action for months and finally was captured by the Germans. He made that awful march across northern France. He was a prisoner of war.

In fact, the mayor told me after this incident, "You know, Reverend, when you face the firing squad three times, it does something to you."

Then I knew what prompted him to put his arms around a dumb beast that had been shot. He, too, had been through it. He, too, had faced seemingly inevitable death. I could then understand his emotional reaction as he picked up that little, old, dirty mongrel dog and put loving arms around it.

Do you know what he said when he came back to the car? The vet had said, "You know, it may cost one hundred dollars to take care of all this."

He [Mayor Pelusso] said, "It doesn't make any difference if it does cost one hundred dollars. You do whatever is necessary. I will take care of it."

You know what? Two thousand years ago, the loving, compassionate, gracious Lord, the Lamb of God, came. You know what He did? He left the throne room. He left it all up yonder. Can you imagine what must have been the conversation of the Triune God, as holy angels looked on, when He took the first step of separation from the Father, came all the way from infinitude, cradled Himself in the womb of a little, Jewish girl, was born in a stable among the animals, and for thirty years worked as a carpenter? Can you imagine what must have gone through the mind and the soul of Jesus Christ of Nazareth?

One day, He looked out on the world. He did not just see a few thousand people there, but with His eye of omnipotence, He saw you and me! He saw me as a little old country boy. And He said, "John, I love you." And He came.

That's how I understood what the mayor was doing. It was the greatest story of the cross that I have ever seen! My friend, when a mayor of a great city will take time to take a mongrel dog in his arms, kiss him, pay the bill, never grumble about it but be glad to do it, bless God, the Christian people of America ought to wake up and realize that Jesus Christ paid the awful debt of the cross, of sin, of hell, and of judgment!

I was wounded, and He healed me. I was lost, and He saved me. I was lonely, and He comforted me. I was broken, and He sheltered me! I was thirsty, and He gave me drink. I was blind, and He gave me sight! I was deaf, and He gave me hearing!

Oh, God, help us tonight! If a mayor would do that for a dog, how in the world can men miss the cross and what it means?

For God so loved the world...!

37

The Fool

For the invisible things of Him [God] from the creation of the world are clearly seen, being understood by the things that are made, even His eternal power and Godhead; so that they [men] are without excuse: Because that, when they knew God, they glorified Him not as God, neither were thankful; but became vain in their imaginations, and their foolish heart was darkened. Professing themselves to be wise, they became fools

—ROMANS 1:20–22

Dr. John faced many battles in his day with atheists. One such debate took place at Indiana University before a crowd of professors. "Men come to reason by facing truth and reality," Dr. John believed, further stating:

> One of my approaches to those atheistic professors was to take them back to the time when they were born. When they first came out of the womb, they didn't know anything. I told them, 'Somebody has messed with your head and impregnated your

mind. You didn't know anything before they bathed you. Do you feel mentally crippled by what someone else told you?'

Listeners did not know how to respond, for he had given them food for thought.

"The Bible tells me where I came from, who I am obligated to, and where I am going," Dr. John said, recounting the story. "Those atheists and agnostics don't even know who they are. I had a chance to be an atheist. Why didn't I choose that? When a man realizes he has an appointment with God, that's one step toward getting things right with God."

Dr. John's statements are a reflection of Proverbs 1:7, which says, "The fear of the LORD is the beginning of knowledge, but fools despise wisdom and discipline." Dr. Jason Lisle of Answers in Genesis, in his book *The Ultimate Proof of Creation,* states, "Knowledge begins with a respectful submission to the biblical God and that rejection of wisdom and biblical instruction leads inevitably to irrationality—to 'foolishness.'"[38] He goes on to say that either we begin with God and His presuppositions as revealed in His Word or we reject them and are reduced to foolishness.

In 1953, Dr. John was invited to host a crusade in Jacksonville, Florida, by pastor George Hodges. During his stay, Dr. John was driving to a radio station to advertise the crusade when he heard an atheist speaking on the radio whose fifteen-minute show was followed by George Hodge's program (when Dr. John would be broadcasting) prior to a Pentecostal broadcast. The atheist continued his program after the Pentecostal show.

Dr. John said to George, his traveling companion, "Have you ever debated him [the atheist]?"

He answered, "Yes. I had a debate with him, but you can't do anything with him. He's one of the leaders in the country, very intelligent."

They soon arrived at the radio station and went into Studio A for their radio show, which was next to Studio B from which the atheist broadcasted.

Dr. John said to a group of singers who were to perform during George's airtime before Dr. John went on air, "I want you to sing one verse of 'How Firm a Foundation,' and you sing to the Lord. Then you let me have it."

The DJ signed the program on. The atheist remained in his studio because

---

38   Dr. Jason Lisle, *Ultimate Proof of Creation.* (Green Forest, Arizona: Master Books, 2009), 40, 146.

he would be back on soon and was preparing for his next show following the Pentecostal program.

After the group sang, Dr. John went on air without introduction and said, "Ladies and gentlemen, my name is John Rawlings. I'd like to give you the name of the man you just listened to in Studio B. The Bible has his name. You find it in Psalm 14:1: 'The fool said in his heart, there is no God.' And I am looking at that fool as I speak to you. Many people profess to be a fool. 'The fool has said in his *heart*, there is no God.' But this fool in Studio B has blabbed it to the public."

Dr. John then began preaching, periodically mentioning the fool in Studio B. There were six telephone lines in the radio station, and every one lit up with listeners calling in and asking for Dr. John to continue preaching. But soon his time was over. The announcer turned on the yellow light; Dr. John had only thirty seconds remaining. He invited listeners to church that evening to hear a continued sermon about the fool in Studio B.

Finally the announcer came on and said, "Ladies and gentlemen, I am sorry. Every line is filled with callers asking to leave Dr. Rawlings on. But I regret to say I have to cut him off." Dr. John had used two minutes of the Pentecostals' time already.

Immediately, Dr. John went into Studio B. The atheist stood as he walked in. Dr. John put his arm around the man's shoulders. His intentions were not to be confrontational; he cared about the man's soul. "Starting out from your mother's womb," Dr. John said, "you didn't know anything. And you've listened to idiots all over the nation. You've read their books; you haven't had one single original thought. You're only telling the people over the radio what somebody else has said. Don't you think for a man of your intelligence it's time to start thinking for yourself? I was born just like you. I didn't know anything. You have become a fool because you're only parroting what somebody else has said."

For fifteen minutes, Dr. John continued speaking with him. And then the yellow light came on; it was time for the fool to be back on the air. Dr. John exited the studio.

The man hesitated, unable to speak even though by now he was back on the air. Finally, he apologized to his radio audience. "I've never had an experience like this," he said. "I owe the audience an apology because I was not prepared for what that minister had to say to me." He then talked about his discussion with Dr. John, who had planted in his mind that we begin our lives without knowing anything.

That night, the church building for Dr. John's crusade was filled, and many people were saved as a result of that single broadcast. Dr. John stood upon the principle that, "Everyone's thoughts are predicated upon someone else's thoughts. We have the sovereign choice to choose which thoughts to take as our own. But as for me," he stated, "my thoughts are based upon this Book."

In calling the atheist a fool, Dr. John was not name-calling but was quoting Scripture. As Jason Lisle writes in *The Ultimate Proof of Creation,* "A fool (in the biblical sense of the word) is someone whose thinking is futile because he has rejected God's revelation (Rom. 1:21; 1 Cor. 3:19; Prov. 1:7). The fool may have very high intelligence, but he refuses to use his intellect in the way that God has designed—in a way that is faithful to God's revelation. As a result, his thinking is reduced to absurdity."[39] Dr. John believed that "Christianity is at odds with secular philosophy," and that "evolution [is] the root cause of why young people reject Christianity."[40]

Dr. John further states that this was the reason Landmark Christian School was founded, starting with kindergarten through high school. Dr. John was once again ahead of his time, predicting the major threat of evolution before thorough studies had been done to show the damaging effect it has on biblical authority. Recent statistics published in the book *Already Gone* confirm Dr. John's forewarning about the destructive teaching of evolution in most schools, even Christian institutions.

For the statistical analysis in the book *Already Gone,* written by Answers in Genesis president Ken Ham and Britt Beemer of America's Research Group, a group of "twenty-somethings" who had left the church were surveyed. The purpose of the study was to discover who was leaving the church, why they were leaving, and what could be done about it. Every person in the sample stated "attended church every week, or nearly every week, when they were growing

---

39   Dr. Jason Lisle, *Ultimate Proof of Creation.* (Green Forest, Arizona: Master Books, 2009), 70.

40   James L. Adams, "Landmark Baptist Temple: Plan it big, keep it simple," *The Cincinnati Post,* (August 21, 1976): 1, 31.

up, but they never or seldom go today."[41] Ken Ham discusses the vicious attack on biblical authority, stating that when a person believes in millions of years and/or evolution, and then reinterprets the biblical account of creation to be over a long period of time, they are undermining the authority from which they get the message of the Gospel. They are undermining the authority of the Word of God by taking man's fallible ideas on the age of the earth and using those ideas to change the clear meaning of the Word of God. It is an authority issue. Ken Ham warns that if we teach such a compromised position to our children, we should be prepared for the great possibility they will open the door of compromise wider and get on "that all too familiar slippery slide of unbelief."[42] Ken Ham further states that a major shift has already taken place in our culture: "The church and the Bible are no longer the places we go to learn historical science. The church gave up that responsibility and relegated it to the world."[43] The book concludes that 70 percent of young people are leaving the church, 90 percent of which do so even before entering college. What Dr. John predicted over thirty years ago in the article above and in his earlier sermons was later confirmed through statistical data. Young people were leaving the church as he foresaw and sadly continue to do so.

Even so, many years ago, Dr. John saw the importance of apologetics and upholding the authority of Scripture, and he never wavered. His presuppositional approach in his biblical worldview was ahead of its time, as today Christian apologetics is a growing and critical ministry in combating secularism in our culture. Again, Dr. John's vision has proven true. He truly has always been a man ahead of his time.

---

41   Ken Ham, Britt Beemer, and Todd Hillard, *Already Gone*. (Green Forest, Arizona: New Leaf Publishing Group/Master Books, 2009), 27.

42   Ken Ham, Britt Beemer, and Todd Hillard, *Already Gone*. (Green Forest, Arizona: New Leaf Publishing Group/Master Books, 2009), 81.

43   Ken Ham, Britt Beemer, and Todd Hillard, *Already Gone*. (Green Forest, Arizona: New Leaf Publishing Group/Master Books, 2009), 85.

38

"In the Beginning, God ..."

Dr. John Rawlings was very strong and unwavering in his convictions. Instead of blindly accepting men's ideas, he saturated himself in the Word of God, which was his foundation. He believed that Scripture is infallible and did whatever he could to take the Gospel message to as many people as possible.

Dr. John's beliefs regarding issues like the biblical account of creation were simple and straightforward. He recognized truth and stood by it unapologetically, and His unwavering belief in the Holy Scriptures shaped his strong leadership qualities, the type that is sorely lacking in today's church. Dr. John recognized the power of the hand that formed the universe and felt it on a personal level and understood God as the God of law and order. "[God] brought light out of darkness," Dr. John preached. "He brought order out of chaos; He caused things to grow, birds to sing. He gave voices to the birds and all the animals." Dr. John communicated such soul-inspiring biblical truths as this in clear and concise ways that everyone could understand.

"We need to understand that God is the Alpha and the Omega!" Dr. John declared in a sermon on February 26, 1978. "That means that He is the first letter in the Greek alphabet; He is the Alpha. He is the last letter in the Greek alphabet; He is the Omega. God had the first word—He [spoke] and worlds were framed—and God is going to have the last word. You and I need to listen to Him when He talks."

Dr. John preached on April 9, 1978, that if you study the Bible, faith comes. He said, "I don't believe Christians are a bunch of zombies and half-wits. I think it is a high mark of intelligence to turn from evolution to the Genesis account of creation. I think it is the only thing that will make sense for any man that is intelligent. How in the world can people believe that matter and force came together? Where in the name of God did matter and force come from? Where did the amoeba come from? It is strange how so-called intelligent people get hung up on that thing. Man, I couldn't swallow that under any circumstances. I am a human being! ... It doesn't make any sense to me! The only thing that makes sense to me is to walk out at night and to see the stars and to know how helpless I am and to know that there has to be a God in back of this creation ... or it could not be. He [upholds] 'all things by the word of His power' (Hebrews 1:3).

"God created this universe and placed it in orbit. It hasn't clashed with anything yet, and I don't expect it to. I am riding this thing, and He said He [is] going to take care of me!

"Every textbook on biology ... that is used in the public school system is on the basis of evolution, that everything has come from the lower species to the level where it is today. That is diametrically opposed to the teaching of the Word of God! The Word of God says that He created life, and that life came from God. We didn't just happen to be, and we are what we are because we happened to be. It isn't evolution; it is *degeneration*.

"How can you people turn to the teachings of evolution, whether it be theistic evolution or the Darwinian theory of evolution? When God [spoke], it was done. God created man in His own image and after His own likeness. [God] breathed into that lump of Mesopotamian clay the breath of divine life, and man became a living soul! That little body growing in the womb of the mother is not man, but the soul within that body. That's you! That body's not you; that's dirt. You live within a body of clay ... Man returns to dust, as Job said, but the soul lives on and on and on in the ceaseless ages of eternity."

Dr. John firmly believed in the sanctity of life, and that life is precious. "God is the giver of life. Any time you take a human life, you murder!" he spoke in another sermon on March 12, 1978. "I don't care who you are. But we are living in that day and age." Of the women in his life, he said, "My dear old grandmother, my granny, had twelve [children], and my mother was one of the twelve. I am so glad she had her [child] and didn't kill my mother while she was in her womb so that she could be grown, married, have a son, and that son could preach the Gospel ... I want to tell you something, men and women.

We need to have a concept of what life is all about—bearing crosses and a right relationship with our blessed Lord Jesus Christ!

"It is thrilling that with all of our advancements in medicine and scientific discoveries, we have been able to save the lives of thousands of infants who might otherwise have died, but then we turn right around and legislate to kill babies in the womb of mothers! It is a crazy generation, isn't it? Just as sure as there is a God in heaven, that baby in the womb of the mother is a human being. Whether it is a baby or a sixty-year-old man you kill, it is still murder. I don't care what anybody says! I can prove it with this Book."

Dr. John never doubted the Bible; he had believed that Scripture is the inspired and infallible Word of God from boyhood. He stated, "Because of my contact with the Bible when I was a little fellow, reading God's Word and then memorizing God's Word, I never ... doubted this Book. I have never had to change a single belief or doctrine. They are all just like they were when I started out forty years ago ... One day, I will have to say good-bye to Earth and this pilgrim journey. But I don't intend, by the help and grace of God, to doubt this Book that I have loved and preached.

"I know I will have to stand before God and give an account—I, John Rawlings—as to whether or not I have been faithful in dispensing God's Word!" He then challenged his congregation, "What are you going to do when you face judgment? There is judgment for every man to face."

39

Serving the Lord

Are you willing to cry out, "Oh, God, take me! Use me! Make me, mold me, shape me, and I will do anything, Lord, you want me to do ... until You say it's enough"?

—CHALLENGE FROM DR. JOHN

On January 29, 1978, Dr. John spoke of a trip to a revival meeting in 1942, a time when the intensity of World War II was mounting. He was driving down the Red River Valley toward a little town called Hornbeck, Louisiana. He described cotton-picking time: "If you have never had the experience of being in the fields of cotton when they harvested it by handpicking it, you have really missed something. My father owned a cotton gin. I grew up picking cotton. I knew the whole background of the scene. It was a beautiful Monday evening. The sun was sinking in the west. The sky was always red in that country when the sun was lowering. There were some streaks of clouds. It was real quiet, no wind blowing. You couldn't drive more than thirty miles per hour. That was the law in those days ...

"I was chugging along down that road. There [were] cotton fields on both sides. They [the workers] were going into the weighing station. They had wagons at different intervals. I looked down at the end of the rows of cotton.

There were perhaps twenty, twenty-two people—all black people. They had picked out to the end of the row ...

"Where the cotton had been picked, the burrs looked brownish, you know. Then where the cotton was not picked, the leaves had mostly fallen off, and there were just white banks out there in the field. It was a beautiful scene. Johnson grass, goat head burrs, prickly pears, and everything were out at the end of the row. It was sandy in that river land.

"Leading the twenty-two people in that row was a tall black man. He must have been about six five. He was a handsome fellow. Those black muscles were showing. He had his shirt cut off. Those long, black arms had muscles like ribbons of steel. He didn't have on a hat. He had his hair cut short. The sweat on [his] bronze face was streaking down. He had a sack eleven and a half feet long full of picked cotton on his shoulder. He had his hand on his hip and the strap of that sack around his neck. He was carrying about eighty pounds of cotton in that sack, going to the weighing station. It was a beautiful sight ...

"I had slowed down. I don't suppose I was going more than twenty miles an hour looking at that scene. There were young men and older people. I saw a gray-haired fellow ... he was stooped. His sack couldn't have been more than seven and a half feet long. The length of the sacks was five and a half, seven and a half, nine and a half, and eleven and a half feet. I saw women, young teenagers, and ... down at the end of the row of people was a little black boy with one gallus. His little overalls had been cut off short, [and] he didn't have on any shirt. His little brown body was just sparkling. He, too, was sweating.

"He had a little sack made out of a fifty-pound flour bag ... He had been out in that field all day with the rest of those people ... That little fellow had about three, four, or five pounds in his sack ... [and was] barefooted, walking on those old prickly pears, thirsty. He was coming way behind with that little, old sack bobbing on his back, carrying it to the weighing station.

"God spoke to my heart that day. He said, 'Son, see that line of people?' I said, 'Yes, Lord, I see them.' He said, 'You see that man up front? That's Billy Sunday, D. L. Moody, and Sam Jones.' You know the Bible [says], 'Lift up your eyes, and look on the fields; for they are ... white all ready to harvest.' I looked at the hundreds of acres in the Red River Valley, white with cotton. I could see yonder in the distance other weighing stations and strips that had been picked by other groups of people. I began to weep. I saw the aged man. I saw teenagers, laughing and throwing cotton bolls at each other. They had their sacks on their back[s] too. But I saw that little fellow coming up the way ...

"I said, 'Yes, Lord, I get the message. I have never had many talents. I've never had much, but that little boy has been out there, and he's been faithful all day ... the same sun that has been shining on D. L. Moody and Billy Sunday has been shining on me ... If I can just pick four or five pounds and be faithful, you will reward me ...'

"God that day spoke to a country boy. Through the long years, sometimes when the cross has been heavy and the night's lonely, I have gone back and said, 'Lord, do you remember that little boy? That's me. I am trying to get my cotton to the weighing station. Let me preach another sermon! Let me drive another bus! Let me win another soul!' That little boy hadn't been standing idle. He had been busy. He had been picking cotton. He didn't know how to do much, but he did what he could ...

"One day, the eastern sky will be split with His [God's] presence. It will be a blaze brighter than the noonday sun, and we will see Jesus—King of Kings and Lord of Lords. If we have been out yonder working in the vineyard, He is going to say, 'Well done, little boy' [or] 'Well done, aged man. Well done.' ... He is ready. Are you ready? Are you willing to cry out, 'Oh, God, take me! Use me! Make me, mold me, shape me, and I will do anything, Lord, you want me to do ... until You say it's enough'?"

40

Lynchburg, Virginia

In 1994, Dr. John announced his retirement from the pastorate at Landmark Baptist Temple. His son Harold, previously co-pastor, became senior pastor in his father's stead. Dr. John moved to Lynchburg, Virginia, where he lived in a hotel for about six weeks while Mrs. Rawlings finished packing their home in Kentucky before they both moved into their new house in Lynchburg. Dr. John then became Chairman of Ministry Training at the Bible Institute of Liberty University, where he worked with Dr. Jerry Falwell, the school's chancellor and his trusted friend, to implement strategic changes for Liberty's growth and spiritual development.

At Dr. John's arrival, Dr. Falwell called Dr. Danny Lovett, the dean of Liberty Baptist Theological Seminary, and said, "I'd like you meet me at the hotel downtown. I want to introduce you to a man named Dr. John Rawlings, my mentor." Dr. Falwell thought the two would hit it off and be able to help one another. At the time, Dr. Lovett had only been at Liberty for about a year but stayed for fourteen years afterward, including the two and a half years that Dr. John spent there. As Dr. Falwell hoped, the two did become good friends, and all three spent the next two years eating with, listening to, and spending time with one another. Danny Lovett recalls these memories fondly as "the best education I ever had. I heard these two spiritual giants discussing what needed to take place for Liberty University to go to the next level."

After their first meeting that morning, Dr. Lovett was appointed the task of taking care of Dr. John. Whatever Dr. John wanted, he got. Dr. Lovett didn't make many friends during this time because he and his new friend wandered the halls of Liberty picking offices, furniture, and making Dr. John comfortable.

Dr. Falwell began to receive calls from everybody, asking, "Who is this young guy and this man, acting like they own the place?"

"They do own the place," said Dr. Falwell. He told Dr. Lovett to show Dr. John around. "Take him down to the president's office and show him the offices." Dr. John could then have his pick of office space.

The president's assistant gave Dr. John a tour of the available spaces, none of which he particularly liked. "Take me to the president's office," he requested. After they had a look around, his next question was, "What's in this next room?"

"The conference office," said the president's assistant. This was a large room that contained a conference table, TV, plenty of shelves, and storage space.

"Who's in here?" Dr. John wanted to know.

"No one."

"Well, I'll take this one then!" Eventually, Dr. John took an office in the seminary, but in the meantime, Dr. Lovett, Dr. Falwell, and Dr. John had many meetings in the spacious conference room almost daily.

Dr. John taught his friends that evangelism and missions should be at the forefront of the campus, and together they assembled a strategy to resurrect pastoral studies and missions. Dr. John played a key role in Liberty's growth by identifying key changes that needed to take place at the school—everything from changing the president to moving Thomas Road Baptist Church up to Liberty Mountain.

Also during his time in Virginia, Dr. John also helped to establish *The National Liberty Journal* and served on the Seminary Committee of the Board of Trustees Committee for Liberty. He occasionally spoke in the ministry chapel to the ministerial students, "the preacher boys," and would open up the end for a question-and-answer session. He often used examples from his childhood on the farm and illustrations using animals. The preacher boys absolutely loved it. Every so often, Dr. John spoke in regular chapel session as well, and the kids would laugh at his stories and soak up his wisdom.

Dr. Falwell once had a discussion with Dr. John about which issue was most important and relevant to today's culture in proclaiming the Gospel. Dr. John told him proclaiming the Gospel from the very first verse of Genesis. Dr. Falwell soon began developing a long-term relationship with Answers in

Genesis (AIG), the largest apologetics ministry in the United States at the time. In 2009, the importance of the creation message and a literal interpretation of the Genesis account were still taught at Liberty University. On September 25, 2009, Answers in Genesis President Ken Ham spoke to eleven thousand students and staff at the Vine Center of Liberty University.

As he had as pastor of Landmark, Dr. John met many interesting people while serving tenure at Liberty University. Supreme Court Justice Clarence Thomas visited the campus at the time Dr. John was on the Board of Trustees. After he spoke, Dr. John gripped Justice Thomas's hand and said, "Was there a specific moment in your life that you asked Jesus Christ to be your Lord and Savior?"

Justice Thomas answered, "Reverend, there was a time in my life that I made that decision. I was eleven years old when I went forward in a Methodist church during a revival and knelt down at the altar to pray."

After speaking with Justice Thomas for a while, Dr. John went to find Jerry Falwell's wife, Macel, who was accompanying Justice Thomas's wife, Virginia Lamp, better known as Ginni Thomas. Dr. John asked Mrs. Thomas the same question he had just asked her husband. She too responded that as a child she had made a decision for Christ in a Methodist church, "Although much of my life I haven't lived it," she said.

In the 1990s, Dr. John began working to establish the Virginia Baptist Bible Fellowship. He was not as well known in the Virginia area as he was in Ohio, Missouri, and Texas. While hosting a revival once in the Washington, DC, area, Dr. John remembered only two children bothered to speak to him until the second or third night of the revival when a lady approached him, saying, "Dr. Rawlings, would you do me a favor?"

"If I can, I will."

"There's a man in our community I have been praying for forty years," she answered. "He's the wealthiest man in this whole area. He needs to know the Lord, and I don't know anybody who would have the nerve to go talk to him until I heard you preach. Would you go talk to him?"

Dr. John nodded and said, "Sure, I'll go talk to him. Give me his address, and I'll go down and talk to him."

The next day, Dr. John set off for the rich man's house and drove half a mile before reaching the big horse farm. As he passed a building, he saw a man getting out of a pickup truck. When he came to the house—a beautiful, stately home on a hill—he knocked on the door, and a lady answered. Before she invited him inside, the man in the pickup pulled into the driveway behind him. "Who are you, and what do you want?" the man demanded as he stepped out of his truck.

"I'm holding a revival in town. My name is Dr. John Rawlings. I just thought I'd come by and see you. This is some place you got here. I'm driving around thinking, 'A man as smart as this, who can acquire wealth to own all of this, must be a pretty smart man.'" Dr. John paused. "But you're not smart enough to keep from going to hell, are you? You can acquire all this, and yet you don't know where you're going to spend eternity."

The eighty-four-year-old man who stood before him hung his head. "I've been thinking about that," he acknowledged somberly.

Dr. John handed him a laminated tract that outlined the ABCs of salvation and the Roman Road. As he read from the small card, he led the man to Christ.

Shortly thereafter, the rich man was checked into a nursing home, and Dr. John went to visit him every week. Each time, the man greeted his new friend with, "How's my preacher Dr. John?"

Dr. John spent two years at Liberty University working with friends and mentees like Dr. Falwell and Dr. Lovett. After he left, Dr. Lovett had the privilege of staying on at Liberty for another twelve years and watched everything that Dr. John had done to grow the school come to fruition. After fourteen years at Liberty University, Dr. Lovett left to assume the presidency of Tennessee Temple University in Chattanooga, Tennessee.

When Dr. John moved back from Lynchburg, Virginia, to Union, Kentucky, he and Mrs. Rawlings moved into a condominium. At this point in his life, Dr. John no longer had what one might call a career. When his son George came to visit him, he was concerned when he found his father sitting in an easy chair in his bathrobe. "You need a job," George told him.

And from that moment, the idea of the Rawlings Foundation was birthed.

41

Around the World with the Rawlings Foundation

"A twenty-first century modern miracle of youth evangelism that really works."
—RAWLINGS FOUNDATION SLOGAN

At the age of eighty-four, when most men would have already retired, Dr. John made the move to Lynchburg, Virginia, where he assisted Falwell in laying the foundation for Liberty University to fulfill its potential. Then, after moving back to Northern Kentucky in 1996, Dr. John and his youngest son George established a new organization called the Rawlings Trust, headquartered in Florence, Kentucky, of which Dr. John became the director and Herb joined him shortly thereafter as administrator.

The original purpose of the foundation was to financially assist start-up churches in North America, but the focus soon shifted to a global mission endeavor. The chief goal became to financially assist mission projects around the world. At that time, Dr. John believed that the most effective and efficient way of reaching the lost was to plant new churches and nurture and strengthen small or struggling ones. Dr. John believed that America itself had become a mission field. He recognized that many mainline denominations were losing members and church numbers. He felt that creating the Rawlings Trust was urgent, so the primary purpose became to help finance the birthing of independent

Baptist churches across America. This financial assistance included purchasing property, paying rent on church buildings, initiating building funds, funding for building repairs, etc.

The Rawlings Trust later became the Rawlings Foundation when it went international. As of 2012, the Foundation has built over eighty million dollars of camps and properties over the world for twelve different camps. Yearly, 268,000 kids come to camp, about 30–40 percent of whom accept Christ, some moving on to become church leaders, pastors, or church planters.

Beginning in 1997, the Foundation hosted nine consecutive annual leadership conferences for the BBFI national and state leaders in the United States. These meetings helped to launch the publication of the *Baptist Bible Tribune* in a number of foreign countries.

During that same year, Dr. John, Dr. Falwell, and a well-known pastor from Manila, Dr. Benny Abante, conducted a meeting at the Civic Center in Manila, where Dr. John was approached by a BBFI missionary, Dennis Ebert, inquiring about the possibility of getting help from the Foundation to construct a youth camp on property he had purchased about three hours to the north. Dr. John sent his son Herb to Iba Zambales to survey the property, which is just off the coast of the China Sea. In a matter of a few weeks, the Foundation's worldwide camping ministry was launched. The Highlands-Philippine camp, consisting of 120 acres with twenty buildings became the prototype for all the future camps to follow and is now the largest of all, annually hosting over 150,000 high school campers, teachers, and school officials.

Between the ages of eighty-five and ninety-eight, when Dr. John "should" have been retired, he continued doing more work for God than most men do in a lifetime. Dr. John gives a great deal of credit to his youngest son, George, a lawyer, businessman, and owner of the Rawlings Group, and his wife, Beverly, for their generous funding of the Foundation's ministries around the world.

Dr. John always knew how to catch a vision and is working toward revolutionizing missions in his later years. He adapted to the changes in the world around him and worked to leave a legacy, establishing youth camps all over the world, building Bible colleges, training young men as pastors, and planting churches. Yet even when Dr. John passes on to receive his reward in glory, he will leave not only his legacy but also work for the believers who come after him.

"No organization rises higher than its leadership," says Bill Aven who served with Dr. John. Because he understands that the youth provide the next generation of leaders, Dr. John saw the camp ministry as the way to make an impact on a city and eventually on a country. Out of that vision came another idea: to build a facility on the campuses to train pastors and missionaries. This became a reality with the construction of a Bible college on the Highlands-Cambodia campus. Young Cambodian men who graduated from the college are now pastors serving in many churches and three missions in towns and villages surrounding the college.

Bill continues, "In all of the camps we are operating now, we have discovered we must have an American missionary in charge, as the nationals do not have the skill to put everything together. But the American missionary can't be effective without the help of the nationals. You bring those two together, and you see the results!"

He continues, describing Dr. John. "The guy's been building all his life. Here he is [in 20012], ninety-eight years old, and guess what? Still building camps around the world."

Dr. John testifies of an example: "My work in the faraway country of Fiji to help to get a college started so those men could reach their own people was a challenge. One night, a little Fijian church—with the only modern thing, electricity—had a group of young men playing guitars and singing praise songs. When the invitation was given, the son of a Fijian pastor came weeping to the altar and surrendered his life to preach the Gospel.

The next day, I visited the couple in their primitive home; in fact, when I walked through the front door, I walked on Mother Earth and not on a floor of wood or concrete. When I knelt on that floor with those beloved people, it was one of the most fulfilling experiences I have ever had. And then the father put his arms around me and thanked me for coming. As I walked away, I turned around and looked back. That Fijian mother stood with her hands folded and apron wrapped around her hands, her dark skin glistening in the sunlight, [and I thought], *What a day of rejoicing it will be when God gathers all His children from every kindred and people and nation and tongue to rejoice together in the city of God because someone cared, someone was willing to pay a price.*"

In 1999, Dr. John traveled with Joe Burress, pastor of Victory Baptist Church in Rochester, New York, who was raised in Cincinnati, led to the Lord by Dr. John while attending the University of Cincinnati, and attended Landmark with his family during his high school and college years. Under Dr. John's leadership and guidance, Joe dedicated his life to serving the Lord.

Traveling from Auckland, New Zealand, to Nadi, Fiji, with their ultimate destination Suva, Fiji, Dr. John and Joe were on an overnight plane. They had been traveling for a long time when an electrical storm struck at about 1:00 or 2:00 a.m. Joe, who had been trying to sleep, saw that Dr. John was still awake. He had noticed before that Dr. John never slept on flights. Joe asked him, "Why are you still doing what you're doing?"

Dr. John answered with a story. "I was with my father on a three-day journey on our mule-drawn, log wagon. We were on our way back home. I was eight years old and snuggled up by my dad, both of us sleepy, as the mules knew their own way home, and it was late, and it was dark. Startled, I woke up as the mules started braying. I asked my dad about it, and he answered, 'They smell home.'"

Dr. John paused. "Joe, that's why I'm here. I can smell home."

Together they traveled to Auckland, New Zealand, to the church pastored by Zane Edwards. Joe was to demonstrate martial arts of which he was an expert. The evening service began at 7:00 p.m., but Joe couldn't find Dr. John, so he searched outside and walked down the street. He spotted "Pappy" in the midst of what appeared to be twenty towering men under the streetlights, talking to them. They discovered later that these men were descendents of the Maori tribe of New Zealand. As Joe approached the group, he heard Dr. John call out, "See that little guy coming down there? He'll kick the sh--t out of you!" Joe thought, *He's just got us killed.* Dr. John continued, "You need to listen to him. Joey, show these punks."

Joe describes the men as very rugged gang members from outside Auckland. When he turned toward them, his eyes were level with their navels. He took the largest man, whom he perceived as the leader, by his pinky finger and, pinching the pressure point, brought him to the ground. He released his grip on the man for a moment and then reapplied the pressure and pushed the man into the group, who staggered backward. The men were apparently impressed because when Dr. John and Joe invited them to the church service, they all attended.

During the service, Joe began his martial arts demonstration and invited some of the men to the stage. One of them went after Joe, but Joe "took him and shook him and threw him to the floor." When asked how big the man was, Joe guessed he was "sumo-wrestler size" of about six hundred pounds. Little did these men know that Joe was a tenth-degree black belt in combat karate and had trained instructors of the different Special Forces who taught the hand-to-hand system. When asked more specifically who he trains, Joe says, "If you knew who they were, they'd have to kill you."

One of the local tribesmen was living with his girlfriend, and when Dr. John found that out, he lectured them both to start living right and get married. The group must have been impressed because each and every one of them was saved that night. About four years later, Joe returned with Dr. John's son Herb to visit the church in New Zealand and discovered that the young man had married his girlfriend and had become the new worship leader with his wife playing the piano. The man whom Joe had taken to the ground came to him and held up his little finger said, "This still hurts real bad." When Herb and Joe arrived, all of the men greeted them with native music. To Joe, it appeared all of the men were faithful in church attendance and were serving Christ as new creations in Him.

Dr. John told the story of a young missionary who came by his office. "I heard the loudest noise beside the window to my office, and I looked out. There was an old car, smoking, just like a shotgun had gone off. A man came after a few minutes. He was a missionary; a fellow from Texas who had married a Yankee girl and was on his way to New England. He was trying to raise money to get to the mission field. Well, you really can't turn your back very well on a missionary. So I called Mr. Willie Holt, who wasn't a Christian at that time, and asked him if he could see about getting a car for the young man. We wound up helping him get a car. Just the other day, I had a letter from this veteran missionary. He started over twenty churches since he has been on the field and a college with an attendance of 150 to 200. It is a remarkable thing how God has used him. Hundreds of people have been saved under his ministry. I'm so glad that we had a part in that man's ministry. One plants, another waters, and God gives the increase so that we may rejoice together (John 4). Many of us will never be missionaries, but do you know what? We can be involved with missionaries that are out yonder, manning the battle stations in other parts of the world. By so doing, you and I will have a part in their ministries."

The islanders of Fiji fell in love with Dr. John and Joe Burress. In fact, Dr. John was named "Chieftain" as recognition for his work in that country. Back then, there was a crossover in Fijian culture since the British had brought Indians from India to harvest sugar cane, so the islanders were made up of their own nationals and the Indians. Although they looked imposing because of their dark skin and strong bodies, they were a very loving people.

When Joe preached in a Fijian church one night, he met a little girl who was part Fijian and part Indian. Dr. John thought by her reaction that she had never seen a white man before, as Joe had blond hair and looked very different from the natives. The beautiful little eight-year-old girl, one of the most beautiful Dr. John had ever seen, was standing close to Joe. When he looked down, their eyes met, and he smiled. She jumped into his arms, threw her arms around his neck, and kissed him. It was a precious moment and a poignant reminder of why Dr. John and Joe had traveled to the island.

One week while visiting a large church of the islanders, Dr. John orchestrated a fake battle for a service. The pastor of the church told Dr. John that when he and Joe left the following day, some of the islanders wanted to see them off. Dr. John knew that could be troublesome for the people of Fiji, as some would have to leave their jobs. But the pastor was insistent, so the next day, about forty islanders accompanied Dr. John and Joe to the airport.

The airport terminal was filled. To Dr. John, there appeared to be nearly two thousand people packed into the space. In typical fashion, Dr. John thought he might as well do something entertaining. Pulling some young people aside from the group, he said, "I want you to put on that mock battle. Scream and make faces and attack each other, like it's real!"

Anxious to do as he asked, after Dr. John had lined them up, they began screaming. A crowd of eight hundred or nine hundred people gathered around, forming a circle around the skirmish.

A white man standing near Dr. John asked, "What the h--l is going on?"

Dr. John answered mischievously, "These young people are doing a mock battle like they do on the islands where they're from. Where are you from?"

"The United States."

"What state?"

"Missouri," the man answered.

"Well, I'm John Rawlings, one of the founders of the Baptist Bible College there."

The man was taken aback. "The h--l you are!" he exclaimed.

"Yes, sir."

The nonreligious man, as he turned out to be, asked if what the islanders were doing was real. In answer, Dr. John walked over to them and stopped them. "Now!" he shouted. He gave the music director a sign, and they began singing religious choruses. After the islanders had sung their choruses, the newlyweds Dr. John had led to Christ gave their testimony, telling how God had saved them, and that they were going back to win their own people to the Lord. Afterward, someone began singing a solo.

Dr. John and his group of friends had stopped everything in the terminal, and many travelers gathered around. In closing, Dr. John spoke for about ten minutes and offered the plan of salvation. He told it colorfully and with excitement, ending with a prayer for all the people there and asking the Lord to not let any plane go down that day. When he gave an invitation, hundreds of hands went up. Looking back on this incident, Dr. John would reflect, "I expect to meet a bunch of them in heaven one day."

Many events at the Rawlings camps around the world have brought many to Christ. An example of God working through the Rawlings Foundation occurred on May 14, 2011, at the 116-acre Highlands Camp in the Philippines. The goal of the event was to share the Gospel with the people of Iba in the Province of Zambales in West Central Luzon, Philippines. As of three days before the event, there had already been 96,560 attendees at the Impact Youth Camp program and 45,329 decisions for Christ. The star of the event was award-winning singer, songwriter, and recording artist Gary Valenciano, known as Gary V. and the "Michael Jackson of the Philippines." As a firm believer in Jesus Christ, Gary V. is blessed and blesses others through his testimony and talent.

God orchestrated a chain of events so that Gary V. agreed to join the evangelistic effort in Iba for the people of Zambales during the May 11 event. Thirteen thousand tickets were sold for the event, and the seats, field, and mango grove were filled with people who would soon hear the Gospel.

Before Gary V. came on stage, the audience enjoyed magic tricks and comedy routines, but soon lightning began to strike, as the Philippines was facing the onset of the rainy season. The crowd dispersed, seeking shelter, as the thunder clapped and the stage cleared to make way for the event's top performer.

However, the rain continued and prevailed for forty-five minutes to an hour. Amazingly, most of the crowd remained. A mic was handed to Gary V., and he said, "If you will be patient and God will stop the rain, we will have the concert you have come for. Too many have worked and prayed for us to give up now." The audience revived and waited out the last thirty minutes of the storm. Then the lights and sound were cued once more, the band began to play, and Gary V. sang one of his best-loved songs. At the end, he walked to the edge of the stage and sat down on the top step. "It is God [who] controls the time and the rain. What has happened here tonight is that God has taken this event away from all of us and taken control. Tonight isn't about us and not about Gary V. Tonight is about Jesus and His love for Iba, Zambales, and for you. You came to see Gary V., but it is about something else. Tonight you are not my fans—you are my friends, and some are my family. Before we leave tonight, many more can be part of that family."

Members of an evangelistic team weaved throughout the crowd while music played softly in the background. Between songs, Gary V. continued sharing his testimony. Finally, the beloved star gave an invitation and those in the crowd who sought Christ could speak with the counselors among them. Seven hundred twenty-three people came to a saving knowledge of Jesus Christ as their Lord and Savior that night and became members of Gary V.'s family—all children of God. Gary V. named the event that night on May 11 "Iba ito," a play on the Tagalog phrase, which means "something else," for truly it was!

42

Mentoring

My dear friend Dr. John Rawlings is one of the last members of that generation of post-World War II preachers and evangelists who dramatically impacted countless lives, including mine. He continues to be on the cutting edge of the ministry today, leading in church-planting efforts worldwide through the Rawlings Foundation. This generation of church leaders ... were fearless representatives of Christ. They continue to inspire me and younger generations today.[44]

—DR. JERRY FALWELL

Many people were influenced and inspired by the character of Dr. John and his ministry. In later years, he became a mentor to many even before the word *mentor* became commonplace. In *Mentoring—An American Management Innovation*, G. S. Odiorne describes mentoring as a recent innovation in American management.[45] The word *mentoring* implies a process involving the

44   Dr. Jerry Falwell, "More about Dr. John." May 5, 2007. *World Net Daily Listen America:* *http://www.wnd.com/index.php?pageId=41456* (March 18, 2009).

45   G. S. Odiorne, "Mentoring - An American Management Innovation." *Personnel Administrator* 30, (1985), 63-65.

transmission of knowledge and wisdom from an experienced elder, or mentor, to his or her younger pupil. As a lifelong pastor, Dr. John was able to transmit his experiences, knowledge, and expertise in the areas of pastoring, preaching, promoting, and more. Dr. John sought to teach his mentees, or "preacher-boys," that they must learn to be creative. "If you are dull, without any imagination—if you don't have dreams—if you care very little about your demeanor, your dress, the people you associate with, and the people [to whom] you are a role model— those will be the determining factors for whether you succeed or fail."

In his book *Basic Baptist Beliefs*, Dr. Harold Rawlings dedicates the work to his parents, John and Orelia Rawlings, stating, "Both of whom by precept and example taught me from my youth to love and learn the central, foundational truths of the Bible." It was in this respect Dr. John also mentored his "preacher boys," preparing each of them how to learn and share God's foundational truths in imaginative and innovative ways. He encouraged these young ministers to hone their skills and "learn how to dramatize and tell a story." He believed preaching to be an art form not only comprised of truth and relevance but also of colorful stories. At the heart of effective preaching is performance with a purpose. He did warn these young preachers to stick to the facts, though, because the more a story is told the more it tends to change and to avoid embellishment for its obviously deceitful nature. He further counseled them not to be "so heavenly minded" that they failed to "do earthly good."

Of course, while Dr. John had a vast and dedicated following, he also had enemies. He could be combative and confrontational at times, especially with fellow preachers with whom he disagreed with or whom he viewed as too liberal. As he aged, when someone walked into his office, they might have heard him speaking into the phone, "Your leadership skills are lacking. The sermon you preached was a failure and definitely not in tune with the needs of the hour." After a pause, he might have said, "You can resent that all you like, but it's the truth." A brave spiritual warrior, he was never afraid to speak the truth and combat any opposition he faced, especially liberalism within the church, such as the Social Gospel, a movement of the early twentieth century involving social justice in the light of Christian ethics.

"The liberal and the modernist [don't] have the answers to the needs of the souls of men," Dr. John believed. "The Social Gospel will not answer that longing of the human heart! The Social Gospel will never make a drunkard sober. The Social Gospel will never make a gambler honest. The Social Gospel will never make a liar go straight! The Social Gospel will never clean the harlot and make her pure so she can go back to her home and tell the people that she has found the Messiah." He asserted that, "a church needs to preach Jesus Christ and Him crucified! The hope of mankind! Paul said, 'For I determine not to know anything among you, save Jesus Christ, and Him crucified.'"

The stories of those who were influenced and inspired by Dr. John are countless, but one family that was profoundly impacted by him was the Kennedy family. Dr. Leland Kennedy, whose father was very close to Dr. John, recalls a story from childhood when Dr. John taught him the lesson of generosity, which greatly influenced his family and entire life.

"I was only a second or third grader at this time, but because of the closeness of the families [the Kennedys and the Rawlingses], we often had fellowship and dinner together. My daddy was a tremendous chef. Dr. John and all the family liked fried oysters. They said that Dad could do them better than anybody. I remember how hard it was [financially]—and I don't know why at that young age I was so mindful of the cost of things ... I felt personally responsible to do what I could do for the family ...

"But I remember Dr. John came, and we had oysters, and it was a good meal. We laughed and talked, and the [Rawlings] boys and I played and enjoyed each other. The parents were having a great time. I remember the laughter. Preachers can really enjoy themselves when they can relax. What I remember most was after they left. I was helping my mother get the kitchen straightened up. I remember taking Dr. John's plate over to Mother to wash it. There was a hundred dollar bill under the plate ... he knew we really, really needed it. That impacted my life to the degree that he was mentoring me then. He was my teacher, and I wanted to be that kind of a person."

Many pastors admired Dr. John's preaching delivery and would often quote him and tell his stories. There were many who also enjoyed imitating Dr. John's raspy voice, which bore much character over his many years of preaching. Pastor Wayne Cox of Florence Baptist Temple was such a man. He was pastor of Dr. John's home church when Dr. John was in his late nineties. He mastered Dr. John's speaking style and was actually able to fool people over the phone. For example, one morning, Pastor Cox saw Dr. John and Dr. Kennedy together, and a mischievous idea took form in his mind. He spotted Carrol nearby and within minutes dialed his number. In his excellent imitation of Dr. John's voice, he rasped, "Carrol, me and Leland are going to breakfast." He then said, "That Wayne Cox fella is a nice guy. Why don't you invite him to lunch someday?" This wasn't the only the time he attempted to catch Carrol off-guard. On a different occasion, he called Carrol's office and asked, again in a voice like Dr. John's, "Carrol, am I there?"

Another time, Pastor Cox called a preacher and, imitating Dr. John, invited him to breakfast and then called a second preacher to join him. Both met for the meal and were completely unsure what to say. They stared at one another across the table, wondering where Dr. John was, their supposed host.

Dr. L. D. Campbell, a pastor in Northern Kentucky, gives this testimony. As a young pastor, he was very impressed and influenced by Dr. John's evangelistic sermons. Around 1970, Dr. Campbell was pastoring a church in Roanoke, Virginia, during which time he listened to Dr. John on the radio each week. He related that he was enamored with Dr. Rawlings's preaching style. When Dr. John was preaching at Thomas Road Baptist Church, Dr. Campbell would drive the fifty miles to the church to hear him speak. When Dr. Campbell later moved to Kentucky, he was then close to Landmark and often visited the church to hear Dr. John. "Dr. Rawlings treated me like I was somebody," Dr. Campbell says. "He treated me like a real preacher. I was only twenty-eight years old at the time."

Dr. Campbell remembers that once when visiting Landmark, Dr. John recognized him from the pulpit and called out, "There's my young Kentucky friend. Do you have any shoes on, son?" Dr. Campbell says, "When Dr. John preached, he could really shuck the corn!"

Dr. Campbell called the church office at Landmark and asked the secretary if he could have some time out of Dr. John's busy schedule.

The secretary answered, "He can give you thirty minutes."

Dr. Campbell met Dr. John in his office. After they spoke for a few minutes, Dr. John called out to his secretary, "Cancel all my other appointments. I'm taking this boy to lunch."

After lunch, Dr. John insisted on paying, although he told Dr. Campbell, "I don't buy lunches." He didn't want the word to spread that he would buy lunch.

They ended up spending one and a half hours together that day.

Dr. Campbell described Dr. John as very innovative and "really on the cutting edge of doing things to grow his church." He said, "Pastors like Dr. Rawlings don't make the papers. He kept his character and integrity and led by example. He didn't mess up morally like some other preachers. He was forthright and did not back up. He was a negotiator and a transformational leader."

In October 2009, Dr. John unexpectedly visited Dr. Campbell's church. Dr. John's approval meant a great deal to Dr. Campbell, as Dr. John was one of his "pulpit heroes." He told one of his congregation members that he wished the other could have heard Dr. John preach in his prime, an outstanding preacher and innovator in developing programs to grow his church. He called Dr. John "a remarkable man" and said, "Faithful preachers like him don't make the news like those who mess up. Faithful pastors like Dr. John should be honored for all they are worth." Dr. Campbell admitted to being nervous preaching in front of Dr. John that October, but nonetheless, he was honored to have Dr. John at his home church.

In Dr. John's later years, many people would come to visit him at his office for his sage advice, wit, and wisdom. Of course, his advice was blunt and could sometimes sting, but there was always truth in what he was saying. One friend and former church member, Hargis Reynolds, before going over to Dr. John's office, would sometimes say, "I might as well take my beatin' from him [now]."

Dr. John's first question for Hargis was always, "Has your wife left you yet?"

Of all Dr. John's mentees, perhaps the most well known would be Dr. Jerry Falwell, who wrote:

> This wonderful man ... has been one of the preeminent church planters, evangelists, missionaries and pastors of the 20th century. For the past six years, since leaving his 43-year pastorate at Cincinnati's Landmark Baptist Temple, Dr. Rawlings and his executive assistant (and eldest son), Herb, have traveled many times to the Philippines, Japan, India, Fiji, Mexico and Brazil—in addition to overseeing an aggressive church planting effort in the U.S. He has preached almost daily and poured millions of dollars from the Rawlings Foundation into these nations, seeking to win souls and to establish Baptist Bible Fellowship International outposts worldwide.[46]

---

46   Dr. Jerry Falwell, "Pray for Dr. John Rawlings." September 2, 2000. *World Net Daily Commentary: http://www.worldnetdaily.com/news/article.asp?ARTICLE_ID=17783* (March 15, 2009).

43

God's Simple Plan of Salvation

As he grew older, Dr. John never lost his zeal for reaching the lost and was never ashamed to share his deep love for the Lord, whether it is with a stranger or an acquaintance, a lost person or a new believer. A friend of the family recalls when Dr. John answered some of her questions and encouraged her and her husband to begin a small group to teach believers how to evangelize. "Go out and do it," he urged.

On soul winning, Dr. John always believed:

> The joy of being a soul winner is incomparable. I do not know of any joy like it. There is not anything that compares with it, to invest in the lives of people! ... Today is the day of destructiveness, of disregard for people and for things. It is a violent, destructive age in which we live. You and I are in the constructing business. We are building a spiritual house, built out of living stones, 1 Peter 2 says. Isn't that beautiful? We are reaching out and bringing men and women to Jesus Christ. By bringing them to Him, they have life, and they have life more abundantly. But this is not all of the story. He not only rejoices "but he calleth together his friends and his neighbors saying unto them, 'Rejoice with Me, for I have found My sheep which was lost.' He not only rejoices within Himself that He has been successful in finding that lost sheep, but He calls His friends and neighbors in ... They rejoice with

Him [that] the lost sheep is found. To be involved in the saving of souls is the greatest life that anyone can be involved in! There is no other life that compares with it! Everything else fades and goes into oblivion, but "he that doeth the will of God abideth forever." (Sermon preached October 30, 1977)

Later in his life, Dr. John put together a pocket-sized, laminated tract, which he took every opportunity to hand out. In witnessing to nonbelievers, Dr. John believed it to be important to be at ease when associating with people from all walks of life, from the businessman to the politician to the athlete. The tract reads as follows:

What Does the Bible Mean to Me?
Where will I be five minutes after death?

1. *I need to be saved. "For all have sinned and come short of the glory of God" (Romans 3:23).*
2. *I cannot save myself. "For by grace are ye saved through faith: and that not of yourselves: it is the gift of God: Not of works, lest any man should boast" (Ephesians 2:8–9).*
3. *Jesus has provided for my salvation. "For God so loved the world, that he gave his only begotten Son, that whosoever believeth in him should not perish, but have everlasting life" (John 3:16).*
4. *Now is the time to accept Jesus as my Savior. "Behold now is the accepted (right) time: behold now is the day of salvation" (2 Corinthians 6:2).*

The backside reads:

Who must I talk to? "Whosoever shall call upon the name of the Lord shall be saved" (Romans 10:13).

5. *Only God answers my prayer. Pray this prayer: "God be merciful to me a sinner, and save me for Jesus' sake. Come into my heart, Lord Jesus, and give me peace with thee" (Luke 18:13).*
6. *God cannot lie. "In hope of eternal life, which God, that cannot lie, promised before the world began" (Titus 1:2).*

Now that I'm saved ... what should I do?

a.   *Tell someone I've been saved (Romans 10:9).*
b.   *Jesus said to be baptized. "Repent and be baptized, everyone of you ..."*
     (Acts 2:38).
c.   *Begin reading my Bible. Start by reading John, Romans, and*
     Ephesians.
d.   *Begin my prayer life. Thank God for blessings.*
e.   *Bring someone with me to church.*

Now, 5 minutes after death, I KNOW where I will be. Heaven will be my home.

Dr. John recalls when he noticed a piece of paper at the towel rack in an airport washroom. "I looked at that, and it had a little tract. It said, 'God's Simple Plan of Salvation.' Do you know who wrote that tract? The late Dr. Ford Porter ... [he] is now in heaven. I helped officiate his funeral some time ago. He was a dear friend of mine ... He had been a great man of God. That tract has gone out, 250 or three hundred million of them, in forty or fifty languages! 'And by it, he being dead yet speaketh.' Somebody is still handing out the tract ... you never know 'how great matter a little fire kindleth.' You do not know ... the lives that you are going to touch. From what you are doing, multitudes will hear the Gospel and be saved! Find that sheep. Then you will rejoice."

At the age of ninety-three, Dr. John read through the Bible eleven times in just one year. A great student of the Bible, he loved searching the Scriptures, discussing certain verses that meant a great deal to him, and thinking about eternity. By this time, he had pastored Landmark Baptist Temple for almost fifty years, served as founder and vice president and then president of the Baptist Bible Fellowship, and led the Rawlings Foundation in helping churches of America and across the world. "On Tuesday, May 16, 2000, Dr. Jerry Falwell presented a plaque to Dr. Rawlings honoring him as the outstanding Baptist Pastor of the 20th century. The Center for Ministry Training at Liberty University had chosen Dr. Rawlings for the recognition."[47]

In previous years, Dr. John had been caring for his ailing wife. As Dr. John put it, he had "not been in the Word" during her time of illness. On February 3,

---

47   "About Dr. John and Landmark." *International Baptist Network: http://www.ibaptist.net/*
     leaders.html (March 5, 2009).

2007, Mrs. Rawlings passed at the age of ninety-four. If she had lived ten more days, she and her husband would have been married for an astounding seventy-five years. Dr. Leland Kennedy and Dr. Jerry Falwell conducted her funeral on February 6 at Landmark Baptist Temple in Cincinnati, Ohio, where she served as a loyal preacher's wife for forty-three years.

44

The Later Years

1990

In his early nineties, Dr. John could be seen walking his neighborhood boulevard wearing shorts and gym shoes but no shirt, which was quite a surprise for people who had only ever seen him wearing his suit and tie, which he had typically worn from dawn until dusk during most of his life.

Even in his later years, Dr. John still went to his office each day and often went next door to White Castle for coffee with a friend. His first question during these conversations would often be something like, "What have you done for Jesus lately?" He never hesitated to "put someone on the spot," or be blunt with them. At times, this bluntness sounded harsh to outsiders, but this was his way to get them to honestly open up about themselves. Dr. John, his sons, and sometimes their wives and other family members would try to meet once a week for breakfast. The family wasn't known for outward expressions of sensitivity to one another, so if others overheard their conversations at the breakfast table, they might have been surprised. But the Rawlings family remained close and united by the goal of reaching the lost for Christ.

At Dr. John's office, his coworkers enjoyed their interactions with him and liked to hear what he had to say about their circumstances and his own. When coworker Vicki Smith asked Dr. John why he pulled out on the road one day in front of heavy traffic, he quipped, "Honey, when you're as old as I am, you don't have time to be patient." Never one to worry about his car being damaged, it wasn't that Dr. John drove fast but rather that he rarely stayed in one spot for more than a moment when he drove. When traffic was stopped, Dr. John became known for going around it, and his vehicles showed the resultant wear and tear. Once Dr. John told Carrol that some damage to the front end of his Cadillac needed to be repaired. When Carrol asked him how it happened, Dr. John replied, "Oh, some curb came out and hit me."

One day, Dr. John invited his grandson Steve and Steve's wife, Melody, to lunch at Izzy's. Not one to plan ahead, Dr. John asked them about a half hour before the lunch hour. When Dr. John asks someone to lunch, he or she drops everything to please him. Dr. John drove the four of them to the restaurant. When he made a wide turn to pull into a parking space, he blocked an SUV. The woman driver glared at him. Grandson Steve had two thoughts. On the one hand, why didn't the lady didn't just go around, as she had enough room? But on the other hand, he saw that his grandfather took up much of the road.

Dr. John looked at his grandson and said coolly, "That woman wasn't too pleased with me, was she?"

Dr. John's great-granddaughters wrote a song to the melody of "Hello Muddah, Hello Faddah" written by Allan Sherman and Lou Busch.

> Daddy's driving
> Is so wild
> Used to be that
> He was mild
> But now he's older
> And it's so bad
> Now he scares me in the car
> Just like his granddad!

On December 29, 2009, Dr. John began driving his new SUV, a white Lexus RX 350. Two years later, Carrol received a call from a manager at the Blue Pantry, a gas station in Union, Kentucky, who was looking for Dr. John because he had not paid for a tank of gas. Carrol phoned his dad and asked, "Did you get caught stealing gas? I was just calling to see if they caught up with you."

At ninety-eight, Dr. John was still filling his own gas tank. He had gone into the store that morning to buy a newspaper. When he handed the clerk his credit card, he failed to mention his pump number, so she only charged him for the paper. He then drove away with a full gas tank, unaware of his crime.

Time could not dull Dr. John's razor wit. Once when Vicki asked how he was feeling, he answered, "I don't know."

"What do you mean, you don't know?"

"When you're my age," he replied, "everybody's either in a rest home, out of their mind, or dead, so I don't have anybody to compare to."

Often when people visited him in his office, he surprised them with outrageous questions, such as, "Is your wife still living with you?" And if so, "How many children do you have that you know of?" Dr. John had quite the sense of humor.

Though he enjoyed going out to eat with friends and family and joking with coworkers, Dr. John wasn't one to entertain at home and would make it quite known when it was time for someone to leave. He jokingly called company "squatters."

45

A Newfound Companion

In the years following Mrs. Rawlings's death, Dr. John experienced a time of loneliness. "I was just sitting around by myself," he said. "I hit a low place in life, and I was thinking, 'Is this all there is?' God answered me and said, 'You don't stop living until you take your last breath.'"

Dr. John and Orelia had enjoyed nearly seventy-five years of marriage. "I had no intention of remarrying," he admitted, "but I was lonely. For a man who loses his mate, his home becomes just a house."

Dr. John received an interesting phone call one day from Bill Aven's wife, Phyllis, from Henderson, Texas. Dr. John had talked to Bill and Phyllis three or four times in recent days about an issue in their church, but this time, Phyllis was calling for a different reason. "Dr. Rawlings, are you standing or sitting?" she asked. "I know you, and I have a personal request."

Until this point, Dr. John had had been under the impression she was going to talk about the church. He gave her the go-ahead to keep talking.

"There's a lady in our church—"

Dr. John's antennae went up.

"—and I've been talking to this lady's daughter-in-law. God has been dealing with her heart. Preacher, write this telephone number down."

Telling this story, Dr. John laughed, "So I wrote the dumb telephone number down of this lady who is called Mary Pruitt. But I figured I could still get out of that corner. I wrote it down on a card and just aimlessly stuck it in my pocket. We talked about the church then, and that ended it."

After a couple of days, Dr. John returned Phyllis's call and asked her to tell him a little bit more about Mary. Phyllis went into detail and then in turn called Mary and told her about Dr. John. Phyllis had been with Mary often during the past few weeks and knew her well. One night she said to her, "Mary, you said when we first came here that you thought you were going to marry a doctor some day. Well, I have a doctor for you." Mary laughed but wanted to know more. Phyllis and Mary's daughter-in-law had decided that Mary needed someone, and Dr. John needed someone, so it was time for them to play matchmaker.

Five days went by since Phyllis's initial phone call to Dr. John. At home one night, Dr. John had come out of the kitchen into the living room and picked up a book. The television was on while he read. He reached into his pocket and felt a card. Without recalling at first what it was, he pulled it out. It was marked with a telephone number and the name "Mary Pruitt."

I think I'll call her, just for the heck of it, he thought. He dialed the number, and a feminine voice answered. Dr. John introduced himself, and the two exchanged small talk. Mary had been married to a man by the name of Pruitt, whose father had pastored the church Dr. John had organized in Henderson, Texas, in 1942. She had been a widow for fourteen years.

As they neared the end of the conversation—"Here's where women are so dominant over men," Dr. John asserts—Mary said, "Would you mind if I called you back?"

"No, I wouldn't mind," Dr. John answered, and she called the next night. "The conversation built up and up," he says. "I don't know how many weeks went by until one evening out of my heart, I said, 'Mary, I think I could love you.'"

Mary answered, "Dr. Rawlings, I can love you."

Dr. and Mrs. Leland Kennedy drove him to Henderson, where he and Mary met on a Tuesday at about two o'clock in the afternoon. The following Saturday, they were married at West Main Baptist Church with Bill Aven officiating.

In anticipation of his meeting his wife-to-be, Dr. John told others that he had to get his pacemaker tuned up, which he did the week before he was married. After the wedding, upon returning to Kentucky with Mary, he said, "I think the Lord has added another five years to my life."

Of course, Phyllis had told Mary ahead of time, "Don't be offended if he says something that sounds cutting because he's like that with everybody all the time." Mary quickly learned how to take Dr. John's humor and quick wit. Phyllis also had warned her, "He likes to deal in projects. If you won't do the job, fine; someone else will step in and do it." This was new to Mary, and it took her awhile to get used to it. But she was able to bring him out of his despondency over the phone, and they fell in love.

Phyllis believed the match between Dr. John and Mary was providential because she knew he couldn't put up with very many women and not very many women could put up with him. Though he and Mary had their issues to sort out, they were able to overcome them. Of this, Phyllis says, "She has a lot of East Texas mannerisms that she has never had to correct. One of the first things Dr. John said was, 'One of the things she is going to get rid of when we are married is the shoe polish on her eyes,'" referring to her makeup.

"Don't even think about it," Phyllis told him. "When we women stand in front of the mirror and see the transformation, you got to like it as well as we like it."

"Well, you may be right, Phyllis," he gave in.

After going through a period of time during which "it was the first time in my life I was really down," Dr. John knew the match with Mary was a God-thing when he received the fateful phone call from Phyllis that morning.

46

Sealed and Settled

Therefore, my dear brothers and sisters, stand firm. Let nothing move you. Always give yourselves fully to the work of the Lord, because you know that your labor in the Lord is not in vain.

—1 CORINTHIANS 15:58

Discussing his life as a preacher, Dr. John would say he was not sure how he would label himself because his accomplishments were many, all done in the name of Christ. As a pastor, he led two of the largest churches in the United States at the time and was one of the key leaders in the founding of the Baptist Bible Fellowship in 1950. His outreach efforts encompassed the globe, as he brought many to a saving knowledge of Jesus and baptized them into the full fellowship of Christ. As a radio evangelist, he preached the salvation message to countless listeners and an unknown number of souls came to salvation through listening to the programming, as it was broadcast to over three hundred radio stations. Throughout his lifetime, he trained many preachers who came up during his ministry (who he called "preacher boys") and helped start many churches and congregations around the world. For already existing churches, he helped rescue approximately five hundred that were having difficulties and contributed to many building programs. In his later years, he founded the

Rawlings Foundation with his sons, George, Herb, and Harold, a ministry with the focus of worldwide evangelism that included mission work and the building of church camps for youth. He was instrumental in founding both Impact Youth Worldwide and the International Baptist Network.

As a pastor, Dr. John was masculine, strong, and resolute; he didn't use "preacher-speak" but spoke in an unpracticed manner that was familiar to the congregation. He was "the real deal," a genuine person, and was the same behind and before the pulpit. He had certitude and was steadfast in his convictions, proclaiming "the Gospel with boldness, unashamedly and unapologetically,"[48] the type of pastor that men and women need according to David Murrow in *Why Men Hate Going to Church.*

In his book, *Why Men Hate Going to Church*, David Murrow discusses what men want and also what they need. Dr. John was the type of pastor who could discern when someone needed tough love. "Men want to be nurtured," Murrow writes, "but they need a good kick in the pants now and then."[49] Dr. John was happy to oblige, but could deliver "a kick in the pants" with biblical authority. As a man of God, he believed in the power of prayer; however, he also believed that "there are some things that you don't need to pray about. Those are things that you just know need to be done." Dr. John's listeners appreciated his forthrightness and honesty. People appreciate this type of truthfulness, and part of Dr. John's charm was that he never "beat around the bush." He knew how to deliver his point without belaboring the topic or using the kind of diplomatic language that would turn people off. Like his Savior, he learned to teach as one having authority. Using stories and illustrations, Dr. John captured the attention of his audience by adding color to his message and making his points applicable to daily life, which he accomplished by staying up on current events by reading many newspapers, magazines, and books. He was a man of information and knew how to relate the current information to the lessons of Scripture. Throughout his life, Dr. John sought out learning experiences and believed that "if you romance learning, you will get a lot more out of life than if you are dull and without imagination, dreams, or vision."

Although Dr. John was a great man of God, most likely the people who knew him as a boy back in Arkansas might never have envisioned him becoming the "Baptist of the Twentieth Century." They probably would never have guessed that someday he would, at age 87, be selected by the Center for

---

48   David Murrow, *Why Men Hate Going to Church.* (Nashville: Thomas Nelson, 2011),171.

49   David Murrow, *Why Men Hate Going to Church.* (Nashville: Thomas Nelson, 2011),173.

Ministry Training at Liberty University as the outstanding Baptist pastor of the twentieth century. But Dr. John always lived according to God's expectations for his life, not man's. Otherwise, he may have lived as a farmer or businessman in Arkansas. Though he could have been successful as such, he would have missed out on God's best for his life. Dr. John counseled others to live their own lives and to not make decisions based upon the expectations of others. He based this principle on the life of the Virgin Mary in Scripture, who pursued God's will despite the opinions of others. She overcame what her family and others expected of her in order to fulfill her God-given destiny: to give birth to Immanuel, the Savior of the world.

Dr. John passed away painlessly and peacefully in his sleep on January 30, 2013, and went home to be with the Lord. Dr. Harold Rawlings penned his father's obituary:

> Dr. John W. Rawlings was born on January 29, 1914, and inherited his heavenly home at the age of 99 on January 30, 2013. He was the husband of the late Orelia Willie Rawlings. He is survived by his second wife, Mary Pruitt Rawlings; four sons, Herbert, Harold, Carrol, and George; nine grandchildren, Steven Rawlings, Jonathan Rawlings, James Rawlings, Catherine Lawrence, Ruth Snell, Joseph Rawlings, Bill Rawlings, Scott Rawlings, Lindsay Rawlings; and 17 great grandchildren. He was born and raised near Cave City, Arkansas. He married Orelia Mobley in 1931, and before she passed away in 2007, they had been married 75 years. He made a commitment to enter full-time ministry at the age of 25 and moved his wife and three young children to Fort Worth, Texas in the summer of 1939. He enrolled in Bible Baptist Seminary, a school founded by Dr. J. Frank Norris, one of the most influential and colorful preachers in the nation at the time. In 1940, Dr. Rawlings became pastor of Central Baptist Church in Tyler, Texas, while still a seminary student. He began with a congregation of 37, and when he left Tyler a little over 11 years later, the church had grown to 1,500 in weekly attendance. In 1951, he accepted a call to pastor Lockland Baptist Church in Lockland, Ohio, a suburb of Cincinnati, where he remained for 43 years. In December, 1963, the church moved three miles north to a beautiful 170 acre location in Evendale, Ohio, and the name

of the church was changed to Landmark Baptist Temple. In the 1970's, the church was considered to be one of the country's ten largest. For almost 30 years, The Landmark Hour radio broadcast blanketed more than half of the U.S., and even reached into some foreign countries. Dr. Rawlings helped found the Baptist Bible Fellowship in 1950 and served two terms as President of that organization. He also helped establish Baptist Bible College in Springfield, Missouri, and served as Executive Vice President of that institution for almost 15 years. By the early 1970s, it would become the nation's largest Bible College. Along with his four sons, he launched The Rawlings Foundation in 1995, and served as administrator of that Foundation until his death. Millions of dollars were funneled into youth camp facilities and Bible Institute campuses around the world during his seventeen-year management of the Foundation. He established the International Baptist Network in 2002, a network of conservative Baptist churches and pastors, the purpose of which was to assist in fulfilling the Great Commission of Jesus Christ. Dr. Rawlings was the recipient of many honorary degrees during his ministry, but his greatest longing was to hear his Master say, "Well done good and faithful servant… enter into the joy of the Lord."[50]

The Village of Glendale, Ohio, remembered his life by lowering the Glendale flag in front of the Village Office to half-mast for three days from February 5 through February 7, 2013. Paige Patterson, the President of Southwestern Baptist Theological Seminary in Fort Worth, Texas, ordered the flag to half-mast in honor of one of the Lord's choicest servants. These acknowledgements were fitting for the lifetime of accomplishments for which Dr. John gave God all the glory. In earlier years, he was presented with the Key to the City of Newport, Kentucky, by Mayor John Peluso; and the Key to the City of Indianapolis, Indiana, by Mayor William H. Hudnut III. At the end of his life, Dr. John was given the Key to the City of Heaven by his Lord and Savior Jesus Christ, from Whom he surely heard the words, "Well done good and faithful servant…enter into the joy of the Lord." Though Dr. John

---

50   Dr. Harold Rawlings, "Dr. John W. Rawlings." February 1, 2013. *Cincinnati.com A Gannett Company:* http://www.legacy.com/obituaries/cincinnati/obituary.aspx?n=john-w-rawlings&pid=162761024 (February 25, 2013).

lived many years after the sermon he preached on October 8, 1978, the words of that message summarize the heartbeat of his existence, his salvation in Jesus Christ:

> I spend my days and nights preaching to stir up the church, my brethren, people who have been born again, to help me reach a lost generation. God knows that the sundial has about run out. I want to tell you something, people. There has never been in six thousand years of human history an hour that is darker, an hour that is so hopeless, an hour that is so helpless as the hour in which we live! Now, for the saved man, that is not true because he is looking up. The King is coming. I believe in the second coming, the imminent return of my Lord Jesus Christ. I have got it made! Whether I am awake or asleep, I will be caught up to meet the Lord in the air. That is sealed and settled!

ABOUT THE AUTHOR

Kaitlyn O. Rawlings is an author, actress, speaker, and world traveller. In addition to her debut work, her great grandfather's biography The Lord is Not Through with Me Yet, she is also the author of the forthcoming fantasy fiction series The Last World Calls. Kaitlyn holds a Bachelor of Arts in English and is currently pursuing further education in acting and performance. She teaches ninth grade English and drama and lives in northern Kentucky with her family. Visit www.kaitlynorawlings.com for more information.